EREBUS

EREBUS

One Ship, Two Epic Voyages, and the Greatest Naval Mystery of All Time

MICHAEL PALIN

GREYSTONE BOOKS
Vancouver / Berkeley

Greystone Books Ltd.
greystonebooks.com

Cataloguing data available from Library and Archives Canada
ISBN 978-1-77164-441-9 (cloth)
ISBN 978-1-77164-442-6 (epub)

Jacket design by Andrew Roberts and Nayeli Jimenez
Maps by Darren Bennett
Typesetting by Integra Software Services Pvt. Ltd, Pondicherry
Printed and bound in Canada on ancient-forest-friendly paper by Friesens

Greystone Books gratefully acknowledges the Musqueam, Squamish,
and Tsleil-Waututh peoples on whose land our office is located.

Greystone Books thanks the Canada Council for the Arts, the British
Columbia Arts Council, the Province of British Columbia
through the Book Publishing Tax Credit, and the Government
of Canada for supporting our publishing activities.

Canada

For Albert and Rose

And indeed, nothing is easier for a man who has, as the phrase goes, 'followed the sea' with reverence and affection, than to evoke the great spirit of the past upon the lower reaches of the Thames. The tidal current runs to and fro in its unceasing service, crowded with memories of men and ships it had borne to the rest of home, or to the battles of the sea ... from the *Golden Hind* returning with her round flanks full of treasure ... to the *Erebus* and *Terror*, bound on other conquests – and that never returned.

Joseph Conrad, *Heart of Darkness*

CONTENTS

At the age of just twenty-two, Joseph Dalton Hooker joined the crew of HMS *Erebus* as assistant surgeon. He went on to become one of the greatest botanists of the nineteenth century.

INTRODUCTION

HOOKER'S STOCKINGS

I've always been fascinated by sea stories. I discovered C.S. Forester's Horatio Hornblower novels when I was eleven or twelve, and scoured Sheffield city libraries for any I might have missed. For harder stuff, I moved on to *The Cruel Sea* by Nicholas Monsarrat – one of the most powerful books of my childhood, even though I was only allowed to read the 'Cadet' edition, with all the sex removed. In the 1950s there was a spate of films about the Navy and war: *The Sea Shall Not Have Them, Above Us the Waves, Cockleshell Heroes*. They were stories of hero-ism, pluck and survival against all the odds. Unless you were in the engine room, of course.

As luck would have it, much later in life I ended up spending a lot of time on ships, usually far from home, with only a BBC camera crew and one of Patrick O'Brian's novels for company. I found myself, at different times, on an Italian cruise ship, frantically thumbing through *Get By in Arabic* as we approached the Egyptian coast, and in the Persian Gulf, dealing with an attack of diarrhoea on a boat whose only toilet facility was a barrel slung over the stern. I've been white-water rafting below the Victoria Falls, and marlin-fishing (though not catching) on the Gulf Stream – what Hemingway called 'the great blue river'. I've been driven straight at a canyon wall by a jet boat in New Zealand, and have swabbed the decks of a Yugoslav freighter on the Bay of Bengal. None of this has put me off. There's something about the contact between boat and water that I find very natural and very comforting. After all, we emerged from the sea and, as President Kennedy once said, 'we have salt in our blood, in our sweat, in our tears. We are tied to the ocean. And when we go back to the sea ... we are going back to whence we came'.

In 2013 I was asked to give a talk at the Athenaeum Club in London. The brief was to choose a member of the club, dead or alive, and tell their story in an hour. I chose Joseph Hooker, who ran the Royal Botanic Gardens at Kew for much of the nineteenth century. I had been filming in Brazil and heard stories of how he had pursued a policy of 'botanical imperialism', encouraging plant-hunters to bring exotic, and commercially exploitable, specimens back to London. Hooker acquired rubber-tree seeds from the Amazon, germinated them at Kew and exported the young shoots to Britain's Far Eastern colonies. Within two or three decades the Brazilian rubber industry was dead, and the British rubber industry was flourishing.

I didn't get far into my research before I stumbled across an aspect of Hooker's life that was something of a revelation. In 1839, at the unripe age of twenty-two, the bearded and bespectacled gentleman that I knew from faded Victorian photographs had been taken on as assistant surgeon and botanist on a four-year Royal Naval expedition to the Antarctic. The ship that took him to the unexplored ends of the earth was called HMS *Erebus*. The more I researched the journey, the more astonished I became that I had previously known so little about it. For a sailing ship to have spent eighteen months at the furthest end of the earth, to have survived the treacheries of weather and icebergs, and to have returned to tell the tale was the sort of extraordinary achievement that one would assume we would still be celebrating. It was an epic success for HMS *Erebus*.

Pride, however, came before a fall. In 1846 this same ship, along with her sister ship *Terror* and 129 men, vanished off the face of the earth whilst trying to find a way through the Northwest Passage. It was the greatest single loss of life in the history of British polar exploration.

I wrote and delivered my talk on Hooker, but I couldn't get the adventures of *Erebus* out of my mind. They were still lurking there in the summer of 2014, when I spent ten nights at the 02 Arena in Greenwich with a group of fellow geriatrics, including John Cleese, Terry Jones, Eric Idle and Terry Gilliam, but sadly not Graham Chapman, in a show called *Monty Python Live – One Down Five to Go*. These were extraordinary shows in front of extraordinary audiences, but after I had sold the last dead parrot and sung the last lumberjack song, I was left with a profound sense of anticlimax. How do you follow something like that? One thing was for sure: I couldn't go over the same ground again. Whatever I did next, it would have to be something completely different.

Two weeks later, I had my answer. On the evening news on 9 September I saw an item that stopped me in my tracks. At a press conference in Ottawa, the Prime Minister of Canada announced to the world that a Canadian underwater archaeology team had discovered what they believed to be HMS *Erebus*, lost for almost 170 years, on the seabed somewhere in the Arctic. Her hull was virtually intact, its contents preserved by the ice. From the moment I heard that, I knew there was a story to be told. Not just a story of life and death, but a story of life, death and a sort of resurrection.

What really happened to the *Erebus*? What was she like? What did she achieve? How did she survive so much, only to disappear so mysteriously?

I'm not a naval historian, but I have a sense of history. I'm not a seafarer, but I'm drawn to the sea. With only the light of my own enthusiasm to guide me, I wondered where on earth I should start such an adventure. An obvious candidate was the institution that had been the prime mover of so many Arctic and Antarctic expeditions from the 1830s onwards. And one that I knew something about, having for three years been its President.

So I headed to the Royal Geographical Society in Kensington and put to the Head of Enterprises and Resources, Alasdair MacLeod, the nature of my obsession and the presumption of my task. Any leads on HMS *Erebus*?

He furrowed his brow and thought for a bit: '*Erebus* ... hmm ... *Erebus*?' Then his eyes lit up. 'Yes,' he said triumphantly, 'yes, of course! We've got Hooker's stockings.'

Actually they had quite a bit more, but this was my first dip into the waters of maritime research, and ever since then I've regarded Hooker's stockings as a kind of spiritual talisman. They were nothing special: cream-coloured, knee-length, thickly knitted and rather crusty. But over the last year, as I've travelled the world in the company of *Erebus*, and come close to overwhelming myself with books, letters, plans, drawings, photographs, maps, novels, diaries, captains' logs and stokers' journals and everything else about her, I thank Hooker's stockings for setting me off on this remarkable journey.

Michael Palin
London, February 2018

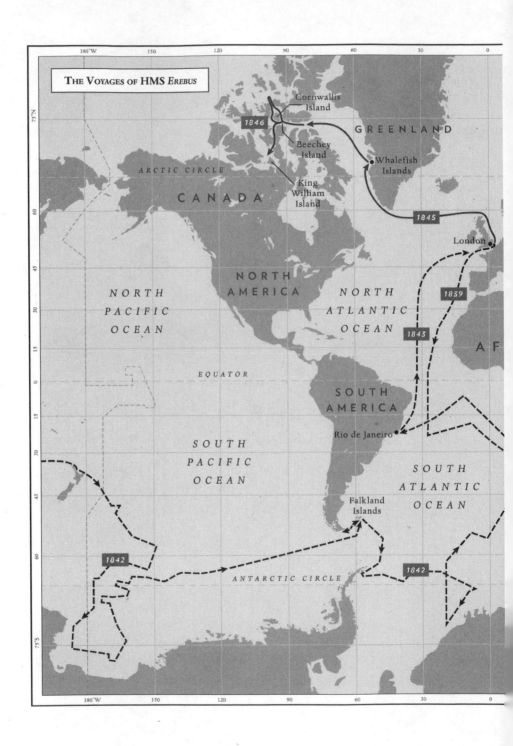

THE VOYAGES OF HMS *EREBUS*

180°W   150   120   90   60   30   0

75°N

Cornwallis
Island
1846
GREENLAND

Beechey
Island

ARCTIC CIRCLE   Whalefish
Islands

CANADA

King
William
Island

60

1845

London

45   NORTH
AMERICA   NORTH
ATLANTIC
OCEAN   1839

30   NORTH
PACIFIC
OCEAN   1843

15   A F

EQUATOR

0

SOUTH
AMERICA

15   SOUTH
PACIFIC
OCEAN

Rio de Janeiro

30   SOUTH
ATLANTIC
OCEAN

Falkland
Islands

45

60   1842   1842

ANTARCTIC CIRCLE

75°S

180°W   150   120   90   60   30   0

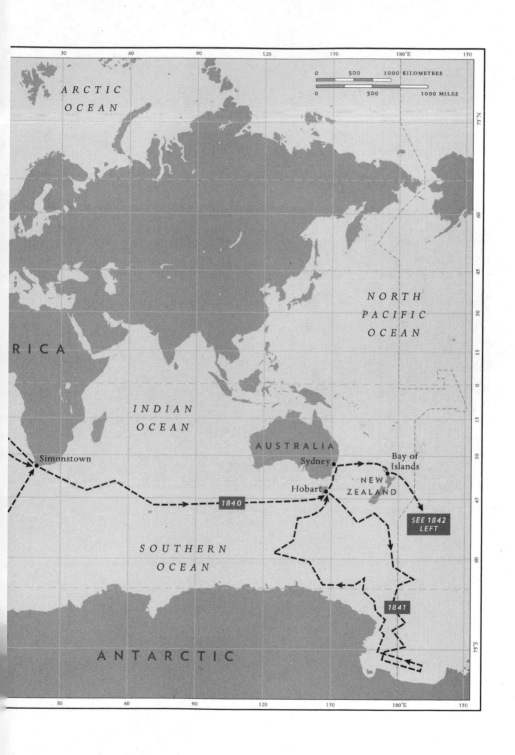

A sonar image, taken in 2014, of the wreck of *Erebus*. She was discovered on a shallow part of the seabed – so close to the surface that her masts would once have peeked out above the waves.

THE SURVIVOR

Wilmot and Crampton Bay, Nunavut, Canada, 2 September 2014. Near the coast of a bleak, flat, featureless island, one of thousands in the Canadian Arctic, where grey skies, sea and land merge seamlessly together, a small aluminium-hulled boat called the *Investigator* is moving slowly, carefully, rhythmically across the surface of an ice-blue sea. Towed behind her, just below the water-line, is a slim silver cylinder called a towfish, not much more than 3 feet long. Inside the towfish is an acoustic device that sends out and receives sound waves. The sound waves bounce off the seabed, are returned to the towfish, transmitted up the tow-cable and translated into images of the seabed below.

There is not much noise on the *Investigator*, save for the monotonous drone of her engines. The weather is quiet, the skies clear and a watery sun is shining onto a glassy-calm sea. Everything is muted. Time is passing, but that's about all.

Suddenly there's a commotion: the towfish has narrowly missed hitting a shoal; the attention of everyone on board switches to making sure their expensive sonar device is safe. At that moment Ryan Harris, a marine archaeologist, casting a brief glance at the screen before going to help, sees something other than sand and stones on the seabed. Something that brings him up sharply.

On the screen is a dark shape: something solid and unfamiliar, lying right there on the shallow seabed, only 36 feet below him. He shouts out. His colleagues crowd around the computer screen. He points to the shape. They can barely believe what they see: below the *Investigator*'s silver towfish, indistinct in detail but unmistakably clear in shape, is a wooden hull. It's broken at the stern as if a bite had been taken out of it, the deck beams are exposed, and all is covered in a woolly coat of underwater vegetation. What they are looking at is a ship. A ship that disappeared off the face of the earth, along with all her crew, 168 years ago. A ship that had one of the most extraordinary lives and deaths in British naval history – and, from this day on, one of the most remarkable resurrections.

She stands proud, so close to the surface that at one time her two tallest masts would have peeked out above the waves. Her hull is solid, apart from some impact-collapse at the stern. Strands of kelp, a large brown algae, cover the outlines of the timberwork like loose-fitting bandages. Her three masts have broken off, as has the bowsprit. Pieces of them lie in the nest of debris scattered around her. Amongst the wreckage, half-sunk in the sand, are two of her propellers, eight anchors and a segment of the ship's wheel. Her three decks have, in some places, fallen in on each other. Many of the main beams that run across the ship appear still to be strong, though the planking above them is mostly stripped away, giving her the appearance – when seen from above – of a half-filleted fish.

A massive cast-iron windlass stands, undamaged, on the upper deck. Nearby are two copper-alloy Massey pumps. Some skylights and the Preston Patent Illuminators that would have given light to the men below are well preserved.

The lower deck, where the life of the ship would have gone on, lies exposed in places, still covered in others. Chests where seamen kept their belongings, and on which they sat at meals, can be made out under the accumulation of silt and dead kelp. There are numbers on the deck beams to mark the positions where hammocks would have been slung. Ladderways and hatches giving access to the decks above lie open and ghostly. The galley stove, on which meals would have been prepared, is intact and in position. In the bows, the outlines of the sickbay can be made out.

Further aft, portions of the captain's cabin, the mess room and several of the officers' cabins are distinguishable through a jumble of collapsed timbers. In one of them is a bed-space, with drawers beneath. The transom – the stern wall of the ship – has suffered most damage, but the captain's bed cabin next to it is in place, as are lockers and a heater. The orlop deck, the lowest of the three, is least damaged, but also the most difficult to penetrate. A shoe, mustard pots and storage boxes have nevertheless been retrieved. Divers have also recovered a set of willow-pattern plates, the stem of a wine glass, a ship's bell, a bronze six-pounder cannon, various decorated buttons, a Royal Marines shoulder-belt plate embossed with a crowned lion standing on a crown, and a thick glass medicine bottle with the name 'Samuel Oxley, London' embossed on the sides. It originally contained a potion made by Oxley from concentrated essence of Jamaican ginger. He claimed it as a cure for 'Rheumatism, Indigestion, Windy Complaints, Nervous Headaches and Giddiness, Hypochondria [I love the idea of a medicine for hypochondria], Lowness of Spirits, Anxieties, Tremors, Spasms, Cramp and Palsy'. This all-too-human cure-all remains, for me, one of the most poignant finds on HMS *Erebus*. A reminder that epic adventures and everyday frailties go hand-in-hand.

For 80 per cent of the year the ice freezes and seals in the ship's secrets again. But when it melts, people like Ryan – who has made more than 200 dives – along with the rest of the underwater team, will be back in the water looking for many more precious details. My dream would be to get to know *Erebus* as intimately as they have done. Just once. What I need is Hooker's wetsuit.

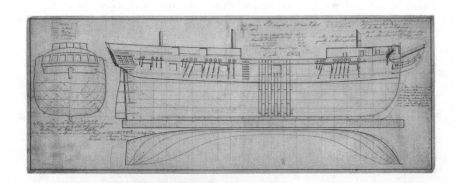

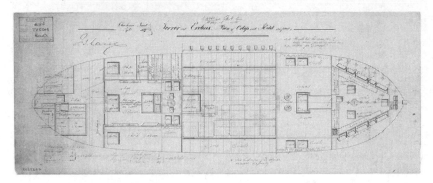

Two contemporary plans showing (above) a typical bomb ship in profile, and (below) the orlop (or lower) deck and hold of *Erebus* and her sister ship *Terror*.

CHAPTER I

MADE IN WALES

7 June 1826, Pembroke, Wales: it's the sixth year of the reign of George IV, eldest son of George III and Queen Charlotte. He is sixty-three, with a quarrelsome marriage, a flauntingly extravagant lifestyle and an interest in architecture and the arts. Robert Jenkinson, 2nd Earl of Liverpool, a Tory, has been Prime Minister since 1812. The Zoological Society of London has just opened its doors. British explorers are out and about, and not just in the Arctic. Alexander Gordon Laing reaches Timbuktu in August, only to be murdered a month later by local tribesmen for refusing to relinquish his Christianity. In north Wales two great engineering achievements are being celebrated, as two of the world's first suspension bridges, the Menai Bridge and the Conway Bridge, open within a few weeks of each other.

At the other end of Wales, in an estuary near the old fortified town of Pembroke, people are gathering on this early June morning for a somewhat smaller celebration. Cheered on by a crowd of engineers, carpenters, blacksmiths, clerks and their families, the stout, broad-hulled warship they have been building for the past two years slides, stern first, down the slipway at Pembroke Dockyard. The cheers rise to a roar as she strikes the waters of Milford Haven. She bounces, bobs and shakes herself like a newborn waterfowl. Her name is *Erebus*.

It wasn't a cheerful name, but then she wasn't built to cheer; she was built to intimidate, and her name had been chosen quite deliberately. In classical mythology Erebus, the son of Chaos, was generally taken to refer to the dark heart of the Underworld, a place associated with dislocation and destruction. To evoke Erebus was to warn your adversaries that here was a bringer of havoc, a fearsome conveyor of hell-fire. Commissioned in 1823, HMS *Erebus* was the last but one of a type of warship known as bomb vessels, or sometimes just 'bombs'. They were developed, first by the French, and later the English, at the end of the seventeenth century, to carry mortars that could fling shells high over coastal defences, doing maximum damage without an armed landing having to be risked. Of the other ships in her class, two were named after volcanoes – *Hecla* and *Aetna* – and the others after various permutations of wrath and devastation: *Infernal, Fury, Meteor, Sulphur* and *Thunder*. Though they never achieved the heroic status of the fighting warships, their last action, the siege of Fort McHenry in Baltimore Harbour in the War of 1812, came to be immortalised in the American national anthem, 'The Star Spangled Banner': 'the rockets' red glare, the bombs bursting in air' refers to the fire from British bomb ships.

It was a proud day for the shipbuilders of Pembroke when *Erebus* went down the slipway, but as she was steadied and warped up on the banks of the Haven, her destiny was unclear. Was she the future, or did she already belong to the past?

The defeat of Napoleon's armies at Waterloo on 18 June 1815 had brought to an end the Napoleonic Wars, which, with a brief lull during the Peace of Amiens in 1802, had preoccupied Europe for sixteen years. The British had been central to the allied war effort and, by the time it drew to a close, had run up a national debt of £679 million, twice her Gross Domestic Product. The Royal Navy had also incurred huge costs, but had outperformed the French, and were now

undisputed rulers of the waves. This brought increased responsibilities, such as patrolling of the slave trade, which Britain had abolished
in 1807, and operations against the pirates off the coast of North Africa,
but nothing on the scale of her war footing. In the four years from
1814 to 1817 the Royal Navy's numbers therefore shrank from 145,000
men to 19,000. It was traumatic for many. Numerous unemployed sailors had to take to begging on the streets. Brian Lavery, in his book
Royal Tars, gives the example of Joseph Johnson, who walked the
streets of London with a model of Nelson's *Victory* on his head. By
raising and lowering his head he would reproduce her movement
through the waves and so earn a few pennies from passers-by. An ex-
Merchant Navy man who could only find work on a warship was
distraught: 'for the first time in my life [I] saw the monstrous fabric
that was to be my residence for several years, with a shudder of grief I
cannot describe'.

There was heated debate about the future of the Royal Navy. Some
saw the end of hostilities as an opportunity to cut defence expenditure and begin to pay off some of the vast debt that the war effort had
accumulated. Others argued that peace wouldn't last for long. The
defeated Emperor Napoleon had been taken to the island of St Helena,
but he had already escaped from incarceration once, and there were
nagging doubts as to whether this latest exile might be the end of
him. Precautions should be taken to strengthen the Navy just in case.

By and large, the Cassandras won. The government authorised
expenditure on new dockyards, including a large complex at Sheerness in Kent and a much smaller yard at Pembroke in Wales. Four
warships, *Valorous, Ariadne, Arethusa* and *Thetis*, were soon under construction in the hastily excavated yards dug out of the banks of Milford
Haven.

The dockyard where *Erebus* was built still exists today, but is now
less about shipbuilding and more about servicing the giant Milford
Haven oil refinery a few miles downstream. The slipway from which

Erebus was launched in the summer of 1826 lies beneath the concrete floor of the modern ferry terminal that links Pembroke with Rosslare in Ireland.

When I visit, I can still get a sense of what it must once have been like. The original layout of roads, running past the few surviving slate-grey terraces built in the 1820s for the foremen and bosses, is quietly impressive. These terraces look as strong and proud as any London Georgian town houses. In one of them lived Thomas Roberts, the master shipwright who supervised the construction of *Erebus*. He arrived in this distant corner of south-west Wales in 1815, when the shipyard was then just two years old.

Sharing responsibility with Roberts for running this new enterprise were Richard Blake, the Timber Master, and James McKain, Clerk of the Cheque. They were not a happy team. McKain's clerk, Edward Wright, claimed in court to have been assaulted by Richard Blake, whom he accused of 'wrenching my nose several times and putting himself in a menacing attitude to strike me with his umbrella'. Roberts quarrelled incessantly with McKain over allegations and counter-allegations of corruption and malpractice. By 1821 McKain could take no more and left to accept a new post at Sheerness Dockyard. He was replaced by Edward Laws. The poisonous atmosphere had begun to clear when the news broke on 9 January 1823 that the Navy Board had shown its continued confidence in the Pembroke yard by placing an order for the construction of a 372-ton bomb vessel, designed by Sir Henry Peake, one-time Surveyor of the Navy, to be named *Erebus*.

She was not to be a big ship. At 104 feet, she was less than half the length of a standard man-o'-war, and at 372 tons she was a minnow compared to Nelson's 2,141-ton *Victory*. But she was to be tough. And more like a tugboat than a sleek and fancy ketch. Her decks and hull had to be strong enough to withstand the recoil from two big onboard mortars, one 13-inch, the other 10-inch. She therefore had to be reinforced with diagonal iron bracing bolted to the planking in the hold, strengthening the hull whilst reducing her weight. She also had to have a hull capacity wide and deep enough to store heavy mortar shells. In addition, she was to be armed with ten small cannons, in case she should need to engage the enemy on the water.

Erebus was built almost entirely by hand. First the keel, most likely made of sections of elm scarfed together, was secured on blocks. To this was attached the stem, the upright timber in the bow, and at the other end of the ship the sternpost, which supported the rudder. The frame, made of oak from the Forest of Dean in Gloucestershire and shipped on barges down the River Severn, was then fitted around these heavy timbers. This task demanded a high level of skill, as the shipwrights had to find exactly the best part of the tree to match the curvature of the boat, whilst taking into account how the wood might expand or contract in the future.

Once the frame was in place, it was allowed time to season. Then 3-inch planking was fitted from the keel upwards, and the deck beams and decking boards were added.

Erebus was not built in a hurry. Unlike her future partner, HMS *Terror*, built at Topsham in Devon in less than a year, it was twenty months before she was ready to go down the slipway. When the work was completed, the Master of the Cheque sent a bill to the Navy Board for £14,603 – around £1.25 million in today's currency.

In all, 260 ships were built at Pembroke. Then, almost exactly a hundred years after *Erebus* rolled down the slipway, the Admiralty decided that the yard was superfluous, and a workforce of 3,000 was reduced, at a stroke, to four. That was in 1926, the year of the General Strike. There was a temporary reprieve during the Second World War when Sunderland flying boats were built there, and more recently warehouses and distribution businesses have moved in to use some of the space in the old hangars, but, as I take a last walk through the grand stone gateway of the old yard, I sense with regret that the glory days are over and will never return.

After her launch at Pembroke, *Erebus* was taken, as was common practice, to a different Admiralty yard to be fitted out. Not yet equipped with a full rig of masts and sails, she would likely have been towed south-west, around Land's End and up the English Channel to Plymouth. There, at the busy new dockyard that would eventually become the Royal Navy's Devonport headquarters, she would have been transformed into a warship, complete with ordnance: two mortars, eight 24-pound and two 6-pound cannons, and all the machinery for storing and delivering the ammunition. Her three masts would have been hoisted, the mainmast towering 140 feet above the deck.

But after this flurry of activity came a prolonged lull. Though armed and prepared, *Erebus* was stood down In Ordinary (the term used to describe a ship that had no work). For eighteen months she rode at anchor at Devonport, waiting for someone to find a use for her.

I wonder if there were such things as ship-spotters then: schoolboys with notebooks and pencils recording the comings and goings around the big yards, as I used to do with trains, in and out of Sheffield. I imagine they could have become attached to the brand-new, chunky-hulled, sturdy three-master that seemed to be going nowhere. She had a touch of style: her bow ornately carved, her topside strung with gun-ports, and at her stern more decoration around the range of windows on the transom, and the distinctive projecting quarter-galleries housing water-closets.

If, however, they'd been about early in the dark winter mornings at the end of 1827, they would have been rewarded with the sight of something stirring aboard HMS *Erebus*: covers being pulled back, lamps lit, barges pulling alongside, masts being rigged, yards hoisted, sails furled. In February 1828, *Erebus* made an appearance in the

Progress Book, which kept a record of all Royal Navy ship movements. She was, it noted, 'hove onto Slip, and took off Protectors, coppered to Load draught'. These were all preparations for service. Hauled out of the water onto a slipway, she would have had the protective timber planking on her hull removed and replaced with a copper covering, up to the level at which it was safe to load her (what was soon to be called the Plimsoll line). Since the 1760s the Royal Navy had been experimenting with copper sheathing to try and prevent the depredations of the *Teredo* worm – 'the termites of the sea' – which burrowed into timbers, eating them from the inside out. Coppering meant that a voyage was imminent.

On 11 December 1827 Commander George Haye, RN stepped aboard to become the first captain of HMS *Erebus*.

For the next six weeks Haye recorded in minute detail the victualling and provisioning of his ship: 1,680 lb of bread was ordered on 20 December, along with 23½ gallons of rum, 61 lb of cocoa and 154 gallons of beer. The decks were scraped and cleaned and the sails and rigging made ready as the crew, some sixty strong, familiarised themselves with this brand-new vessel.

The first day of *Erebus*'s active service is recorded, tersely, in the captain's log: '8.30. Pilot on board. Unmoored ship, warped down to buoy.' It was 21 February 1828.

By the next morning they had passed the Eddystone Lighthouse, which marked the wreck-strewn shoal of rocks south-west of Plymouth, and were headed towards the notoriously turbulent waters of the Bay of Biscay. There were early teething troubles, among them a leak in the captain's accommodation that merited plaintive mentions in his log: 'Employed every two hours bailing water from cabin', 'Bailed out all afternoon'.

For a broad, heavy ship, *Erebus* made good progress. Four days after setting out, they had crossed the Bay of Biscay and were within sight of Cape Finisterre on the north coast of Spain. On 3 March they had reached

Cape Trafalgar. Many on board must have crowded the rails to gaze at the setting of one of the British Navy's bloodiest victories. Perhaps one or two of the older hands had actually been there with Nelson.

For the next two years *Erebus* patrolled the Mediterranean. From the entries in the log that I pored over in the British National Archives, it seems that little was demanded of her. Headed 'Remarks at Sea', the notes do little more than laboriously and conscientiously record the state of the weather, the compass readings, the distance travelled and every adjustment of the sails: 'Set jib and spanker', 'Up mainsail and driver', 'Set Top-Gallant sails'. One never senses that they were in much of a hurry. But then there was not a lot to hurry about. International rivalry was between rounds. Napoleon had been knocked out, and no one had come forward to pick up his crown. True, in October 1827, a few months before *Erebus*'s deployment, British, Russian and French warships, in support of Greek independence from the control of the Ottoman Empire, had taken on the Turkish Navy at Navarino Bay, in a bloody but ultimately decisive victory for the allies. But that had proved a one-off. Amongst the Great Nations there was, for once, more cooperation than conflict. The most that merchant ships in the Mediterranean had to contend with were Corsairs – pirates operating from the Barbary coast – but even they were less active, after a naval campaign against their bases.

All *Erebus* had to do was show the flag, remind everyone of her country's naval supremacy and annoy the Turks, wherever possible.

Erebus sailed from Tangier along the North African coast to Algiers, where the British garrison marked her arrival with a 21-gun salute, returned in kind by *Erebus*'s own cannons. Here, Commander Haye notes, rather intriguingly, six bags were taken on board, 'said to contain 2652 gold sequins and 1350 dollars, to be consigned to several merchants at Tunis'. As they left Algiers, there is the first mention of punishment on board, when John Robinson received twenty-four lashes 'for skulking below when the hands were turned up'.

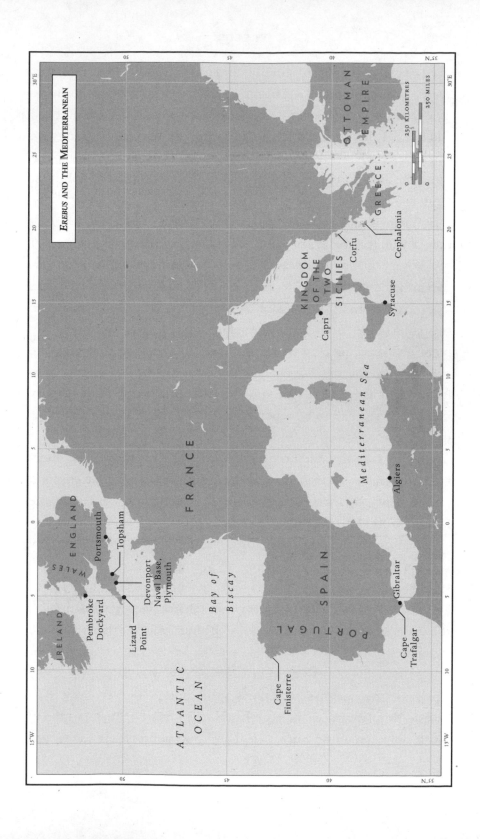

EREBUS AND THE MEDITERRANEAN

ATLANTIC
OCEAN

IRELAND
WALES
ENGLAND
Pembroke
Dockyard
Portsmouth
Topsham
Lizard
Point
Devonport
Naval Base,
Plymouth

Bay of
Biscay

FRANCE

SPAIN

PORTUGAL

Cape
Finisterre

Gibraltar
Cape
Trafalgar

Algiers

Mediterranean Sea

Capri
KINGDOM
OF THE
TWO
SICILIES
Corfu
Syracuse
Cephalonia

GREECE

OTTOMAN
EMPIRE

250 KILOMETRES
250 MILES

Laziness, or failing to jump to orders, was considered a serious breach of discipline, and Robinson would have been made an example of, in front of the entire crew. He would have had his shirt removed and been lashed by his wrists to a grating put up across a gangway. The boatswain would probably have administered the whipping, using the feared cat-o'-nine-tails, a whip with nine knotted flails that scratched like a cat.

Some men took pride in surviving a flogging, preferring ten minutes of pain to ten days in prison below deck. Michael Lewis, author of *The Navy in Transition 1814–1864*, even suggests that 'there was a certain art in being flogged ... a fine marine in good practice would take four dozen with a calmness of demeanour which disassociated the operation of the lash from the idea of inflicting pain by way of punishment and warning, and connected it up in people's mind with the ordinary and routine'. But change was in the air. Just a few years later, in 1846, following persistent efforts by the MP Joseph Hume, every flogging at sea had to be reported to the House of Commons. This had an immediate effect. More than 2,000 floggings were meted out in 1839; by 1848 this had been reduced to 719. Use of the cat-o'-nine-tails was outlawed in the Navy in around 1880, though corporal punishment with the cane was administered until well after the Second World War.

Robinson's whipping apart, time passed uneventfully, each day being a ritual of eating, sleeping, manning the decks and endless scrubbing and washing. The obsession with 'scrubbed hammocks and washed clothes' was, of course, more than a matter of cleanliness. It was a matter of routine, for without routine there was no discipline.

Occasionally something more interesting would happen. On 7 April 1828 the captain's log reports a ship bound for New York from Trieste being boarded and searched. On 24 June, '1 Russian Line of Battle Ship and a Brig came in sight. 13 gun salutes were exchanged and a covered Jolly Boat took the captain across to what turned out to be a Russian Admiral's flagship.' On the same day the log notes: 'Jolly Boat returned. Opened cask of wine, No 175. 24 and one-eighth gallons.'

Once *Erebus* was on station around Greece and the Ionian islands, the 'Remarks at Sea' read more and more like a holiday brochure. Endless days of 'Light Breeze and Fine Weather', and an itinerary to die for: Cephalonia, Corfu, Syracuse, Sicily and Capri. *Erebus*'s posting could hardly have been more idyllic. Unless you were Caleb Reynolds of the Marine Artillery, given twenty-four lashes for 'uncleanliness and disobedience of order'; or Morris, Volunteer First Class, given '12 lashes over the breach for repeated neglect of duty and disobedience of orders'. Considering where she was, *Erebus* doesn't sound to have been a happy ship.

Things began to change as she entered her second year of duty in the Mediterranean, with the appointment of Commander Philip Broke. The son of Rear-Admiral Sir Philip Bowes Vere Broke, who made his name with the audacious capture of the USS *Chesapeake* in 1813, his approach seems to have been rather different from Haye's. Certain rituals continued much as they had before – the log continues to record the mundane details of washing and cleaning and holy-stoning of the decks, the state of the provisions, wind directions and reefing of the sails – but the beatings appear to have declined. Broke had a different way of instilling discipline in the ship's crew, or at least a different set of priorities for his ship. Weekly, and latterly almost daily, the log is now filled with artillery exercises. On 13 April 1829: 'Exercised a division of seamen at the Great Guns, and Marine Artillery at small arms.' On 20 April, off the island of Hydra: 'Exercised a division of seamen with broadswords.' On 6 May: 'Exercised a division of seamen firing at a target with pistols.' Whether it was just another way of dealing with the perennial problem of boredom or in response to some specific instruction from the Admiralty, Broke seemed more keen than his predecessor to see *Erebus* as a fighting machine. But he never had the chance to show what she could do, for by May 1830 *Erebus* was on her way home, having never fired a gun in anger.

Two rather heart-warming late entries follow: 'Lowered a boat for the ship's company to bathe' and, on reaching Gibraltar on 27 May, 'Hove to, to bathe.' Bathing, rather than flogging, seemed to be more to the liking of the crew's new captain.

Three weeks later *Erebus* was within sight of the Lizard Lighthouse. On 18 June her artillery and Great Guns were rolled out by Commander Broke for the last time, and on 26 June 1830 she reached Portsmouth, furling her sails and lowering her flags in respect for King George IV, who had died that morning. (Respect that was not afforded to him by his obituary in *The Times*: 'There never was an individual less regretted by his fellow creatures than this deceased king. What eye has wept for him. What heart has heaved one throb of unmercenary sorrow.') He was succeeded that day by his younger brother, who became William IV. William's ten years in the Navy had earned him Nelson's praise and the affectionate title of the 'Sailor King'.

As the British Crown changed hands, Commander Broke and the crew of *Erebus* were paid off. Despite her captain's best efforts at mustering his men to roll out the Great Guns and flash their broadswords, *Erebus* would never again be a warship.

A triumphant moment in polar exploration: James Clark Ross's discovery of the North Magnetic Pole in 1831.

CHAPTER 2

MAGNETIC NORTH

If the years in which *Erebus* patrolled the Mediterranean were ones of comparative idleness for the Royal Navy, there were certain benefits. Press gangs became a thing of the past. Men could choose their ships. The Navy became more specialised, more professional. And with the Napoleonic Wars over, a non-militaristic area of maritime activity started to open up, offering opportunities for the able, the adventurous and the better-qualified to use Britain's naval superiority to pursue new goals: to extend man's geographical and scientific knowledge by exploration and discovery.

The impetus for this new direction came largely from two remarkable men. One was the polymath Joseph Banks, the embodiment of the Enlightenment. An author and traveller, botanist and natural historian, Banks had circumnavigated the globe with Captain Cook in 1768, bringing back a huge amount of scientific information as well as mapping previously unknown corners of the planet. The other was one of Banks's protégés, John Barrow, an energetic and ambitious civil servant, who in 1804, at the age of forty, had been appointed Second Secretary at the Admiralty.

Barrow and Banks formed around them a circle of enterprising scientists and navigators. Much inspired by the work of the German naturalist Alexander von Humboldt, their aim was to assist an international effort to chart, record and label the planet, its geography, natural history, zoology and botany. They were to set the agenda for a golden period of British exploration, motivated more by scientific enquiry than by military glory.

Barrow's priority was the partly explored Arctic region. Ever since John Cabot, an Italian who settled in Bristol, had discovered Newfoundland in 1497, there had been keen interest in discovering whether there might be a northern route to 'Cathay' (China) and the Indies to compete with the southern route via Cape Horn (dominated at that time by the Spanish and Portuguese). From his desk at the Admiralty, John Barrow championed the cause, using every conceivable contact and pursuing every line of influence to make it happen. If the Navy could discover a Northwest Passage linking the Atlantic and Pacific Oceans, he argued, the advantages to Britain in terms of safer and shorter journeys to and from the lucrative East would be immense.

Around 1815, the year of Waterloo, whalers – the forgotten men of polar exploration, but the only ones to keep a regular eye on Arctic and Antarctic waters – returned from the north with reports of the ice breaking up around Greenland. One of them, William Scoresby, was of the opinion that if one could get through the ice-pack that lay between latitudes 70 and 80°N, there was clear water all the way to the Pole, offering the tantalising prospect of a sea passage to the Pacific. He backed this up with evidence of whales harpooned off Greenland appearing, with the harpoons still in their sides, south of the Bering Strait.

Barrow, attracted by the idea of an ice-free polar sea, persuaded the Royal Society to set a sliding scale of rewards for penetration into Arctic waters. These ranged from £5,000 for the first vessel to reach 110°W, to a £20,000 jackpot for discovering the Northwest Passage itself. With the backing of Sir Joseph Banks, he then approached the First Lord of the Admiralty, Robert Dundas, 2nd

Viscount Melville, along with the Royal Society, with a view to commissioning two publicly funded Arctic expeditions: one to search for a sea passage from the Atlantic to the Pacific, and the other to make for the North Pole to investigate the reports of clear water beyond the ice.

For Robert Dundas, this suggestion must have seemed a heaven-sent opportunity. A Scot whose father had enjoyed the dubious distinction of being the first minister ever to be impeached for misusing public funds, he had been at the Admiralty for six years, where he had spent much of his time resisting cuts to the Navy. Barrow's proposals offered a means of keeping some existing ships busy, and thus fending off any criticism that the Navy had considerably more than it knew what to do with. He therefore took kindly to Barrow's new proposals.

To lead one of the expeditions the Admiralty turned to a Scottish mariner, John Ross. The third son of the Reverend Andrew Ross, he came from a family who lived near the town of Stranraer in Wigtownshire, whose fine natural harbour would have been a regular port of call for Royal Navy vessels. It was common then for families to let their children join the Navy as part of their general schooling, and John had joined up as a First-Class Volunteer at the age of nine. By the time he was thirteen he had been transferred to the 98-gun warship *Impregnable*. A distinguished career, in and out of battle, followed. In late 1818, when he received the letter appointing him leader of the Admiralty-backed expedition to search for the Northwest Passage, he was forty years old, well regarded and had spent most of his life in service.

Ross was given command of HMS *Isabella* and proceeded to use a little nepotism to bring on board his eighteen-year-old nephew, James Ross. Inspired and encouraged by his uncle's example, James had joined the Navy at the age of eleven, and had served an apprenticeship under his uncle in the Baltic and the White Sea, off northern Russia.

He joined *Isabella* as a midshipman, traditionally the first step to becoming a commissioned officer.

James was tall and well built, and his education in the Navy had served him well. He had learned a lot about the latest scientific advances, especially in the field of navigation and geomagnetism. The ability to understand and harness the earth's magnetic forces was one of the great prizes of science in the early nineteenth century, and one in which James Clark Ross (he added the 'Clark' later, to distinguish himself from his uncle) was to become intimately involved.

In charge of HMS *Trent*, one of the ships entrusted with reaching the North Pole, was another career sailor, thirty-two-year-old John Franklin. Like John Ross, he had seen action during the Napoleonic Wars, being thrown in at the deep end aboard HMS *Polyphemus* at the Battle of Copenhagen when he was only fifteen, before being taken on as a midshipman with Matthew Flinders as he mapped much of the coast of Australia (or New Holland, as it was then). Young Franklin learned a lot from Flinders, who had himself learned a great deal from Captain Cook. Before he was twenty, Franklin had gained further battle experience as a signals officer on HMS *Bellerophon* at the Battle of Trafalgar. He was a lieutenant by the time he was twenty-two. When the strikingly handsome James Ross first encountered the round-faced, chubby, prematurely balding John Franklin at Lerwick in the Shetlands in May 1818, as *Isabella* and *Trent* prepared to set out for the Arctic, he must have regarded him as something of a hero. He can have had no idea that their paths would cross again in the future, or that they would be the two men to become most closely associated with the dramatic career of HMS *Erebus*.

Like many of the senior naval men of the time, Franklin was a well-educated polymath with a particular interest in magnetic science. This was his first Arctic commission and he took it seriously.

Andrew Lambert, his biographer, assesses his state of mind at the time: 'He might not have a university pedigree, or the status of a Fellow of The Royal Society, but he had been round the world, made observations and fought the king's enemies. He was somebody, and if this venture paid off he could expect to be promoted.' Unfortunately, the voyage, which he had hoped would eventually reach the far east of Russia, never got past the storm-driven icebergs around Spitsbergen, and John Franklin was back in England within six months.

The John Ross expedition to the Northwest Passage was initially more successful. Having reached 76°N and safely crossed Baffin Bay, *Isabella* and her companion *Alexander* found themselves at the head of an inlet on the north-western side of the bay. This was the mouth of Lancaster Sound, later to become known as the entrance to the Northwest Passage. But it was also the place where Ross made a serious error that was to prove a lasting blot on his reputation. When looking west down the inlet, he came to the conclusion that there was no way through, because there appeared to be high mountains ahead. In fact they were thick clouds. So convinced was he, however, that not only did he fail to bring his officers up on deck to confirm what he thought he'd seen (they were below, playing cards), but he even gave the imaginary range a name, Croker's Mountains, after the First Secretary to the Admiralty. It was a bizarre episode. Ross, on his own initiative, then ordered the ship to turn and head for home, though not without adding insult to injury by naming an imaginary gulf Barrow's Bay. When the error was revealed, Barrow was furious and never trusted John Ross again.

But the lure of the Northwest Passage remained strong and Barrow's largesse next fell upon William Edward Parry, captain of the Ross expedition's second ship, *Alexander*, who was duly invited to lead a fresh attempt. At thirty, Edward Parry, as he was usually known, was of a younger intake than John Ross or John Franklin, though he had been with the Navy for more than half his life, having joined when he was thirteen. James Clark Ross was once again engaged as midshipman. One of his fellow officers on the *Alexander* was a well-regarded Northern Irishman, Francis Rawdon Moira Crozier. He and James Ross were to become lifelong friends and, like Ross, Francis Crozier would go on to play a major role in the destiny of *Erebus* and that of her sister ship, *Terror*.

Parry's expedition took two ships, *Hecla* and *Griper*, on what proved to be one of the most fruitful of all Arctic voyages. Not only did they pass through Lancaster Sound, removing Croker's Mountains from the map, but they also penetrated deep into the Northwest Passage. They took the unprecedented step of over-wintering on a bleak and previously unknown island far to the west, which they named, after their sponsor, Melville Island. Fortunately, they were well prepared. Each man was issued with a wolfskin blanket at night and great care was taken with the supplies, which included Burkitt's essence of malt and hops, and lemon juice, vinegar, sauerkraut and pickles to stave off scurvy. By the time Parry and his ships arrived back in the Thames estuary in November 1820, they had penetrated hundreds of miles of previously unknown land.

Meanwhile John Franklin, despite his underwhelming achievement on the North Pole expedition, had been offered another chance by Barrow. Along with George Back and Dr John Richardson, he was given command of a land expedition to map the north-flowing Coppermine River to its mouth in the Arctic Sea. It was wild and difficult country, and as Franklin's working life had so far been spent at sea, he was not perhaps the ideal man for such demanding terrestrial exploration. Moreover he was encumbered by the heavy equipment that was needed to fulfil the scientific obligations of the mission.

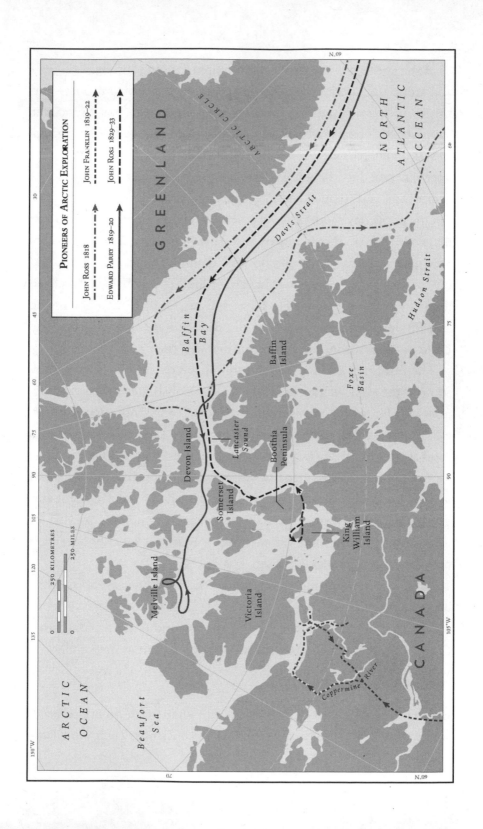

In the event, much new land was mapped, along the river's course and along the Arctic coast, but Franklin left his return too late and his men were caught in vicious weather conditions as winter approached. Their food ran out and they were reduced to eating berries and lichens wherever they could find them. Franklin recalled later that one day 'the whole party ate the remains of their old shoes [moccasins of untanned leather] to strengthen their stomachs for the fatigue of the day's journey'. The dreadful conditions produced bitter divisions. Ten of the accompanying Canadian voyageurs (fur traders who also acted as scouts and porters) died on the march home, and one of those who survived, Michel Terohaute, was believed to have done so by cannibalism. He then shot an English member of the expedition, Midshipman Robert Hood, before being shot in turn by Dr John Richardson, second-in-command of the party.

The disorganised chaos at the end of the expedition was seen by some at the time as the result of Franklin's obstinacy and unwillingness to listen to the voyageurs or the local Inuit. More recently, the editor of a 1995 edition of Franklin's journals summed him up as 'a solid representative of imperial culture, not only in its many positive aspects, but in its less generous dimensions as well'. But when he arrived back home a year later and told his side of their fight for survival, his book became a bestseller and, far from being criticised for jeopardising himself and his men, John Franklin quickly became a popular hero: The Man Who Ate His Boots.

Barrow's multi-pronged attack on the Northwest Passage had brought results and, even when unsuccessful, had so firmly gripped the public imagination that men like Parry and Franklin and James Clark Ross were becoming shining lights in a new firmament – a world in which heroes fought the elements, not the enemy.

In 1824, as *Erebus* was being carved into shape in a quiet corner of south-west Wales, two of her fellow bomb ships, *Hecla* and *Fury*, were once more to go into action against the ice. Impressed by their sturdy design and reinforced hulls, Edward Parry, the explorer of the moment, chose them to spearhead yet another assault on the Northwest Passage.

This new journey represented a step up for the young James Clark Ross, he of the tall, straight back and leonine thatch of thick dark hair, for he was appointed Second Lieutenant on the *Fury*. But the expedition itself was not a success. First, the ships were held up by thick ice in Baffin Bay. They attempted to warp themselves through by driving anchors into the ice and pulling themselves along using the ships' hawsers, but it was a dangerous technique, which, as Parry himself admitted, could go quite violently wrong: on one occasion, he recorded, 'three of *Hecla*'s seamen were knocked down as instantaneously as if by a gunshot, by the sudden flying out of an anchor'. Then *Fury* was driven ashore and had to be abandoned on the coast of Somerset Land. After just one winter, the decision was taken to return home.

Barrow, however, remained convinced that Parry could do no wrong. With the strong support of Sir Humphry Davy of the Royal Society, he therefore entrusted him with an attempt on the North Pole. The other man of the moment, James Clark Ross, was appointed as Parry's second-in-command. Also on board were Ross's friend Francis Crozier and a new assistant surgeon, Robert McCormick, who would go on to play an important part in Ross's subsequent adventures.

The expedition reached Spitsbergen in June and from there the men headed off on reindeer-drawn sledges, aiming to make about 14 miles a day on their way to the Pole. They continued north, travelling by night and resting by day to avoid snow blindness. Unfortunately, the reindeer proved less than ideal for towing the sledges and were later killed and eaten; and by the end of July the party's progress had slowed to one mile in five days. The decision was taken to turn back.

A loyal toast was drunk, and the standard they had hoped to run up at the Pole was hoisted.

Even though they hadn't achieved their goal, Parry and his men had scored a considerable achievement. They had reached a new furthest north of 82.43°, some 500 miles from the North Pole, a record that was to stand for nearly fifty years. As for Ross, he had survived forty-eight days in the ice and had shot a polar bear. Yet the fact remained that another attempt on the North Pole had failed, leading *The Times* to state in a prescient editorial: 'In our opinion, the southern hemisphere presents a far more tempting field for speculation; and most heartily do we wish that an expedition were to be fitted out for that quarter.' That, however, was to be a long time coming.

On his return in October 1827, James Ross was promoted to commander, but, with no immediate prospect of further work, was stood down on half-pay. Thanks to his uncle, however, he didn't have to kick his heels for long. Just a few months later John Ross, who had been cold-shouldered by Barrow and most of the Admiralty after the Croker's Mountains fiasco, won financial support for a new polar expedition from his friend Felix Booth, the gin distiller. One of the conditions Booth imposed was that Ross should involve his nephew – a condition that the bluff and curmudgeonly John swiftly agreed to, even though he hadn't asked James first. He even promised that James would serve as his second-in-command. Fortunately for everyone, James, now in the prime of life and in need of money, accepted.

Booth agreed to invest £18,000 of his gin fortune in fitting out *Victory* – not the legendary flagship of Lord Nelson, but an 85-ton steam-driven paddle-steamer, previously employed on the Isle of Man–Liverpool ferry service. Ross's idea was that because the *Victory* was not wholly dependent on sail power, it would be able to push its way more easily through the thicker ice. The principle was sound enough, but the crew began to have trouble with the engine the morning after they left Woolwich. Even with it working flat out, they could only make three knots. Before they had left the North Sea they discovered that the boiler system was leaking badly (one of its designers suggested they stop up the hole with a mixture of dung and potatoes). And they were still within sight of Scotland when one of the boilers burst – as did John Ross's patience, on being told the news: 'as if it had been predetermined that not a single atom of all this machinery should be aught but a source of vexation, obstruction and evil'. In the winter of 1829 they dumped the engine altogether, to general relief.

Despite these teething problems, they went on to have their fair share of success. John Ross, perhaps a little sheepishly, sailed *Victory* through the non-existent Croker's Mountains and out the other side of Lancaster Sound. En route he mapped the west coast of a peninsula to the south, which he named Boothia Felix, shortened later to Boothia, but still the only peninsula in the world named after a brand of gin. They made contact with the local Inuit, to the benefit of both sides. One of the Inuit was particularly impressed that Ross's carpenter was able to fashion him a wooden leg to replace one he'd lost in an encounter with a polar bear. The new leg was inscribed with the name 'Victory' and the date.

Their greatest achievement was still to come. On 26 May 1831, two years into what was to be a four-year expedition, James Clark Ross set off on a twenty-eight-day expedition by sledge across the Boothia Peninsula, with the intention of pinpointing the North Magnetic Pole. Just five days later, on 1 June, he successfully measured a dip of 89°90'. He was as close as it was possible to get to the Magnetic Pole. 'It almost seemed as if we had accomplished everything we had come so far to see and do,' John Ross later wrote; 'as if our voyage and all its labours were at an end, and that nothing now remained for us but to return home and be happy for the rest of our days.'

The raising of the Union Flag and the annexing of the North Magnetic Pole in the name of Great Britain and King William IV should have been the prelude to a hero's return, but the capricious Arctic weather refused to cooperate. The ice closed in and the expedition's survival began to look increasingly precarious. As the prospect of a third winter trapped in the Arctic turned into reality, elation gave way to bitter resignation. In June, James Ross had been triumphant. Just a few months later his uncle John wrote with feeling: 'To us, the sight of the ice was a plague, a vexation, a torment, an evil, a matter of despair.'

It was worse than anyone could have expected. Had it not been for their close contact with the local Inuit, and the adoption of a diet that was rich in oil and fats, they would surely have perished. Indeed, it was to be nearly two years before the Rosses and their companions, 'dressed in the rags of wild beasts ... and starved to the very bones', were miraculously rescued by a whaling ship. This turned out to be the *Isabella* from Hull, the ship that John Ross had commanded fifteen years earlier. The captain of the *Isabella* could scarcely believe what he saw. He had assumed that uncle and nephew had both been dead for two years. So many had despaired of ever seeing them again that there was national astonishment when they sailed into Stromness in the Orkney Islands on 12 October 1833. When they arrived in London a week later, their reception was nothing less than triumphal. Their remarkable fortitude in surviving four years in the ice, their scientific achievements and their skills as explorers were all praised and celebrated. This near-disaster, far from deterring future expeditions, ensured that the Arctic would remain a potent target for the Admiralty's ambitions and, years later, would profoundly change the course of many lives.

John Ross, now rehabilitated, was awarded a knighthood. His moment of triumph was, however, marred by an unpleasant falling-out with his nephew over who should receive credit for the discovery of the North Magnetic Pole. James claimed sole recognition, for pinpointing its position. His uncle insisted that if he had known his nephew was intending to go for the Pole, he would have accompanied him. To official eyes, it was James who was the coming man. Alongside his prickly and impulsive uncle, he appeared dependable and decisive – a safe pair of hands. At the end of 1833 he was promoted to post captain and given the task of conducting the first-ever survey into the terrestrial magnetism of the British Isles.

He had barely begun the work when word came of twelve whaling ships and 600 men trapped in the ice in the Davis Strait, between Greenland and Baffin Island. The Admiralty agreed to a rescue mission and, predictably, turned to James Clark Ross to lead it. He chose a ship called *Cove*, built in Whitby, and picked Francis Crozier as his First Lieutenant.

As Ross and Crozier made their way north from Hull to Stromness and into the North Atlantic, the Admiralty looked around for suitable back-up vessels, should extra effort be required. Of the two bomb ships that had been converted for Arctic travel on Parry's expeditions, one, HMS *Fury*, had been dashed against the rocks on Somerset Island, and the other, *Hecla*, had been sold a few years earlier. That left HMS *Terror*, one of the Vesuvius Class, built in 1813, with plenty of active service behind her; and the as-yet-untried and untested *Erebus*. On 1 February 1836 a skeleton crew was despatched to Portsmouth to dust *Erebus* down and haul her round to Chatham to await the call. *Cove*, meanwhile, ran into ferociously bad weather, one gale battering her so severely that it was generally reckoned it was only James Ross's cool, calm captaincy that saved the ship from going under. After returning to Stromness for repairs, Ross, Crozier and the *Cove* set out again for the Davis Strait. By the time they reached Greenland they learned that all but one of the whalers had been freed from the ice.

Despite this, the rescue efforts were seen as heroic. Francis Crozier was promoted to commander (confusingly, the rank below captain) and James Ross was offered a knighthood. Much to the dismay of his many supporters, he turned it down, apparently because he felt the title of Sir James Ross would mean that he might be mistaken for his pugnacious and recently ennobled uncle.

'The handsomest man in the navy' – according to Jane Griffin, the future wife of John Franklin – was, however, rather less successful in his private life. In between his many journeys, Ross had met and fallen in love with Anne Coulman, the eighteen-year-old daughter of a successful Yorkshire landowner. Ross had done the decent thing and written to her father, expressing his feelings for Anne and hoping that he might visit her at the family home. Coulman had written back indignantly, firmly shutting the door on the liaison and expressing his shock that Ross should harbour such feelings 'for a mere schoolgirl'. His opposition was multi-pronged. 'Your age [Ross was thirty-four] compared with my daughter's, your profession and the very uncertain and hazardous views you have before you, all forbid our giving any countenance to the connection.'

Anne, however, was as much in love with James as he was with her. For the next few years they continued to meet secretly. Coulman's stubborn opposition to their relationship drove Ross to write to Anne in angry frustration: 'I could not have believed it possible that worldly emotions could have had so powerful an influence as to destroy the most endearing affections of the heart, and cause a father to treat his child with such unfeeling hardness and severity.' Fortunately, one of James Ross's great qualities was his determination. Once he had set his mind on something, he was not easily deflected. He continued to keep in contact with Anne, and she with him. Their perseverance was eventually rewarded.

HMS *Terror* was soon in action on another mission, leaving the Medway in June 1836 as the flagship of George Back's latest ambitious expedition to extend his survey of the north-west Arctic. By September she was beset in the moving ice and was severely knocked about throughout the winter. She eventually broke free of the ice-pack and, still encased in a floe, drifted into the Hudson Strait. With her hull damaged and secured with a chain, *Terror* just about made it to the Irish coast, where she unceremoniously ran aground.

Before disaster struck, George Back had some kind words for *Terror* that could have been applied to all the bomb ships: 'Deep and lumbered as she was, and though at every plunge the bowsprit dipped into the water, she yet pitched so easily as scarcely to strain a rope-yarn.' His description of her in fine weather made the frog sound like a prince: 'The royals and all the studding-sails were for the first time set, and the gallant ship in the full pride of her expanded plumage floated majestically through the rippling water.'

Erebus had no such chance to impress. Though she had come tantalisingly close to seeing some action, in the end she had merely exchanged one dockyard for another. De-rigged at Chatham and back In Ordinary again, she was becoming the 'nearly ship' of the British Navy.

Throughout the early nineteenth century, the Antarctic remained *terra incognita*. James Weddell's 1822–4 voyage in search of the South Pole – depicted here in his 1825 memoir – penetrated further south than any previous ship, but failed to sight land.

CHAPTER 3

MAGNETIC SOUTH

When the recently formed British Association for the Advancement of Science met in Newcastle in the summer of 1838, terrestrial magnetism was high on the agenda. Now, it was felt, was the time to seize the moment – to claim the prize. Once the earth's magnetic field was understood and codified, compasses and chronometers could be set with absolute precision, and navigation would no longer be an erratic process dependent on clear skies and guesswork. The result would be a nineteenth-century equivalent of GPS.

One of those pushing hardest for such research was Edward Sabine, a Royal Artillery officer who had sailed with Ross and Parry to the Arctic. For the last ten years, as Scientific Advisor to the Admiralty, he had argued vigorously that Britain should use her naval superiority to gather valuable information on the earth's magnetic field. But he also agreed with the influential Alexander von Humboldt, a Prussian nobleman who had made the first studies in geomagnetism on a celebrated voyage to South America in 1802, that only if countries worked together could the world be reduced to a set of clear, empirical, scientific principles.

The theory that linked geomagnetism and navigation had already been developed by Carl Friedrich Gauss, an astronomer at Göttingen University. To make progress towards putting these ideas into practice, Sabine and others argued for a network of observation stations to be set up across the globe, which would report simultaneously. James Clark Ross had discovered the North Magnetic Pole and established its variation from true north. Now, the logical next step was to turn attention to those parts of the earth that remained largely unexplored, in particular the remote southern hemisphere.

Up until now, Antarctic exploration had never been taken very seriously. Much of what was known about the southern lands came from Captain Cook, who in the 1770s had twice crossed the Antarctic Circle – and he had not been overwhelmingly enthusiastic. It was a realm, he wrote, of 'thick fogs, snowstorms, intense cold and every other thing that can render navigation dangerous'. For the most part, the region had been left to individual whalers and seal-hunters.

Nevertheless, such descriptions as came back fed a growing popular fascination. For the Romantics, the Antarctic represented the mystery of the unknown and the untamed. Samuel Taylor Coleridge's 'The Rime of the Ancient Mariner', for example, which was published in 1798, depicts a cursed ship drifting helplessly into the Southern Ocean:

> *The fair breeze blew, the white foam flew,*
> *The furrow followed free;*
> *We were the first that ever burst*
> *Into that silent sea.*

In Coleridge's poem the voyage ends in abject disaster. The hero of Edgar Allan Poe's only novel, *The Narrative of Gordon Pym of Nantucket* (1838), finds the Southern Ocean a place of all kinds of danger and depravity, from shipwreck to cannibalism. A place of infernal cold and darkness. A place where souls in torment are driven to destruction. The sort of place the Greeks had a word for: Erebus.

As artists and poets were busy frightening themselves and the public, the scientists – as scientists do – were going in the other direction, the direction of learning and logic, of exploration and explication. In the spirit of the Enlightenment, the existence or non-existence of a Southern Continent was another mystery to unravel. Now the demands of science and a newly aroused sense of human potential were coming together to begin the unravelling.

There were other motives, too. The eminent astronomer Sir John Herschel pressed the case for the practicalities of a southern expedition at a meeting in Birmingham, laying on something more than mere science. 'Great physical theories,' he argued, 'with their trains of practical consequences, are pre-eminently *national* objects, whether for glory or utility.' With this chauvinistic nudge, Herschel's committee produced a memorial of resolution, which was presented to the Prime Minister, Lord Melbourne.

Over the winter the arguments went one way and the other, but on 11 March 1839, Lord Minto, First Lord of the Admiralty, finally informed Herschel that permission had been granted for an Antarctic expedition. It was to be a prestigious enterprise. It therefore demanded a leader of the first rank. Fortunately, among those most pre-eminently qualified to lead it were two notable polar explorers: James Clark Ross and John Franklin. One was the man who had turned down a knighthood. The other was The Man Who Ate His Boots.

Ross's recent career had been covered in glory. Franklin's, too, had been successful, if a little more muted. In 1825, three years after his first Arctic voyage, he had launched a second overland expedition. During the winter months he had absorbed himself in painstakingly thorough scientific observations. When conditions improved, he had led his men on an exploration of 400 miles of unsurveyed coastline, west of the Mackenzie River. And at the end of the season, having learned from previous experience, Franklin had decided not to risk his men by pushing further, but had returned to London.

Knighted in 1829, and with his reputation as a navigator and expedition leader much enhanced, Franklin was then commissioned in August 1830 to take charge of HMS *Rainbow*, a 28-gun, 500-ton sloop, with orders to proceed to the Mediterranean. What followed was a safe, solid and successful tour of duty in many of the seas from which *Erebus* had recently returned. *Rainbow* had a 175-strong crew and was a much bigger, more impressive ship than any he had commanded before. Franklin, the most affable and sociable of men, was seen as an accessible and humane captain. Life on board was so congenial that the ship acquired nicknames like 'Franklin's Paradise' and 'The Celestial Rainbow'.

Franklin's social skills also helped nurture Britain's relationship with the newly independent Greek state and ease local factional disputes, at a time when the Russians, previously an ally of Britain and France, were supporting an unpopular provisional government, and the allies were looking to install their own man as the new king of the country. After a prolonged search the British and French head-hunted an eighteen-year-old Bavarian prince called Otto, the son of King Ludwig of Bavaria, and by all accounts a bit of a drip. He did, however, award Franklin the Order of the Redeemer, for his help.

Franklin enjoyed everything he saw of Ancient Greece during his tour of duty, but was profoundly unimpressed by the new Greece, which he regarded as corrupt and leaderless. Having done his best to adjudicate on various local disputes, he must have been relieved to get back home to Portsmouth at the end of 1833, just in time for Christmas. Virtue had its reward, though: in appreciation of his efforts, the new king, William IV, decorated him with Knight Commander of the Guelphic Order of Hanover.

Franklin's private life during these years had been marked by tragedy. In 1823 he had married the poet Eleanor Anne Porden, and they had had a daughter (also called Eleanor), but just five days after he sailed on his second Arctic expedition, his wife had died from tuberculosis. By all accounts a remarkable, much-admired woman, she had known that she wouldn't survive, but had insisted that her husband should press ahead with his plans. Four years later, on 4 November 1828, he had married again. Jane Griffin, the daughter of a lawyer, was quick, clever and energetic, and had been a close friend of Eleanor's. Franklin's biographer, Andrew Lambert, speculating as to what she saw in the portly explorer, concluded: 'a romantic hero, a cultural icon, and it was perhaps this image that she married.' And it was protecting and elevating his image that was to preoccupy the rest of Jane's life.

Back from the Mediterranean, Franklin was respected, happy in his new marriage – but at a loose end. There was no new posting to go to, and for the next three years he was effectively unemployed. It must have been a deeply frustrating time for him. Then, in 1836, a new opportunity arose, in the form of the lieutenant-governorship of Van Diemen's Land. It was, admittedly, something of a poisoned chalice. The previous governor, George Arthur, had brought in social reforms that had upset many of the small community there, and left it unhappy and divided. But for Franklin and his ambitious wife, the offer must have come as something of a godsend. After several years of enforced idleness, here at last was a new opportunity for him to display his talents. He accepted with alacrity, and the couple set sail later that year, arriving in Hobart in January 1837.

What Franklin wasn't to know was that just over a year later the Admiralty would be looking for an experienced polar explorer to lead an expedition to the Antarctic. Had he been aware, would he have accepted the post in Van Diemen's Land? As it was, his absence from England at the critical moment effectively ruled him out as a candidate. The Admiralty had no hesitation in offering the job to James Clark Ross, whose Arctic experience and discovery of the North Magnetic Pole embodied the navigational and scientific qualifications they were after. And he was available.

★★★

Having secured Ross's services, the Lords of the Admiralty looked around to find ships worthy of this ambitious venture. Bomb vessels had been the Royal Navy's craft of choice for extreme exploration as long ago as 1773, when two bomb ships, *Racehorse* and *Carcass* (the name for an incendiary shell), had been converted for an expedition to the North Pole. They had reached the Barents Sea before being turned back by the ice. By now, there were only two bomb ships left as realistic candidates for Antarctic duty. One was HMS *Terror*, strengthened and rebuilt after a ten-month battering in the ice on George Back's Arctic expedition in 1836 and 1837. The other, currently riding on the River Medway at Chatham, had never been further than the warm waters of the Mediterranean. But she was slightly bigger and more recently built than *Terror*, and she became the unanimous choice to be the flagship. After nine years of premature retirement, and nearly fourteen years after she had been cheered down the slipway at Pembroke, HMS *Erebus* was set to become one of the most famous ships in history. On 8 April 1839, James Clark Ross was appointed her captain.

Within two weeks of the expedition being confirmed, *Erebus* was put into dry dock at Chatham to have the coppering on her hull, which had been in place since her Mediterranean patrol duty, removed and replaced. The traditional trappings of a warship were dismantled to give her cleaner, more functional, more weather-resistant lines. Three levels on the top deck were reduced to one, with the removal of the raised quarterdeck and forecastle, giving a single flush deck. This would provide extra storage space for the nine auxiliary boats that *Erebus* was to carry. These ranged from 30-foot-long whale-boats to a 28-foot-long pinnace, two cutters and a 12-foot gig, intended essentially to serve as the captain's private taxi. More space was created by dispensing with most of *Erebus*'s weaponry. Her twelve guns were reduced to two and the redundant gun-ports filled in.

Her transformation from warship to ice-ship was supervised by a Mr Rice at Chatham Dockyard. So thorough was it, and so impressed was James Clark Ross, that he included Rice's memorandum of work on *Erebus* in his published account of the expedition. Which is how we know that her hull was strengthened with 6-inch-thick oak planking, increasing to 8 inches at the gunwale, to make a 3-foot-wide girdle around the ship; and that the deck was reinforced with 3-inch-thick planks laid fore and aft, and with additional planks laid diagonally on top. 'Fearnaught, dipped in hot tallow' was laid between the two surfaces (fearnaught was a thick felt, installed as insulation). Lower down the hull, the doubling narrowed to 3-inch-thick English elm. The remainder of the ship's bottom, down to the keel, was doubled with 3-inch Canadian elm. Extra-thick copper was used to cover the bow from water-line to keel. Anything projecting from the stern was removed, including the overhanging quarter galleries. The ornately patterned carving on her bow, which was a feature of all warships, however humble, was stripped away. Decoration was sacrificed to utility and durability.

During the summer of 1839, as the sawyers and ropers, sailmakers, carpenters and smithies worked away at Chatham, James Ross was busy picking his officers. His unsurprising choice for his second-in-command and captain of the *Terror* was the Ulsterman, Francis Rawdon Moira Crozier, with whom he had sailed so often on bruising Arctic expeditions that it was said Ross was one of the very few people allowed to call Crozier 'Frank'.

Crozier, three years Ross's senior, was one of thirteen children from Banbridge in County Down, a few miles south of Belfast. His birthplace, a handsome Georgian townhouse built in 1796, still stands. His father had made money in the Irish linen industry, and Francis would have had a comfortable, strongly religious upbringing (in time his father changed his allegiance from Presbyterian to the Protestant Church of Ireland, moving from radicalism to the establishment).

One of Francis's brothers became a vicar and the other two went into the law. But because his father was keen to get one of his sons into uniform and was prepared to pull some strings at the Admiralty, Francis himself was taken into the Royal Navy on 12 June 1810, at the age of thirteen.

Over the years he impressed all who worked with him. No less a figure than John Barrow endorsed him warmly: 'A most zealous young officer, who, by his talents, attention and energy, has succeeded in working himself up to the top of the service.' That Crozier never quite reached the top is a mystery. Something in his personality seems to have held him back: a lack of sophistication, perhaps, a lack of confidence ashore, an awareness of his limited formal education. His biographer, Michael Smith, describes him as 'Rock solid and reliable', but goes on to say, 'Crozier was born to be a number two.'

Edward Joseph Bird, thirty-seven, was chosen as First Lieutenant of *Erebus*. He too had sailed with Ross, latterly as second-in-command on HMS *Endeavour* on one of Parry's expeditions. Bird was described by Sir Clements Markham, a Victorian geographer and explorer and for many years President of the Royal Geographical Society, as 'an excellent seaman, unostentatious and retiring'. He was bearded, with prematurely receding hair brushed forward and a marked resemblance in build and general chubbiness to John Franklin. Ross trusted him implicitly.

In June, Crozier wrote to Ross in some frustration, concerned that no First had yet been chosen to accompany him on *Terror*. He seemed not to want to take the decision himself. 'I myself know not one of any standing who would suit us, however there must be plenty,' he wrote, adding, somewhat enigmatically, 'we do not want a philosopher'. At that time the words 'philosopher' and 'scientist' were often indistinguishable, so it's not clear whether Crozier was merely indicating a preference for a naval man or signalling discomfort with intellectuals. Eventually Archibald McMurdo, a capable Scot, was chosen to be Crozier's First Lieutenant. He knew *Terror*, having been Third Lieutenant on her when she narrowly avoided destruction in the ice on Back's expedition of 1836. Charles Tucker was chosen as master of *Erebus*. He would be the man in charge of navigation.

Others on board with Arctic experience were Alexander Smith, First Mate, and Thomas Hallett, purser, both of whom had served with Ross and Crozier on *Cove*. Thomas Abernethy, who was appointed gunner, was a reassuring presence all round. Though his artillery duties were largely honorific, he was a big, powerfully built man who had been one of Ross's closest and most trusted companions on many Arctic forays. Indeed, he had been at his side when he reached the North Magnetic Pole.

Thankfully for future historians and researchers, two appointments on *Erebus* went to men who recorded her adventures in minute detail: Robert McCormick and Joseph Dalton Hooker. McCormick, who had been on the *Beagle* with Charles Darwin, was the ship's surgeon and naturalist, a combination that may seem strange today, but was understandable in this pre-pharmaceutical age, when doctors made their own medicine and plants were the main ingredient – in fact, the Apothecaries Act of 1815 had made the study of botany a compulsory part of medical education. He was, as they say, a character, and quite full of himself. On the *Beagle* McCormick had become increasingly irritated by the freedom that Captain Fitzroy accorded Darwin, who, despite having no official naval status, was often allowed ashore to naturalise whilst McCormick had to stay on board. In the end McCormick got himself invalided off the expedition, to no one's great disappointment. The irritation had clearly been mutual. 'He chose to make himself disagreeable to the Captain,' tutted Darwin, adding, '. . . he was a philosopher of rather an antient date'.

McCormick was certainly well read in natural history, geology and ornithology and had at some point impressed – or perhaps pestered – Ross enough to have been assured of a post. So here he was, settling himself and his books, his instruments and his specimen cases onto HMS *Erebus*. Opinionated as he may have been, his diary offers a precious source of information about her four years in the Antarctic.

Joseph Dalton Hooker was the son of William Jackson Hooker of Norwich, who, through the influence of the ubiquitous Sir Joseph Banks, had been appointed to the Chair of Botany at Glasgow University. William realised from very early on that his son had a precocious talent. At the age of six he had correctly identified a moss growing on a Glasgow wall as *Bryum argenteum*. By the time he was thirteen he was an obsessive botanist, able to recite long lists of Latin names.

William Hooker, through his wide range of contacts, had heard of the proposed Antarctic expedition and, sensing the potential for a budding naturalist to make his name, used all his influence to get an assignment for his son. This was, after all – for reasons both scientific and commercial – a golden age for botany. As Jim Endersby, Hooker's biographer, writes, 'Much of the wealth of Britain's empire rested on plants' – from timber and hemp for the ships, to indigo, spices, tea, cotton and opium that they carried. Understanding how, where and why things grew where they did was of immeasurable benefit to the government. It made sense, therefore, to have a botanist aboard the expedition.

As it turned out, the only official position open to Hooker was that of assistant surgeon, and to this end Joseph rapidly qualified as a doctor. But it was clear where his true interests lay. 'No future botanist will probably ever visit the countries whither I am going and that is a great attraction,' he wrote to his father. On 18 May 1839, six weeks before his twenty-second birthday, Joseph Hooker received the news that his appointment as second surgeon on HMS *Erebus* had been confirmed. He would be the youngest man on board.

Throughout the expedition, like his immediate superior McCormick, Hooker kept copious journals, probably encouraged by the example of Charles Darwin. (He told his father that he slept with a set of proofs of *The Voyage of the Beagle* under his pillow.) As was the practice on publicly financed expeditions, all diaries and notebooks kept on board were seen as the property of the Admiralty and had to be surrendered at the end of the voyage. And, as M.J. Ross, biographer and great-grandson of Sir James, points out, there were no professional scientists on this expedition: all the officers and crew were members of the Royal Navy and were therefore subject to these restrictions. Letters home, however, were exempt from examination, making young Hooker's copious correspondence with his family all the more valuable. It offers an informality and openness that no official report could contain.

After receiving his commission, Hooker was ordered to report to Chatham Dockyard where, as he records in his journal, 'I spent nearly four tedious months ... waiting until the ships should be fully ready and equipped'. He was quartered, or 'hulked' as they called it, on an old frigate called HMS *Tartar*. It was common then to use retired warships as temporary accommodation. Some, like Turner's famous 'Fighting Temeraire', were used as prison ships and had a reputation for being indescribably filthy.

A number of other crew members were similarly hulked on the *Tartar*, including Sergeant William Cunningham, who was in charge of a squad of Marines, consisting of a corporal and five privates, allotted to HMS *Terror*. A similar detachment would have been aboard *Erebus*. The Royal Marines' role was rather like that of a police force. They were charged with maintaining order and discipline on board, searching for and returning deserters, carrying out punishments, collecting and despatching mail, rationing out spirits, securing the ships when in port, and providing a guard for visiting dignitaries. In addition to all these duties, Sergeant Cunningham kept a daily diary, or memorandum book, throughout the voyage. From his initial entry, we know that he and his men arrived on the

Medway on 15 June 1839 and were immediately put to work fitting out the ships.

By the beginning of September, *Erebus* was fully crewed up, with twelve officers, eighteen petty officers, twenty-six able seamen and seven Marines, making up a complement of sixty-three. About half the personnel were First Entry men – who had never before served in the Royal Navy, but in many cases had seagoing experience on whalers. Provisions and equipment were also brought on board, including warm clothing of the best quality. Last to be loaded was food for the voyage, including 15,000 lb of beef and 2,618 pints of vegetable soup.

On 2 September, *Erebus* and *Terror* were inspected by the Earl of Minto, First Lord, and three senior Lords Commissioners of the Admiralty. Final instructions were received from the Admiralty on the 16th, and three days later *Erebus* and *Terror* moved downriver to Gillingham Reach, where compasses were adjusted and last provisions taken on board. Ross's mother and father had come down from Scotland to see him off and they stayed on board as the ship continued down the Thames. Unfortunately, they had only reached Sheerness when they ran aground in low water and had to be towed the next morning to Margate by the steamship *Hecate*. Here they remained waiting for the westerly winds to abate, and for one of the anchors to be replaced – Ross fulminating, justifiably, but hardly succinctly, against 'the gross negligence of those whose duty it was to ascertain the soundness of that, on which, under different circumstances, the ship, and lives of all on board, might have ... depended'. It was not an auspicious start.

For the people of Margate, the presence of this great expedition so fortuitously becalmed on their doorstep was quite an attraction. They came out in numbers to gaze at the ships, and some were invited aboard. No one can have been more warmly welcomed than the naval pay clerks who arrived on the 25th to issue three months' pay in advance. The rest of the crew's wages were to be passed directly to their families until their safe return.

On the last day of September 1839 the wind swung round to the east and they could at last head down into the English Channel, dropping their pilot at Deal and continuing south-west, in what McCormick described as 'boisterous weather'. It would be almost four years to the day before any of them saw the English coast again.

Sailors who had never previously crossed the Equator were traditionally subjected to a line-crossing ceremony. William Cunningham, aboard *Terror*, vividly described his own experience on 3 December 1839: 'I was sat down on the Barber's chair, and underwent the process of shaving by being lathered with a paint brush – and lather composed of all manner of Nuisance that could be collected in a Ship.'

CHAPTER 4

FAR-OFF SHORES

Erebus was never a graceful ship. Functionally barque-rigged, with square sails on the fore and mainmast and a fore and aft sail on the mizzen, she was not quick, either. With a full wind in her sails, seven to nine knots was about the maximum. But in the expert opinion of her captain's great-grandson, Rear-Admiral M.J. Ross, she was 'an excellent seaboat', which 'rolled and pitched a great deal, but easily, so that there was little strain on [the] rigging or spars'.

She was soon put to the test. Four days into the journey, while passing close to Start Point, the southern tip of Devon, on 4 October 1839, she ran into thick fog, followed by a gale and heavy rain. The next morning *Terror* was nowhere to be seen. Less than a week at sea and already the Admiralty's clear instruction that both ships stay together at all times had fallen foul of reality. This didn't seem to worry Ross unduly. As Lizard Point, the last sight of the coast of England, disappeared astern, he was in high spirits. 'It is not easy to describe the joy and light-heartedness we all felt,' he wrote later, '... bounding before a favourable breeze over the blue waves of the ocean, fairly embarked in the enterprise we had all so long desired to commence, and freed from the anxious and tedious operations of our protracted but requisite preparation.'

James Clark Ross was a serious and experienced mariner, cautious with emotion. He'd been through all this many times before, but nowhere else does he reveal quite as intensely his great relief at being on the move, away from pettifogging civil servants and pompous ceremonies, with sixty men around him and a job to do. He was heading south for the first time – and a long way south: if all worked out, further south than any other ship had been before. The challenge that lay ahead was formidable, but one that he relished. As he swung *Erebus* south-south-west, he was indeed master of all he surveyed.

Life on board ship settled into a time-honoured pattern. The day was divided into four-hour watches marked by the ringing of the ship's bell. Eight bells would be rung at midday, followed by one bell at half-past, two bells at one o'clock, three bells at half-past one, and so on, until eight bells were reached again at four o'clock, when the whole process would begin again. The crew would work four hours on and four hours off, through day and night. The boatswain would stand at the hatches, calling 'All Hands!' as the watches changed, and the men would muster on deck before going off to their various stations.

The days began early. Shortly after four in the morning the cook would light the fires in the galley and start to prepare an early pre-breakfast. This would have been some kind of porridge, which would have been downed with ship's biscuit. The five o'clock watch washed the decks and polished the planks with holystone, whilst others followed up with brooms and buckets, swabbing the decks.

By seven-thirty all hammocks would be stowed, and at eight bells the captain would inspect the work and, if that was approved, the boatswain would pipe for breakfast. (The boatswain's whistle was a vital part of life on board: it served as the equivalent of a modern PA system, with different cadences conveying different orders.) The main meal would be taken at midday and generally comprised something like hardtack biscuit, salt beef, cheese and soup. A grog ration

– a quarter-pint of rum and water for each man – was served with it. At that time, too, if the skies were clear, and with the sun at its highest point above the horizon, measurements would be taken to determine the ship's latitude. Various other tasks filled the rest of the day, including the checking of stores and equipment, sail-handling and the washing of clothes. In the evening more grog would be served, the fiddles would come out and songs would be sung and jigs danced.

The accommodation on the ship was segregated according to rank, with captain's, officers' and warrant officers' cabins towards the stern, and other ranks further forward. The captain's cabin ran the entire width of the ship. At the stern end he would have had five lights – or windows – to look out of, each about 3 feet high with quarter-panes doubled up – one frame on the inside, one on the outside. Fanning out from his quarters were the cabins for individual officers: on the starboard side, next to the captain's bed cabin, was one each for the surgeon and the purser, both about 6 feet by 5 feet 5 inches, with a washbasin in one corner, a table in another and a bed-place with drawers underneath; on the port side were four similar cabins, three occupied by the lieutenants and one by the master. Next to them, running forward, were four single but smaller cabins, accommodating the captain's steward, the steward's pantry, the First Mate and the Second Master. They would have had little more than a seat, a cupboard, a scrap of a table and narrow bed-places. Further forward on the starboard side were small individual cabins for the purser's steward, the gun-room steward and the assistant surgeon (both with bed-places but no washbasins). Next to them, the master gunner, boatswain and carpenter shared a mess room and adjoining communal sleeping quarters, with two bunks and a single bed-space.

Between the rows of cabins was the wardroom, where the officers dined together, served by their own stewards and sometimes joined by the captain. The officers contributed to mess rations out of their own pockets, which ensured that their menu was more varied than that doled out to the rest of the crew. The better-off would have had their own wine and other delicacies. The purser and mates ate separately in their own mess room, also known as the gun-room. A ladderway and main hatch were situated amidships, and beyond them, in the forward third of the ship, was the forecastle, an open area where petty officers, Marines and sailors ate and slept. All except the officers and warrant officers slept in hammocks.

The men would have eaten at tables of four, squeezed either side of the long Sail Bin, where spare sails were stored. They would have used their own seaman's chests both for seating and for storage of their gear.

Beyond the forecastle was the galley and finally, in the bows, the Sick Room. From the plans of the ship, it seems there were only two water-closets with cisterns. These were located at the stern, flanked by two hen coops, and next to the Colour Boxes, where all the various signal flags were kept in neat compartments. There must have been other toilets, but only the captain's and officers' privy is marked.

All in all, there was little room on board and, if you weren't an officer, almost no privacy at all, but this would have been true of any ship, and indeed of many of the homes that the men came from and which they shared with their often-large families. The key to life at sea was regular activity, scrupulous cleanliness, respect for orders and for the officers who gave them. If that broke down, as it famously did with Captain Bligh on the *Bounty*, then there was the risk of mutiny. Which is why the detachment of seven Marines on both ships was so important. There were no Marines on the *Bounty*.

For the most part, however, men on board ship seem to have got on well with one another. A chaplain on HMS *Winchester*, quoted by Brian Lavery, describes how 'One peculiar characteristic of society on shipboard is the tone of hilarity, often kept up to a pitch which might elsewhere appear inconvenient and overstrained', though he adds, 'It would be, however, a great mistake to conclude, from any apparent levity of disposition, that sailors are a peculiarly thoughtless class. On the contrary, few men are more prone to moods and deep and serious reflection.' Constant close proximity on board *Erebus* and *Terror* inevitably caused some tensions, even among the officers. On Christmas Eve 1839, for example, McCormick, his cabin 'having become filled to overflowing with the Government collection of specimens of natural history', got the Second Master to take some of it away and store it in the hold, only to find that First Lieutenant Bird, 'to whom everything connected with science is a bore ... ordered it up again, as having no abiding place there'. But such moments of disagreement were the exception rather than the rule.

Ross was the man in charge, but he was still a servant of the Crown, paid by the government and obliged to follow the most thorough set of instructions ever drawn up by the Admiralty. The precise route was carefully prescribed, determined as it was by the programme of scientific observations that lay at the heart of *Erebus*'s mission. The number-one priority was to visit the locations that would enable measurements of terrestrial magnetism to be taken. After that, there was work to be done making detailed observations of ocean currents, depths of the sea, tides, winds and volcanic activity. Other studies covered such disciplines as meteorology, geology, mineralogy, zoology, vegetable and animal physiology and botany. The one thing the crew were not allowed to do was to engage in the activity for which *Erebus* had originally been built: 'In the event of England being involved in hostilities with any other power during your absence, you are clearly to understand that you are not to commit any hostile act whatever; the expedition under your command being fitted out for the sole purpose of scientific discoveries.'

Erebus had been across the Bay of Biscay before, and this time she seems to have avoided the nightmare weather for which it was famous. 'During our passage across the Bay of Biscay we had no favourable opportunity of determining the height of its waves, as we experienced no violent storm,' Ross noted, rather regretfully. *Terror*, on the other hand, was having a less happy ride, having come close to disaster during the storm that separated the two ships off the Devon coast. According to Sergeant Cunningham's memorandum book, three members of the crew had been pulling in the flying boom – a spar to which extra sail could be attached – when they 'nearly lost their lives in consequence of the violent manner in which she pitched ... flying boom men and all completely under water'. It took four days for *Terror* to catch up with *Erebus* at their first stop – not a good omen for the voyage ahead.

Nevertheless on 20 October, nearly a month after setting out, the two ships reached their first port of call, the island of Madeira, some 550 miles off the African coast. Here various readings were taken, including the measurement of Madeira's highest point, Pico Ruivo. A Lieutenant Wilkes of the United States Exploring Expedition (who, like Ross, was headed for the Antarctic) had recently done his own calculations, and Ross was rather surprised to find that these differed from his own by some 140 feet: 'much greater than we should expect from the perfect and accurate instruments employed on both occasions'. Later in his voyage Ross would have further reason to question information gathered by Wilkes – and would be rather less polite about the lieutenant.

Erebus stayed in the roads of Funchal for ten days, but her crew were far from idle. Her auxiliary boats were constantly being lowered and raised, ferrying provisions in from the town. One was appropriated by Surgeon McCormick, who proceeded to make several exploratory walks around the island with a local man, Mr Muir.

On 31 October the two ships weighed anchor and made for the Canary Islands. Progress was uneventful, though Ross did record that their trawl nets came up with an entirely new species of animalcula, which, he enthused, 'constitute the foundation of marine animal subsistence and by their emitting a phosphorescent light upon disturbance, render the path of the ship through the waters on a dark night surprisingly brilliant'. Their time at Santa Cruz, Tenerife, was similarly unmarked by incident, the highlight arguably being the hoisting on board of 'one live cow', as recorded by Cunningham. But a passing remark he makes about the next island they visited shows that these islands were not havens of peace and tranquillity. Cunningham may have been able to buy 'good wine' and oranges on St Jago, but his note that its inhabitants 'are or have been, slaves' serves as a reminder of how recently this appalling trade had dominated the region. Though the trade in slaves had been illegal in the British Empire since 1807, slavery itself had only been banned in 1833. And at the time *Erebus* and *Terror* visited, the Royal Navy was still patrolling the waters off the West African coast to intercept slaving vessels – a role that must often have been as horrible as warfare. Christopher Lloyd describes in his book *The Navy and the Slave Trade* how one officer, boarding a slave ship in 1821, found her crammed so full below decks that her human cargo was 'clinging to the gratings to inhale a mouthful of fresh air and fighting each other for a taste of water, showing their parched tongues, and pointing to their reduced stomachs as if overcome by famine'.

As *Erebus* and *Terror* approached the Equator, they entered the latitudes between the north-east and south-east trade winds. 'Violent gusts of wind and torrents of rain alternate with calms and light baffling breezes,' observed Ross, 'which, with the suffocating heat of the electrically-charged atmosphere, render this part of the voyage both disagreeable and unhealthy.' If Ross, in his spacious stern cabin, found it uncomfortable, one can only imagine how much worse it must have been below decks, even with the hatches opened.

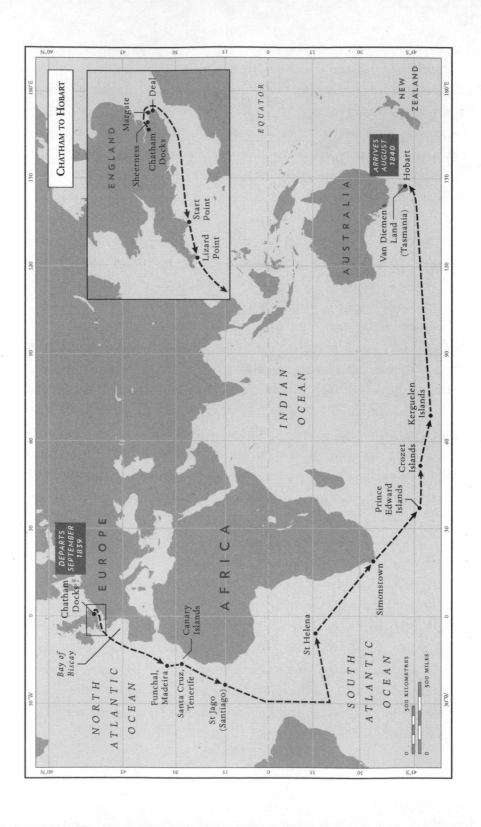

CHATHAM TO HOBART

ENGLAND

Sheerness
Margate
Chatham Docks
Deal

Start Point

Lizard Point

EUROPE

Chatham Docks
DEPARTS SEPTEMBER 1839

NORTH ATLANTIC OCEAN

Bay of Biscay

Funchal, Madeira
Santa Cruz, Tenerife
Canary Islands

St Jago (Santiago)

AFRICA

EQUATOR

INDIAN OCEAN

SOUTH ATLANTIC OCEAN

St Helena

Simonstown

Prince Edward Islands

Crozet Islands

Kerguelen Islands

AUSTRALIA

Van Diemen's Land (Tasmania)

Hobart
ARRIVES AUGUST 1840

NEW ZEALAND

500 KILOMETRES

500 MILES

On 3 December 1839, *Terror* crossed the Equator ahead of *Erebus*. William Cunningham, who had never done this before, was, as a 'greenhorn', subjected to the ritual line-crossing ceremony at the hands of his fellow crewmen, dressed as King Neptune and his attendants, and duly recorded the event in his diary:

> I was sat down on the Barber's chair, and underwent the process of shaving by being lathered with a paint brush – and lather composed of all manner of Nuisance that could be collected in a Ship (not excepting Soil [excrement]). The fire engine was playing on the back of my neck the whole time with its utmost force. After being well scraped with a piece of an iron hoop I was tumbled backwards into a sailfull of water ... and had a good sousing ... after which I have the pleasure of seeing nearly 30 others go through a similar process.

At midday they spliced the main brace (this being the term for a special ration of rum) and 'after Dinner turned the hands up to dance and skylark'.

Their first Christmas away from home was celebrated with traditional enthusiasm. After prayers and a sermon from Captain Ross, thirteen of the officers sat down in the gun-room to a dinner of pea soup, roast turkey and ham, parsnips, plum pudding and pumpkin tart. Two days later they had freshly caught dolphin for breakfast, and five days after that the men of *Erebus* saw out the old decade 'with all hands on deck, stepping out to the fiddle'. Aboard *Terror*, on the stroke of midnight, Captain Crozier sent for the bosun to pipe all hands to splice the main brace, 'and I must say,' wrote Cunningham, 'I never saw a body of men turn out so smartly before'. The fiddler struck up 'Rule, Britannia!' and, with dancing and conviviality lasting until two in the morning, they welcomed in the 1840s: 'all finished with three hearty cheers.'

★★★

The expedition appeared to be going well, but it was also going slowly.

The need for constant comparative observations forced both ships into a meandering, indirect course. They had crossed the Magnetic Equator on 7 December, when Ross had noted with satisfaction that the needle on his Fox dip circle (a device used to measure the angle between the horizon and the earth's magnetic field) was perfectly horizontal. He had seen it point directly upwards at the North Magnetic Pole and, assuming the expedition was successful, would witness it point straight down when they reached the South Magnetic Pole. Now, observations indicated that they were on or around the line of least intensity: the magnetic doldrums. And because Ross was keen to explore this phenomenon, he continued on a zigzag course, constantly criss-crossing the line. Eventually, though, to the relief of the sailors, if not the scientists, they made landfall at the island of St Helena on 31 January 1840.

This was the open prison to which Napoleon had been brought after his defeat at Waterloo. Mindful that he had already escaped from one island, Elba, it had been considered that this speck in the middle of the Atlantic was about as safe a place of confinement as anywhere in the world. And, sure enough, this was where he had died, less than twenty years earlier.

McCormick, ever the one for excursions, secured a horse and trotted up the mountain to see where Napoleon had spent his last days. The great French emperor had been reduced to living at incongruous addresses with names like 'The Briars', before finally settling in the rather grander Longwood House. McCormick, to his evident distress, found Longwood rundown and abandoned. 'Napoleon's billiard room is now filled with bearded wheat,' he sadly recorded in his journal. In what had been Napoleon's sitting room he found a threshing machine. He continued on through the dilapidated house, displaying awe and a certain sense of regret. 'This apartment opens into the bedroom, under the second window of which the great Napoleon's head rested when he took his last breath on earth.' One can almost sense his voice falling to a whisper. The next day he visited Napoleon's tomb, around which ducks were 'irreverently waddling'.

For Joseph Hooker, meanwhile, *Erebus* was proving a good home. 'I am very happy and comfortable here,' he wrote to his father. 'Not very idle.' Because they shared a similar interest in the sciences, Hooker got on well with Ross. The captain had given him space in his cabin for his plants, and 'one of the tables under the stern window is wholly mine'. A letter to his sisters offers an intimate glimpse of their relationship. 'Almost every day I draw, sometimes all day long and till two or three in the morning, the Captain directing me. He sits at one side of the table, writing and figuring at night, and I, on the other, drawing.' Ross had ordered nets to be hung overboard to collect sea creatures – another plus for Hooker. 'McCormick pays no attention to them, so they are therefore brought at once to me.' Hooker's one regret was that the expedition was progressing so slowly. Perhaps not surprisingly, he didn't blame Ross's obsession with following magnetic lines for this. Instead he criticised the *Erebus*'s sister ship: 'The *Terror* has been a sad drawback to us, having every now and then to shorten sail for her [to allow her to catch up].'

Terror certainly seems to have been the more relaxed and less cerebral of the two ships at this time. In his diary, Cunningham notes the high point of the day: 'Killed a Bullock in the afternoon and the offal which was throwed overboard attracted a Shark which we caught about 10 PM with a hook and a bait of the Bullock's tripe. He made great resistance on being hauled inboard. He was of the blue specie and measured 9 feet 5 inches.' The next day he noted, 'Dissected Mr Jack Shark . . . and every man on board had a splendid Blow out [feast] of his carcase; his flesh was white as milk and not the least rank.' Next day the weather was 'extremely fine going free . . . Eat the last of the Shark for supper.'

By 26 February they had slowed down yet again, but Cunningham seemed unconcerned. 'The latter part of the day becalmed,' he wrote. 'Felt particularly cheerful – can't account for it.'

There was great excitement aboard *Erebus* on 6 March, when, hove-to for one of their routine sea-depth measurements, the weighted line dropped a full 16,000 feet, the greatest depth recorded on the journey thus far. As they drew closer to the Cape, Ross's journal records frequent sightings of albatross, one of the largest of all sea-birds, with up to 10-foot wingspans and capable of speeds of 50 miles an hour. The settled weather conditions began to change. On 11 March the fog was so dense that *Terror* had to fire one of her cannons to ascertain the position of *Erebus*. She fired back, but later, in a very heavy swell, which Cunningham thought 'the heaviest since we have been at sea', the two ships were separated once again. *Terror* was not the laggard this time. She arrived at Simonstown on the Cape of Good Hope a full twenty-four hours before *Erebus*.

McCormick was on deck at dawn on Friday the 13th and described his excitement at seeing Table Mountain as only a geologist could. 'At 5.40 a.m. I saw Table Mountain on the port bow ... The horizontal stratification of the white silicious sandstone forming the summit of the hills above their granite base is seen to great advantage from the sea.' Fit that on a postcard.

Simonstown naval base, originally built by the Dutch, but taken over by the British in the 1790s, lay on the western shore of Simon's Bay, a few miles south of Cape Town. As soon as they had settled in the bay, Ross began organising the construction of a magnetic observatory, whilst McCormick went off to climb the horizontal stratification of white siliceous sandstone and visit the Constantia vineyards. Joseph Hooker wrote to his father of the relationship between the two surgeons. 'McCormick and I are exceedingly good friends and no jealousy exists ... He takes no interest but in bird shooting and rock collecting. I am nolens volens [willingly or unwillingly] the Naturalist for which I enjoy no other advantage than the Captain's cabin, and I think myself amply repaid.'

Marine Sergeant Cunningham was meanwhile having trouble with a perennial naval problem: deserters. Able seamen Coleston and Wallace had absconded, before being found and brought back by a constable (the two men turned out to be serial deserters, jumping ship again in Hobart a few months later). Despite the rigours of the voyage, very few men jumped ship in the four years they were away. This could have been because they were well looked after and comparatively well paid. But then desertion rates generally reflected the agreeableness of the location. In 1825 Captain Beechey in HMS *Blossom* recorded fourteen of the crew deserting at Rio de Janeiro. There would certainly have been few incentives to jump ship in Antarctica.

Cunningham did get some time off, however. On the last day of March he went ashore to enjoy himself. 'Beer ... was served out at the rate on one quart [two pints] per "biped" which was said to disorder some of the people's attics.' Of all the euphemisms for drunkenness, I think 'disordering the attic' one of the most poetic.

On 6 April 1840, after a three-week stay, the expedition left Simonstown. Not a moment too soon, if Cunningham's diary is anything to go by. Three days after the beer and the shore leave, three 'very large' bullocks had been brought aboard. One of them had run amok, goring a Mr Evans in the thigh. That same evening, perhaps not coincidentally, Cunningham reported 'a very troublesome first Watch on account of several of the Boat's crew getting Drunk'. Time to go.

They headed out of the harbour towards the open sea, passing HMS *Melville*, the flagship of Admiral Elliot, commander-in-chief of the Simonstown Station, whose crew climbed the rigging to give them three cheers as they sailed by. Nature wasn't as friendly. A west wind came on so hard that *Terror* was left behind and had to be towed out of the harbour. By the time she reached open ocean, she'd lost sight of *Erebus*. Despite firing rockets and burning blue lights all night, she received no response from her sister ship.

The hostile conditions were familiar to mariners off the South African coast. The Indian and Atlantic Ocean currents meet here, above a 200-mile extension of the continental shelf known as the Agulhas Bank, creating what Ross described as 'a harassing jobble of a sea. Winds blowing from almost every point of the compass.' To avoid it, he took *Erebus* southwards, leaving behind two of their precious sea thermometers, which had been torn off their mooring lines. Ahead of them lay a long haul east to Tasmania, or Van Diemen's Land, as it was still officially known: more than 6,000 miles across some of the stormiest seas in the world, already known then, by their latitude, as the Roaring Forties.

Fierce, persistent westerlies blew relentlessly across the Southern Ocean, with no land masses to break them. The combination of strong following winds and massive swells was a mixed blessing. It enabled the *Cutty Sark* to cut the time between London and Sydney to less than eighty days, but could prove treacherous, too. For Ross, the challenges were rather different. His scientific and surveying agenda meant that rather than race ahead of the wind, he had to keep turning against it to investigate islands on the way. It was not always possible. They only had time to glimpse the shores of the Prince Edward Islands, on which McCormick registered his astonishment at seeing a cove 'literally enamelled with penguins', before a shrieking storm had blown them past with no chance of a landing.

The sheer power of the elements surprised even someone as well travelled as *Erebus*'s captain. At one point Ross experienced 'the heaviest rain I ever witnessed ... thunder and the most vivid lightning occurred during this great fall of water, which lasted without intermission for more than ten hours'.

The strength of the ship and the skill of her crew were put to their fiercest test so far as the wind, now blowing at Force 10, kept changing direction, veering so violently that 'we spent the night in great anxiety, and in momentary expectation that our boats would be washed away by some of the broken waves that fell on board, or that from the frequent shocks the ship sustained ... we should lose some of the masts'.

It seems astonishing that there should be anyone living in these storm-tossed latitudes, but there were, and Ross had been asked to take provisions to some of them: a group of eleven elephant-seal hunters, stranded on Possession Island in the Crozet archipelago. The wind looked likely to blow *Erebus* past the island, but with considerable effort Ross managed to turn about and beat up to the west. Unable to get a boat to shore, they anchored a little way off, and six of the sealers came out to meet them. Ross wasn't impressed. 'They looked more like Esquimaux than civilized beings ... Their clothes were literally soaked in oil and smelt most offensive.' McCormick was less judgemental. He described Mr Hickley, the spokesman for the beleaguered sealers, as 'their manly-looking leader who was an ideal "Robinson Crusoe" in costume'. To young Hooker, Hickley was rather splendid, 'like some African Prince, pre-eminently filthy, and withal a most independent gentleman'. They left the sealers with a chest of tea, bags of coffee and a letter from their employer, which, McCormick noted, 'seemed to disappoint the leader of the party ... who evidently had been anticipating a ship for their removal, instead of fresh supplies'.

Ross, mindful of his instructions from the Admiralty, continued on to their next, official destination. Once again, magnetic observation was the prime reason for the choice. 'It is probable that Kerguelen Island will be found well-suited to that purpose,' the Lords of the Admiralty had laid down. It certainly wasn't well suited for much else. First discovered by a Frenchman, Yves-Joseph de Kerguelen-Tremarec, in 1772, the Kerguelens are definitively remote: according to the opening sentence on one travel website I looked at, they are 'located 2,051 miles away from any sort of civilization' (it's the 'any sort' I find so tantalising). They are also covered with glaciers, and far south enough for Ross to have recorded the expedition's first sighting of Antarctic ice. Not surprisingly, Captain Cook christened Kerguelen the 'Island of Desolation'.

As *Erebus* approached this bleak fortress, McCormick's journal entry for 8 May 1840 tells the sad story of the demise of one of the smallest of her crew, Old Tom, a cock brought out from England with a hen, for the purpose of colonising the island they had now reached – the establishment of new species on remote islands being one of the aims of the mission. 'Tom ... died today,' he wrote, 'in the very sight of his intended domain; had his body committed to the deep by the captain's steward – a sailor's grave.'

Better news came with a cry from the crow's nest as they were beating up towards Kerguelen's Arched Rock to make a landing. The sails of HMS *Terror* had been spotted, the first sight of her for a month. But such was the power of a heavy rolling sea that it took three days for *Erebus*, after a series of twenty-two tight tacks, to gain the harbour mouth, and a further day before *Terror* joined her. It then took another two days for both vessels to warp their way to the head of the harbour, where they were able to drop anchor and get boats ashore with building materials for an observatory.

Certain days had been decreed by the international community as simultaneous magnetic-measurement days, or term days. Ross was scrupulous in making sure that wherever he was, he had instruments ready to record the magnetic activity in that place at the same time as others elsewhere on the globe were noting their findings. This required secure solid housings for the measuring equipment. Two observatories, one for magnetic and the other for astronomical observations, were therefore set up on the beach in Christmas Harbour in time for the term days of 29 and 30 May. There was much excitement when the results were coordinated later. Activity detected on Kerguelen was found to be remarkably similar to that observed and measured in Toronto, around the same latitude, but at the other end of the earth.

Joseph Hooker was excited by the challenges of Kerguelen Island for rather different reasons. Captain Cook's expedition had identified only eighteen plant species, but Hooker found at least thirty in one day. Even when he couldn't get out, he turned the constant buffeting of the gales to his advantage. 'Could I but tell you the delight with which I spent the days when I was kept on board by foul winds ... In spite of the rolling of the ship I have made drawings for you all,' he wrote home. The great excitement was finding the wonder-vegetable *Pringlea antiscorbutica*, a cabbage that grew on Kerguelen Island and which had been identified by Captain Cook's botanist, Mr Anderson, as a miracle food for sailors. With a horseradish-tasting root and leaves that resembled mustard and cress, it had such powerful anti-scorbutic properties that it had been served for 130 days on Cook's expedition, during which time no sickness had been recorded. Ross's expedition put the wonder-cabbage to use straight away, and to general approval. Cunningham was one of those who registered enjoyment. 'Like[d] the taste of the wild cabbage much.'

On 24 May 1840, they celebrated the twenty-first birthday of Queen Victoria with the firing of a royal salute, servings of plum pudding, preserved meat and a double allowance of rum at night. The very next day they were forcibly reminded of just how far away they were from an English summer, as falling snow was whipped into a ferocious blizzard. As darkness fell, Cunningham wrote of 'a complete hurricane' blowing. 'I never heard it blow so hard as it has done this night.'

Surgeon McCormick shared Hooker's enthusiasm for Kerguelen Island, but more from a geological perspective. 'This, and Spitzbergen in the opposite hemisphere constitute, I think, the most striking and picturesque lands I've ever had the good fortune to visit,' he noted enthusiastically in his journal. And this despite the fact that 'neither the Arctic nor Antarctic isles have tree or shrub ... to enliven them'. What excited McCormick was not what was to be found now on the black basalt rocks of this lonely island, but what had been there thousands of years before. 'Whole forests...of fossilized wood lie entombed here beneath vast lava streams,' he marvelled, uncovering beneath the debris a fossilised tree trunk with a girth of 7 feet. He was exercised by the whole question of how to explain this phenomenon. Back in England, he had been fascinated to find corals and other forms of tropical life embedded in the limestone of north Devon. Now he was equally intrigued to discover forests of coniferous trees entombed on the now-treeless island of Kerguelen. 'I have wondered how they could ever have existed there.' It was another seventy years before Alfred Wegener made the audacious suggestion that the continents themselves might have moved over time, and another fifty years after that before the theory of plate tectonics was finally proven.

So far as the wildlife of the island was concerned, McCormick seems to have regarded it principally as a form of target practice. It's impossible to turn a page of his extensive journals without marvelling, or perhaps despairing, at his appetite for admiring God's creatures, then shooting them. On 15 May he identifies the chioni, or sheathbill, a 'singular and beautiful bird ... so fearless and confiding, [it] seems peculiar to the island to which its presence gives a charm and animation, especially to a lover of the feathered race like myself'. This is followed next day by the succinct entry, 'I shot my first chioni.' A week later, accompanying Captain Ross and an exploring party, he 'shot two and a half brace of teal and tern and returned ... at five p.m.' The day after that, 'I shot a gigantic petrel ... and a young black-backed gull flying overhead.' On the 30th, 'I went on shore about noon, shot a black-backed gull from the dinghy, and a shag at the landing place.' And he wasn't finished for the day. On his way back to the ship, after calling on Captain Ross at the observatory, he 'shot two chionis, two gigantic petrel, two shags, and a teal flying round the point'.

McCormick liked a challenge, but in the course of one onshore expedition his adventurous spirit nearly lost him his life. Having been on a mineralogical foray and having packed his haversack with 'some of the finest specimens of quartz crystals ... weighing in all some fifty pounds', he found himself, as night fell, cut off by torrential waterfalls. He abandoned the haversack, and eventually made his way to the bottom of a cliff before realising that he wouldn't be able to get to the ship from there. 'The darkness of the night,' he recalled a little later, 'only relieved by the fitful glare from the white, foaming spray the torrents sent upwards, the terrific gusts of wind, accompanied by a deluge of rain, combined together with black, overhanging, frowning precipices, to form a scene of the wildest description.' When he did finally make his way back to the ship, he was fed tea with, perhaps appropriately, some stewed chionis on the side, which 'our thoughtful, kind-hearted boat's crew had caught in my absence'.

Activity was the key to survival on any closely packed ship, but particularly in these wild and inhospitable places, where it must have been only too easy to lose any sense of purpose. Captain Ross always made sure there was work to do, building and operating the observatories. Of course from a personal point of view, the scientific imperative of the expedition – whether it was in natural history, zoology, botany or geology – was clearly something that motivated and excited him as much as it did the likes of McCormick and Hooker.

To know how the ordinary seaman responded, we have only Sergeant Cunningham's diaries to go by. They convey a pretty miserable portrait of men doing their best in dreadful conditions. Gales blow on forty-five of the sixty-eight days they spend in the Kerguelens. Wind, rain and snow rake the harbour as they struggle to get equipment ashore and back. The nearest Sergeant Cunningham comes even to recording contentment is a day on which he shoots and cooks several shag. These, he notes, prove 'capital eating'. Otherwise his diary entry for Sunday 19 July can stand for most of the others: 'high and bitter cold: Divine service in the forenoon. I may put this down as another of those miserable Sundays a man spends in a ship of this description.'

At least it was to be his last Sunday in the Kerguelen Islands, for the next morning, 20 July, after days of being blown back by the winds, *Erebus* and *Terror* finally extricated themselves from what Ross described as 'this most dreary and disagreeable harbour'. Joseph Hooker tried, rather unconvincingly, to look on the bright side. 'I was sorry at leaving Christmas Harbour: by finding food for the mind one may grow attached to the most wretched spots on the globe.' Not one for the Tourist Board.

Today, the Kerguelen Islands are part of the French Southern and Antarctic Lands, and can only be reached by a ship from the island of Réunion, which sails four times a year. The sole year-round occupants are scientists. *Plus ça change.*

Christmas Harbour might have been dreary and disagreeable for the crew of *Terror* and *Erebus*, but at least it had provided some shelter. Now back in the open ocean, they were once again exposed to the full force of the Roaring Forties. A series of deep depressions rolled in day after day and, with icebergs looming on the horizon and fifteen hours of darkness through which to navigate, enormous pressure was put on the master and quartermaster to hold them on course.

In the driving rain and the unremitting turbulence, it was not long before *Terror* once again disappeared from sight. The disparities between the two ships still rankled with Ross. He rather testily records having to keep *Erebus* under moderate sail whilst he searched for her older sister ship, 'to our great inconvenience, the ship rolling heavily in consequence of not having sufficient sail to steady her'. Eventually he gave up and *Erebus* carried on alone.

Ironically, it was on one of the few fine days that the worst happened.

The crew were busy mopping up and men were in the rigging spreading the sails out to dry, when the boatswain, Mr Roberts, was struck by a swinging staysail sheet and, as an eyewitness remembered, 'whirled overboard'. A lifebuoy and various oars were immediately flung out to him, but the ship was making six knots at the time and he slipped quickly astern. Two cutters were lowered into the sea, but as they'd had to be tightly lashed down against the storms, precious time was lost in launching them. The whole tragedy was witnessed by Surgeon McCormick, who was walking the quarterdeck at the time. 'The last I saw of him was as he rose on the top of a wave, where a gigantic petrel or two were whirling over his head and might have struck him with their powerful wings or no less powerful beak, for he disappeared all at once between two seas.'

One of the rescue cutters was hit by a cross-wave and four of her crew were thrown into the water. It is unlikely any of them could swim, there being a superstition among sailors that learning to swim was bad luck – an admission that things could go wrong. The rescue attempt could therefore have led to a multiple drowning, had it not been for the sharp reactions of Mr Oakley, the Mate on *Erebus*, and Mr Abernethy, the gunner, in the other, returning boat. They immediately pushed back from the ship and managed to pluck all four men out of the rolling sea, 'completely benumbed and stupefied by the cold'. The now-overloaded cutter ran alongside the ship for some time, taking on more and more water before it was finally plucked aboard.

Roberts's cap was recovered, but that was all. The boatswain is so central to the life of a ship that his demise must have been a shock to everyone. His piping and shout of 'All Hands!' would have been as common a sound as the ship's bell. The expedition had sustained its first loss of life, just short of the first anniversary of its launch.

On 12 August they caught a glimpse of a cloud-shrouded coast line. Charts and sextant readings told them they were off the south-westerly point of New Holland (what is now Western Australia). This must have raised hopes that the worst was over, but the most destructive storm of all was still to come. The very next day it struck with more fury than any they had yet experienced. The ship was engulfed and the wind blew with such demonic intensity that the main topsail was ripped to shreds and the staysail wrenched off, leaving only the bare pole from which it once hung. 'One vast, swelling green mountain of a sea came rolling up astern,' McCormick recalled, 'threatening to engulf us, sweeping over the starboard quarter-boat, in upon the quarter-deck which it deluged, drenching me to the skin, as I clung to the mizzen-mast catching hold of some gear to avoid being washed overboard.' His graphic account continues with a memorable description of his skipper, roped in place on the deck, defying the elements, evoking Captain Ahab in *Moby-Dick*: 'Captain Ross maintained his position on the weather quarter by having three turns of the mizzen topsail halyards round him for support.' The heavy seas persisted, and although the wind abated, the hatches had to remain battened down the whole of the next day, 'with lighted candles in the gunroom' to dispel the gloom below decks.

On the night of 16 August, under a bright full moon, Ross records, with what can only have been almighty relief, 'we saw the land of Tasmania ahead of us'.

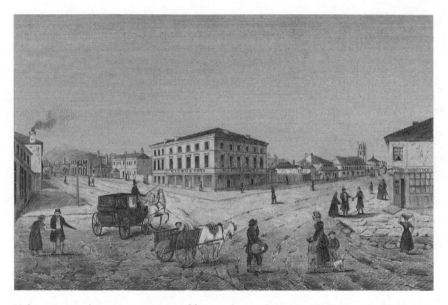

Hobart in 1840, home to a mixture of free settlers and convicts. *Erebus*'s arrival in August of that year caused huge excitement locally.

CHAPTER 5

'OUR SOUTHERN HOME'

In 2004, on a visit to Tasmania, I read Matthew Kneale's book *English Passengers*. Though there is dark humour and fine description in the story of a mid-nineteenth-century emigrant to Tasmania, it is also a powerful indictment of the rigidity and cruelty of Victorian imperial certainties – the same certainties that motivated Barrow and Ross and Sabine and Minto, and Melville and von Humboldt and Herschel, and all the great men who dominate the life and times of HMS *Erebus*. These were men of intelligence and intellectual curiosity, stimulated by the spirit of the Enlightenment to search and discover, to push back the boundaries of knowledge, convinced that the more they measured and traced and calculated and recorded, the more beneficial it would be for mankind. But this sense of purpose also contained within it an implicit sense of superiority, which, when misused, fed the dark side of Britain's increasing self-confidence. And nowhere was the light and shade of Victorian Britain more sharply defined than in the self-governing colony on whose shores HMS *Erebus* arrived more than three months after leaving Cape Town. Van Diemen's Land had a population of 43,000; and 14,000 of them were convicts.

On board HMS *Erebus* as she made her way up Storm Bay, past the Iron Pot Lighthouse and into the shelter of the Derwent estuary, were men who had distinguished themselves on many journeys and in many fields, who had mastered the art of sailing ships through the fiercest waters on the planet, and who carried with them cases – and, indeed, cabins – full of scientific evidence. On land were many thousands of men and women who had been forcibly removed from their home country because they were judged to be born criminals, morally unsalvageable, incapable of rehabilitation. Thomas Arnold, the famous headmaster of Rugby School, embodied this unforgiving attitude and expressed it uncompromisingly in one of his letters: 'If they will colonize with convicts, I am satisfied that the stain should last, not only for one whole life, but for more than one generation; that no convict or convict's child should ever be a free citizen ... It is the law of God's Providence which we cannot alter, that the sins of the father are really visited upon the child in the corruption of his breed.' The recipient of this letter was now the Lieutenant-Governor of Van Diemen's Land, Sir John Franklin.

As *Erebus* sailed towards Hobart harbour in mid-August 1840, her captain expressed his relief, contrasting 'the rich and beautiful scenery on both sides of the expansive and placid waters of the Derwent' with 'the desolate land and turbulent ocean we had so recently left'. McCormick, too, saw only a pleasing prospect: 'The approach to Hobart Town is very picturesque.' Sergeant Cunningham's reflections, on the other hand, hit a rather different note: 'This being Van Dieman's [*sic*] Land, I could not help thinking ... how many unfortunate beings has seen it ... with a full heart and a melancholy boding that they were to terminate their existence in it, outcasts from Society and aliens from their fatherland, separated from wives, parents, friends and from every tie that links man to this vain and sublunary world. I turned from the scene with a thankfull remembrance how much better off I was than some thousands of my fellow men.'

The debate as to whether the place they had landed in should be called Van Diemen's Land or Tasmania was officially settled in Tasmania's favour fifteen years later, in 1855. But there had been an earlier name: Lutruwita, which was the name by which the Aboriginal inhabitants knew the island, and had done for a thousand years or more. It was now redundant. As the convicts were brought in, the indigenous population was booted out. By the time the Ross expedition arrived, the brutal process of clearing the original inhabitants from their land was almost complete. Those who were left alive were confined to an Aboriginal mission on Flinders Island, off the north coast, where they were taught English ways.

The educated people of Hobart – those familiar with English ways – would have heard of the Antarctic expedition long before it arrived. The local newspapers had been following its preparations with great interest. It would, after all, be one of the boldest and most prestigious undertakings they had witnessed since the colony had been officially established, sixteen years earlier. There had been almost daily speculation about the expedition's aims – finding the South Magnetic Pole, discovering a new continent, penetrating further south than anyone had been before – and their chances of achieving them. *The Hobart Town Courier* went into wondrous detail about the state-of-the-art instruments on board the two ships, not least the walking sticks hollowed out so as to carry nets for catching insects. 'The ferrule at the bottom is removed, and the nets are drawn forth ready for instant use,' it marvelled.

Now it had all come true. The expedition was here.

Erebus moored up at five in the afternoon of Monday 17 August. *Terror* was already safely anchored, and Captain Crozier and the officers came aboard to welcome their sister ship, and to bring letters from home that had been awaiting their arrival. Not one to waste a moment, Surgeon McCormick took some of his fellow officers out to celebrate their arrival by going ashore for the last night of a play called *Rory O'More* at the Theatre Royal. Rory O'More was an Irish Catholic hero, a persistent rebel against the English, who put a price of £1,000 on his head. His head was duly delivered and displayed at Dublin Castle to deter other rebels.

For Joseph Hooker, landfall had brought little cause for celebration. A letter from his father, edged in black, informed him of the death of his elder brother from yellow fever, whilst on missionary work in the West Indies.

Few people could have been happier to see the two embattled vessels safely moored in the Derwent estuary than the Lieutenant-Governor of Van Diemen's Land. Sir John Franklin was overjoyed at being reunited with his friend and fellow explorer, James Clark Ross. They made a contrasting pair. Franklin, fourteen years older, was short, at 5 feet 6 inches, and famously affable, whereas Ross was tall and dashing and took himself rather seriously. In a movie he could have been played by Errol Flynn, himself a Tasmanian.

'In 1836,' writes his biographer, Andrew Lambert, 'Franklin was fifty, famous and fat.' And he was in Van Diemen's Land because there had been nothing better on offer. Advancement in the Royal Navy followed a strict rota system, which ensured that senior positions only became available after those who held them died. Fame and success could not leapfrog anyone into promotion. So Captain Franklin had looked around for other positions concomitant with his talents, his experience and his evangelical sense of mission.

Having been offered, and turned down, the governorship of Antigua, he accepted the more lucrative position of Lieutenant-Governor of Van Diemen's Land, largely because he felt it his duty to put his talents, achievements and wide experience in the service of the great new colonial initiative, and because his forceful second wife, Jane – a vigorous, sociable woman, with considerable networking skills – felt it to be a very useful rung on the social and political ladder, which she was determined to help him climb.

But things had not gone according to plan. Sir John's request that the flow of convicts to Van Diemen's Land should be stemmed, if there was to be any chance of achieving some improvement in the lot of the free islanders, was ignored by the Colonial Office, whose response was to increase the numbers. When New South Wales was granted self-government, its share of the transported convicts was diverted southwards. In 1842 alone, 5,663 convicts arrived in Van Diemen's Land.

To make matters worse, Sir John was no politician, and although popular with most of the islanders, found himself in the uncomfortable position of having to please the Colonial Office by saving money, and the colonists by spending it. In theory, much of the political burden should have been carried by John Montagu, a very capable, shrewd and ambitious public servant who had served in Van Diemen's Land for some years, but that role was increasingly usurped by Jane, who, with the advantage of having her husband's ear, proceeded to implement what she thought was right for the colony. This included diverting government funds to her own pet projects, such as a college for boys to train in the Christian faith; convict education; and various art projects. Her interference made a bitter enemy of Montagu and his supporters, who described her as a 'man in petticoats'. As the geographer Frank Debenham says, it must have been a 'great strain' for Sir John and Lady Franklin 'to govern a community of which one part was tasting the freedom and independence characteristic of a pioneer settlement and the other part was bound and shackled by a penal system of extreme severity'. But making an adversary of John Montagu was a mistake that was to have profound consequences for both Jane and her husband.

Jane Franklin found Hobart short of men of consequence. Sir John was simply missing his own kind. As a letter from Jane to her father makes abundantly clear, the Franklins could hardly wait to throw open the door of Government House for the glamorous Captain Ross and his intrepid officers: 'The arrival of Captains Ross and Crozier added much to Sir John's happiness . . . ,' she wrote. 'They all feel towards one another as friends and brothers and it is the remark of people here that Sir John appears to them in quite a new light, so bustling and frisky and merry with his new companions.' Lady Franklin was taken aboard *Erebus* and couldn't help noticing that Captain Ross had Negelin's portrait of her husband hanging in his cabin (it's one of the best: Franklin is in uniform, smiling jovially, with epaulettes like small waterfalls on each shoulder). Back on dry land, she showed indefatigable interest in all aspects of the expedition, inviting both senior and junior officers to attend the local Science Society, in which she was much involved and where she would quiz them about their work. Of course, given that ladies were present, certain proprieties had to be observed: on one occasion she noted that when 'some drawings and descriptions of the position of the young in the pouch of some marsupial animals' were shown, it was necessary that 'the gentlemen withdrew to the library' to inspect them.

Not that the ladies of Hobart were exactly prudish. The contemporary Tasmanian historian Alison Alexander describes how the local rumour mill sought to account for the childlessness of their governor and his wife, leading to some forthright gossip during a meal at which Jane and John Franklin were clearly not present. 'The ladies when they retired ... were wondering why Sir John had no family. "Dear me," said one of them ... "don't you know! I always heard his members got frostbitten when he went to the North pole".'

Captain Ross, though top of many guest lists, was not one to fritter time away, and made it clear that his most urgent priority was to get an observatory up and running. The Franklins, keen to oblige, had anticipated this and had already assembled stores and materials, from plans sent out from England. The next morning Ross and Franklin selected a suitable spot. A small quarry-working near Government House had revealed a deep bed of sandstone rock, which Ross judged to be the perfect base for the observatory, as sandstone has no magnetic properties

Joseph Banks, friend of Captain Cook and champion of polar exploration.

John Barrow, Second Secretary to the Admiralty and polar enthusiast.

John Ross, prickly and impulsive Arctic pioneer.

'Passage through the ice', from John Ross's *A Voyage of Discovery* (1819).

A scale model (1:40) of *Erebus*, as she was in 1826.

James Clark Ross, 'the handsomest man
in the navy'

Robert McCormick, *Erebus*'s surgeon and bird dispatcher.

Francis Crozier, 'better suited for a second than a first'.

Christmas Harbour, Kerguelen Islands, painted by John Davis, Second Master on *Terror*.

Right: The wonder cabbage *Pringlea antiscorbutica*, which Joseph Hooker found in the Kerguelen Islands. An engraving from his *The Botany of the Antarctic Voyage* (1844).

Below: The Adélie penguin, as depicted in *The Zoology of the Voyage of HMS Erebus & Terror* (1844–75). Penguin featured on the menu a number of times during Ross's Antarctic expeditions.

Pringlea antiscorbutica, *Hook fil*

EUDYPTES ADELIÆ *(Homb. & Jacq.)*

The Rossbank Observatory, Hobart: a painting by the convict artist Thomas Bock, based on an original sketch by John Davis. In the centre are (from left to right) John Franklin, James Ross and Francis Crozier.

Left: A page from Joseph Hooker's Antarctic journal, with his watercolour of an iceberg.

Below: A chronometer used on *Erebus*.

'Part of the South Polar Barrier', 2 February 1841,
a watercolour by *Terror*'s John Davis.

'Bringing in the year 1842', by John Davis.

'HMS *Erebus* passing through the chain of bergs', 13 March 1842,
by John Davis.

Jane Franklin, aged 24.

John Franklin, aged 42.

Right: Eleanor Franklin's invitation to the *Erebus* and *Terror* ball.

Below: Erebus and *Terror* in New Zealand, August 1841, as imagined by the marine painter John Wilson Carmichael a few years later.

that might interfere with the readings. That very afternoon a party of 200 convicts was set to work to dig the foundations.

Erebus and *Terror*, meanwhile, were moved upriver to a small, quiet cove away from the main bustle of the harbour and conveniently close to the grounds of Government House. It was later given the name Ross Cove, and it hasn't changed much.

I'm there in 2017. It's June, a couple of months before *Erebus* and *Terror* would have been in port, and I'm spending several days in Hobart, staying at the Henry Jones Art Hotel, one of a row of low and harmonious nineteenth-century buildings beside the harbour, with stone-dressed walls and low-pitched red roofs. Set back from the water, the façades look attractive in scale and colour, almost Venetian in the low morning sunlight. The remains of chunky painted lettering on the wall read: 'H Jones and Co Pty Ltd. IXL Jams'. This was once the factory for one of Hobart's most successful export businesses. The 'IXL' trademark was a play on founder Henry Jones's motto, 'I excel at everything.'

And the business lived up to the motto. Tinned fruits from Tasmania were sent all over the world, exuberantly described and brightly labelled: Choice Cling Peaches, Sliced in Heavy Syrup; Boomerang Brand, Tasmanian Fancy Apples. It was Britain joining the European Union and abandoning Commonwealth trade preferences that did for H. Jones, and the company no longer exists.

To get to Ross Cove, I walk a half-mile or so by the side of the busy Tasman Highway that links Hobart with the airport. I have to stop and get my camera out to take a shot of some eye-catching street art – two functional junction boxes painted in riotously colourful designs, featuring penguins and seals and albatrosses and long-haired vampy ladies. Antarctic chic. Art is booming in Hobart, stimulated by the huge success of MONA, the Museum of Old and New Art, displayed in multi-level caves dramatically excavated out of the cliffs a few miles up the Derwent.

Peeling off the main road, I cross a car park and scramble down towards a stretch of railway line running parallel with the water. My companion, Alison Alexander, fount of all knowledge on the history of Tasmania, and clutching her handbag, beckons me to follow her onto the track. It's not used that often, she assures me, as she holds back a wire fence for me to squeeze through. A little way down the railway line, we turn off and cut through a small grove of newly planted trees to the waterside. 'This is Ross Cove,' Alison tells me. 'They chose to moor up here because' – she turns and points up to a flagpole on some turreted rooftops, which I can just see peeking over the trees – 'it was the closest they could get to Government House. For unloading everything.' And for getting Ross and Crozier to their dinners, no doubt.

I stand for a while at the water's edge, trying to coax my imagination back 177 years. Nothing has been built here in all that time, which surprises me, given its proximity to the centre of Hobart, and how the city seems to be thriving and expanding. The beach, a thin strip of loose stones between the river and the grass, must have been much the same when the ship's cutters rode up against it, as they ferried materials to and from the ships out on the water. Behind me, the long protective ridge of Mount Wellington, rising more than 4,000 feet to the west of the city, would have been the same dominating landmark. The main harbour is a half-mile away. Stretching down to the water are the sheds, jetties and a newly built complex containing an upmarket hotel and a big new cruise-ship terminal. In the 1840s there would have been much more activity. Ships bringing convicts and hopeful settlers in, and taking wheat and wool out. Fishing boats and whalers, too, for these were plentiful waters for southern right whales, which were caught and killed here in their thousands. How times have changed. Tasmanians now pride themselves on being protectors of the environment, and would no more kill a whale than raise an oil well in the estuary.

The ships that ply the Derwent these days are more likely to be the catamaran ferries taking people to and from MONA, or cruise liners on their way around the world. And, of course, ships on their way south. Hobart is Australia's gateway to the Antarctic, and as I walk around the quayside on the night I arrive, I linger beneath the broad rust-red bows of a contemporary Antarctic explorer, the ice-breaker and survey ship *Aurora Australis*, into which *Erebus* could fit three times over. She is drawn up at a jetty, looking tired and travel-worn. I later learn that she has just this month been retired from active duty.

A short way up the slope behind Ross Cove is the rather magnificent Government House, which dates from 1856. In its predecessor, Jane Franklin held her famous dinner parties. She never tired of showing off Captain Ross, though not always uncritically. Writing to her friend Mrs Simpkinson, she enthused: 'Captain Ross has the wildest bushy grey head!', but qualified this with a note of disappointment, 'He looks much older than when I saw him last.' She was never afraid to speak her mind. At another of her gatherings at which Ross was present, she was similarly disparaging about the artistic gifts of a local guest, a Captain Cheyne, 'who,' she noted, 'did not escape me with his frightful drawings of Govt. House'.

At that same gathering, over the brandy, Ross explained to them all the importance of his magnetic observatory, one of a chain of eighteen to be set up in different parts of the world. He went out of his way to compliment the Admiralty on their preparations for the expedition, saying that he had received almost everything he'd asked of them. His one disappointment, he said, was not to have been able to secure his candidate for Gunnery Lieutenant, a very able man named Fitzjames, who was making a name for himself in charge of gunnery on HMS *Ganges* in the eastern Mediterranean. Sir John Franklin, nodding affably at the head of the table, was not to know that within a few years he and Lieutenant Fitzjames would sail *Erebus* into oblivion.

The efforts of the convicts working on the Rossbank Observatory could not be faulted, and within nine days construction was advanced enough to install the measuring equipment for the term-day observations on 27 and 28 August.

As the onshore work progressed, the crews had time to explore the town. Sergeant Cunningham liked Hobart. 'The town is very pleasantly situated. Quite Englified,' he wrote, though he added a word of caution: 'A stranger must be particular selecting his company, as you don't know convicts from free people.' Ross was relaxed enough to allow for plenty of out-of-hours socialising between the sailors and the military garrison. Cunningham, for example, spent a lot of time with his counterpart, Sergeant Cameron of the 51st Infantry Regiment, going to concerts at the theatre, playing quoits at the barracks and going on climbing expeditions. And while Hooker seems to have found the social scene almost arduous ('The myriads of invitations to dinners, balls and routs that have literally been showered on us all'), his immediate senior, Robert McCormick, clearly revelled in it. In just his first week in Hobart he went aboard an Australian packet ship preparing to return to Sydney; made himself known at the Colonial Hospital; tasted, 'for the first time in my life', kangaroo soup; and entertained a steady stream of local worthies on board *Erebus*, including a Dr Wingate from the convict ship *Asia*, Mr Anstey, a barrister, and Mr Bedford, a surgeon. Dr Clarke, the Inspector-General of the Forces, came aboard for lunch with him one day, and that same evening McCormick received an invitation card to dine at Government House: 'Twenty sat down to table.' There he received yet another invitation, from a fellow guest, Mr Gregson, who lived in a picturesque spot on the other side of the Derwent. Taking it up the next day, McCormick was clearly delighted to be close to nature again. 'Saw several paroquets and shot two blue titmice and a lark returning.'

Francis Crozier, meanwhile, had fallen deeply in love with Franklin's niece and Lady Franklin's trusted friend, confidante and secretary,

Sophia Cracroft. His affections were returned with flirtatious inconstancy. To rub salt into the wound, Sophy made little secret of her much stronger attraction to the glamorous Ross than to the decent, steadfast Crozier, whom she described with disdain as 'a horrid radical and an indifferent speller'. Lady Franklin, who developed a protective fondness for Crozier, was shrewd enough to see that his relationship with the mercurial Sophy was doomed. The tragedy is that Crozier never saw this himself.

But while the crews of *Erebus* and *Terror* were busy enjoying themselves – or having their hearts broken – and the ships themselves were being caulked, repainted and their decks whitewashed, news had arrived that made Ross realise they faced competition.

Earlier in the year the elaborately forenamed French explorer Jules Sébastien César Dumont d'Urville had arrived in Hobart. Known to the British public as DuDu, he was something of a legend, famous for having found the Venus de Milo in a field in Greece. A private man, but an enthusiastic scientist and explorer, he ruffled Ross's feathers by claiming to have discovered not just Venus, but the coast of the Antarctic continent as well. His two ships, *Astrolabe* and *Zélée*, he said, had followed a coastline for 150 miles and he and some of his officers had gone ashore and claimed it for France, naming it Adélie Land, after his wife (Adélie is now better remembered for lending her name to the Adélie penguin, one of the smallest and feistiest of the species, which gather to breed in huge numbers). His ships had then followed a 60-mile-long wall of ice, which he believed overlay solid land. To this he gave the name Côte Clairée. D'Urville admitted that his real purpose had been to beat Ross to the South Magnetic Pole, but despite offering 100 francs reward to every crew member if they reached 75°S, and five francs for every degree after that, his ships – unstrengthened for the ice, and with an outbreak of scurvy on board – had failed to reach it. They had retreated to Hobart, with the loss of sixteen men.

As if d'Urville's claims weren't irritating enough, Charles Wilkes, in command of the American Exploring Expedition vessel *Vincennes*, had also registered a claim to have seen and mapped an Antarctic coastline a few months earlier.

Ross was publicly polite, but privately peeved. 'That the commanders of each of these great national undertakings should have selected the very place for penetrating to the southward, for the exploration of which they were well aware ... the expedition under my command was expressly preparing ... did ... greatly surprise me,' he later wrote.

Though there was no open rivalry, Ross made it clear that he was not going to be taking any advice from Johnny Foreigner. As he subsequently argued in his account of the expedition: 'Impressed with the feeling that England had ever led the way of discovery in the southern as well as in the northern regions, I considered it would have been inconsistent with the pre-eminence she has ever maintained if we were to follow in the footsteps of the expedition of any other nation.' Personal pride and patriotism had both been piqued, and Ross set about replanning his course to the Antarctic, deliberately avoiding any suggestion of following the competition.

After nearly three months in Van Diemen's Land, the crews were getting restless. The longer the stay, the greater the potential for a breakdown of discipline. One evening in October, Cunningham was called to the Police Office to deal with two deserters, Thomas Farr and William Beautyman, who had been captured in the bush, outside the town. On the very next day, 8 October, three seamen from *Terror* attacked a police constable, knocking him to the ground and stealing a dollar. On the streets, it seemed, the love affair with the expedition was coming to an end.

But if other ranks might be misbehaving, the popularity of the officers was growing by the day. On 30 October, the *Hobart Town Courier* ran an account of a ball held in the expedition's honour at the Customs House, now Tasmania's Parliament House and still one of the finest buildings in Hobart. After noting that 'the town was disturbed from its uniform aspect of settled dullness', the *Courier* stepped up the hyperbole. 'The fame of this expedition is ... like lightning, it is electrical, it vibrates simultaneously from north to south. At the very moment Captains Ross and Crozier are engaged in making observations in this spot ... men of science are making the same observations in various parts of the world ... It is, as it were a mighty scientific machine, constructed so as to evolve a grand secret – a sort of imitative planetary system ruling us frail creatures on earth.' And there was more: 'It is not therefore to be wondered at, that wherever this expedition goes, it is hailed as a star of men's worship.'

'We are now, November 9th, all ready for sea,' Joseph Hooker wrote to his sister Maria, the chattiness of his tone belying the vast distance between them. 'The ship is as full as an egg,' he went on, 'we can hardly stir in our mess ... When we shall return here again no one, not even the captain knows; it may be in 6 months, or not for 18: it will all depend on what we found at the Southward [the unexplored south].' Hooker seemed anxious to talk about anything other than the risk and scale of what lay ahead. He was particularly exercised about living costs. 'The funds of the mess are very low, so low that I have to lend all I do not spend to pay off the debts. All tailoring, soap, candles and books are extravagantly dear and, as we each have to lay in 18 months stock, I fear that some I.O.U's will be left behind.' Life at sea was expensive for the officers, who were expected to buy their own personal luxuries and contribute to the overall mess bill. Young Joseph, it seems, was better able to ride it out than others. His farewell sounds a note of rather desperate cheerfulness. 'Do you want me to bring home any live small parrots for you? Very beautiful and quiet.'

Before they left for the Antarctic, there were some last-minute changes in personnel. Lieutenant Henry Kay, Franklin's nephew, who had come out from London on *Erebus*, was chosen to stay behind to run the Observatory with the help of Scott from *Terror* and Dayman, one of Hooker's messmates. Two men had successfully deserted. 'I am glad of it,' wrote Hooker on hearing this, 'as we want none but willing hands.' Most tragically, Edward Bradley, Captain of the Hold on *Erebus*, whom Ross rated 'one of our best men', had been killed in an accident whilst cleaning out the tanks on board. He had fallen and become trapped in a tank in which a fire was burning.

Under this cloud, the expedition finally caught the tide in the early hours of Thursday 12 November. Sir John Franklin came aboard *Erebus* to see them off. Judging by Hooker's account, it was an emotional moment: 'the good old gentleman shed tears when going over the side; and as he shook hands with each of us and said "God bless you all", it was really quite affecting'. Sir John then boarded *Terror* to wish them well. Sergeant Cunningham was impressed. 'He is a nice fatherly old man,' he wrote, 'and is much interested in our welfare: we manned the rigging and gave him three hearty cheers, and one more for coming up.' When he had seen them safely south of the Iron Pot Lighthouse, Franklin disembarked, along with the pilot, onto the government yacht *Eliza*.

It must have been a bittersweet farewell for Sir John. He was a seaman, not a civil servant, and it can't have been easy for him to watch the sails disappear over the horizon. Lady Franklin was equally sad to see them go, but didn't accompany her husband, explaining in a last letter to Captain Ross, 'To tell you the truth, though I wished to see you fairly launched in the Southern Ocean, yet I had misgivings as to my desire to take any further leave of you.' Then, as if checking herself, she reverted to the royal 'we': 'Our hearts are with you and our constant prayer will be that God in his mercy will protect and bless you and restore you to us safe, happy and successful. Believe me ever, very affectionately and very truly yours, Jane Franklin.'

There is no indication as to whether or not Ross reciprocated Lady Franklin's heartstring-tugging farewell. Captain Crozier, on the other hand, had, just before they left, asked John Davis, Second

Master of the *Terror*, to sketch himself, Ross and Sir John standing together in the gardens of the Observatory, and had sent her the result as a parting gift. Lady Franklin referred to it in another of her letters to Ross as 'one of the prettiest thoughts that ever entered into Captain Crozier's head', though she couldn't resist adding, 'its accuracy as a portrait more than compensates any defects it may possess as a picture – I almost think I hear the frogs croaking as I look at it'.

Before I leave Tasmania, I'm invited to a meal by Alison Alexander and her husband, James, a retired lecturer in psychology at the University of Tasmania. They represent, I suppose, the present-day cultural elite of the city. Alison can claim descent from the original convict families, which, in Tasmania, is the nearest you get to aristocracy. She has tried to re-create for me the sort of meal that might have been served to the officers from *Erebus* in the winter of 1840: good thick vegetable soup, lamb joint with fried onions, potatoes and broccoli, served by candlelight on a lace tablecloth. One of her other guests embodies the new Tasmania. Bob, tanned, bearded and ex-Merchant Navy, made a lot of money from abalone fishing and is now looking to buy a vineyard. His wife Chris went to the same school as Alison, opposite the Anglesea Barracks where sailors and officers of the Ross expedition spent many an evening with their army colleagues.

Later, I take a walk before turning in. It's something I always do when I'm abroad – like beating the bounds. I walk along the quayside near my hotel and look out towards the sea. It's getting very cold. Far down the Derwent, a red light pierces the darkness. It's Iron Pot Lighthouse. Seeing its light stab out across the water I can easily indulge my imagination and feel the connection between then and now. Between *Erebus* and me. And I find myself wishing her good luck on a really big adventure.

Joseph Hooker described how the sight of this live, 12,500-foot volcano 'caused a feeling of awe to steal over us, at the consideration of our own comparative insignificance and helplessness'. Ross, appropriately, decided to name it Mount Erebus. This engraving is based on a watercolour by John Davis, second master of *Terror*.

CHAPTER 6

'FARTHER SOUTH THAN ANY (KNOWN) HUMAN BEING HAS BEEN'

As human contact receded astern, squally rain lashed the ship and a helpful breeze propelled her south. It had been nearly fourteen months since the officers and crew of HMS *Erebus* had left London, and although the voyage had been eventful and often dangerous, they had at least been in well-charted waters where, no matter how remote, someone had been before them. Soon they would be going beyond the known, into a part of the world for which there were no maps.

The routine of life at sea was re-established. There were sails to be rigged and decks to be scrubbed, food to be prepared and watches to be maintained, but although it may have looked like business as usual, Surgeon McCormick certainly sensed that these were far from normal times. A greater destiny lay ahead of them. 'Our future for the next few months,' he wrote in his journal, 'is so exceptionally novel, so full of interest, so promising in the prospective of great discoveries in a region of our globe, fresh and new as it was at creation's first dawn.' What Ross would have made of this kind of talk around the captain's table is not known. Heroics and high emotions were not for him. His mind would have been concentrated on the practicalities.

And particularly the consummation of what one historian has called the 'Magnetic Crusade'. A few hundred miles south, a lifetime's ambition lay waiting to be realised. If all went well, James Ross would complete a most extraordinary feat: planting a British flag at the South Magnetic Pole as he had done at the North Magnetic Pole ten years earlier. This, he felt convinced, was his destiny.

Around 50°S, Australasia peters out in a chain of small uninhabited volcanic islands. The Aucklands had been discovered in 1806 by a whaler, Abraham Bristow, who had been working for the Enderbys, a whaling family whose ships were mapping the Southern Ocean long before Barrow and the Admiralty made Antarctic exploration into official business. Now, on 20 November 1840, they were the first port of call for *Erebus* and *Terror* on this new leg of their journey.

Landing was a nightmare, and it took Ross and the master five hours of fighting fierce winds to gain the harbour – known, deceptively, as 'Sarah's Bosom'. The first things Ross noticed on the windswept beach were two poles with boards nailed to them. He took a boat through the crashing surf to investigate.

One of the boards bore details of a recent visit to the island by Dumont d'Urville, the last sentence of which must have stuck in Ross's craw: '*Du 19 Janvier au 1 Février 1840, découverte de la Terre Adélie et détermination du pôle magnetique Austral!*' (from 19 January to 1 February 1840, discovery of Adélie Land and determining of the South Magnetic Pole). Ross, of course, knew by now that d'Urville had not in fact reached the South Magnetic Pole, but this reminder that the Frenchman might so easily have beaten him must have raised a shudder. To add insult to injury, the second board bore the message that one of the ships involved in Wilkes's expedition, the US brig *Porpoise*, commanded by a Lieutenant Ringgold, had also been here 'on her return from an exploring cruise along the Antarctic circle'. There was even a bottle with a message in it, to the effect that *Porpoise* had coasted along the ice-barrier. The only comfort Ross could draw from it all was that there was no mention of Wilkes, or his claim to have discovered an Antarctic continent.

With these slights absorbed, the by now well-practised ritual of landfall took place. All hands were called upon to clear trees and dig foundations for the construction of an observatory. While this was going on, the terminally curious McCormick took the opportunity to explore the island. He noted that 'throughout this excursion I met with scarcely any signs of animal life'. But when he did, of course, he put a gun to it, bagging a shag, a black-backed gull and 'a fine falcon' before he returned to the ship.

Hooker, meanwhile, was having a wonderful time. Far south though they were, the climate here was a mild and humid one, where mosses, lichens and ferns grew large and luxurious. Before they left the Auckland Isles, eighty species of flowering plants had been discovered, more than fifty of which had never been classified before. 'The whole land seemed covered with vegetation,' Hooker enthused. Captain Ross seemed equally taken with the botanical profusion, noting how fortunate it was that the medical officers had no sick to attend to and could spend their time collecting. He registered wholehearted approval when Hooker brought a 4-foot tree-fern onto an already-crowded ship.

Ross was attracted by the islands for other reasons, too, seeing in them great potential for an enormous penal settlement. Convicts from the now-free colonies of New South Wales, New Zealand and Van Diemen's Land could all be accommodated here. He would get in touch with Franklin about it. There were also rich stocks of black and sperm whales around the islands, which he felt could be commercially exploited, and he was pleased to hear later that Charles Enderby's whaling business had applied for permission to do just that.

Nowadays our inclination would be to leave the natural beauty of such islands untouched, but the motive of Ross, and those who commissioned his expedition, was to expand and improve and enlighten.

What we might now see as shameless exploitation, they saw as bringing, wherever possible, the benefits of science to a savage and benighted world. McCormick shot birds so that he could better understand them. Ross, like Abraham Bristow before him, decided to leave livestock on Auckland Island, because he felt it was his duty to those who would inevitably come after him to begin the process of cultivating wild places, and to continue the process of spreading Western values across the globe. Pigs, chickens, goats and rabbits were accordingly offloaded from the ship, along with some strawberry and gooseberry bushes that Franklin had given Ross in Hobart. Today most of the descendants of the livestock have either died out or been removed, and Auckland Island remains uninhabited. Ironically, in view of McCormick's activities, it is now a bird sanctuary.

With the magnetic observations completed, *Erebus* and *Terror* weighed anchor and headed 160 miles south-east to Campbell Island. It was another promising anchorage, with a large, deep-water harbour and plentiful supplies of wood and water, but for the first time since the embarrassment of that initial day at Sheerness, both *Erebus* and *Terror* ran aground, misjudging a muddy shoal near the harbour entrance. Those aboard *Erebus* warped her free by hitching ropes to the trees onshore, but *Terror* was left high and dry, and her crew spent the night pumping fresh water out of her tanks and unloading stores, so that she could be lifted off at high water the next morning.

Whilst Ross measured the rise and fall of the tides, McCormick marvelled at the sheer number of nesting albatrosses on the island, 'their beautiful white necks seen above the grass . . . studding the hills in all directions'. He found only one egg per nest, several of which he took out and back to the boat. He was pleased with himself for despatching three Arctic skua, the albatross's foe, as he called them, but next day several of them fought back and 'fiercely attacked me, circling round my head and darting with open beak at my face'. From the deck of the re-floated *Terror*, Sergeant Cunningham marvelled at the sight of thousands of penguins 'ranged along [the beach] like soldiers'. There were plants in abundance, too: with the help of Captain Ross, Hooker collected more than 200 species in the two days they were there. It was as if the natural world was putting on one last bravura display of profusion and fecundity. On 8 May 2018, Campbell Island witnessed a bravura display of a different kind; when the tallest wave ever recorded in the southern hemisphere broke onto her beaches. It was measured at 78 feet high.

At nine o'clock on the morning of 17 December, anchors were weighed and the sails were set. A fresh wind became a gale and Campbell Island, their final landfall before the Antarctic, had vanished from sight by midday.

Erebus and *Terror* were now in waters that only a handful of people had ever crossed before. British interest in these far southern waters was almost entirely due to the demand for whale oil, which kept the nation's lamps lit and hands washed. The Enderby Company encouraged her captains to explore as far south as they could. One of them, John Biscoe, had circumnavigated Antarctica between 1830 and 1832, reaching 67°S, and in 1838 John Balleny, engaged by the Enderby Company on a sealing expedition, found a small archipelago near latitude 66°S and 163°E, later named the Balleny Islands.

Ross had much in common with the whaling captains. He, too, was a practical man. His account of the atmosphere on board as they headed south is unromantic and businesslike. It is also defiantly positive. 'We were in possession of the best of human means to accomplish our purposes,' he wrote. 'Our ships were in every respect most suitable for the service, with three years provisions and stores of the best kind, and supported by officers and crews in whom I had reason to entertain the utmost confidence.' Looking around him, as the temperatures dropped and rain became sleet, then sleet became snow, he saw that 'Joy and satisfaction beamed in every face.'

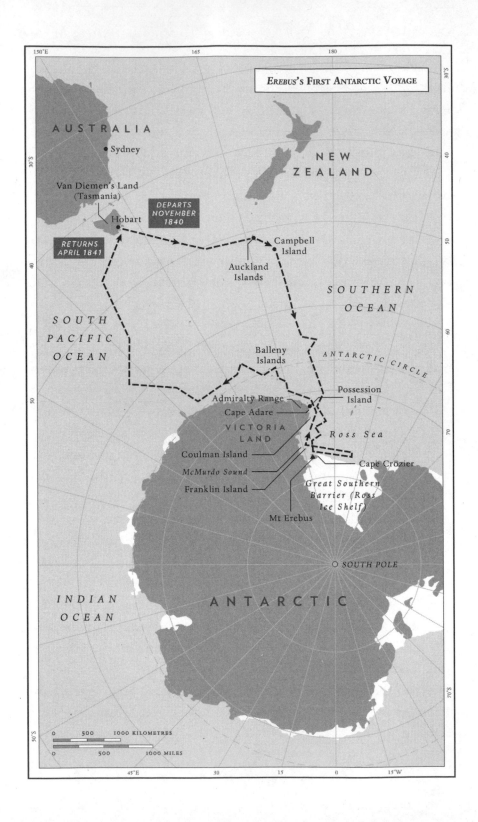

Erebus's First Antarctic Voyage

150°E · 165 · 180

30°S

AUSTRALIA

• Sydney

Van Diemen's Land
(Tasmania)

**DEPARTS
NOVEMBER
1840**

• Hobart

**RETURNS
APRIL 1841**

40

NEW
ZEALAND

40

SOUTHERN
OCEAN

50

Auckland
Islands

Campbell
Island

SOUTH
PACIFIC
OCEAN

Balleny
Islands

ANTARCTIC CIRCLE

60

50

Admiralty Range

Cape Adare

VICTORIA
LAND

Coulman Island

McMurdo Sound

Franklin Island

Mt Erebus

Possession
Island

Ross Sea

Cape Crozier

Great Southern
Barrier (Ross
Ice Shelf)

70

INDIAN
OCEAN

ANTARCTIC

○ SOUTH POLE

70°S

0   500   1000 KILOMETRES

0   500   1000 MILES

45°E · 30 · 15 · 0 · 15°W

Their second Christmas Day at sea was spent in the teeth of a northerly gale. 'A very disagreeable day,' Cunningham recorded, before adding more cheerfully, '[we] had plenty to eat and drink'. McCormick spent the day, as he had done every day since they left Campbell Island, skinning birds, drying plants and then arranging and stowing away the recent additions to the expedition's natural-history collections. In order not to miss an opportunity to augment these collections, he was working on a technique for shooting passing birds so that they fell onto the deck and not into the water. On 30 December he added a snow-white Antarctic petrel to the specimen cases.

The days were getting colder and the icebergs were getting bigger. Late on 28 December, Cunningham described one of them as having 'Something after the shape of a dismasted Ship'. He reckoned it was 2 miles in circumference and 100 feet high. Ross, who'd had plenty of experience of Arctic icebergs, saw their southern counterparts as being very different: much more monolithic, with less variety of form, and being on the whole larger and taller. They also passed a lot of whales, mainly sperm and humpbacks, of unusually large size, in such profusion and so tame that the ships could sail by without disturbing them.

I greatly envy their opportunity to see so many of these hypnotically watchable creatures. When I made a journey to the Antarctic Peninsula in 2014 the sight of a single whale was enough to bring everyone out on deck, reaching for cameras and binoculars. Sometimes, if you were very lucky, two or three would surface. Watching them was both compulsive and strangely soothing. Of all God's creatures, they seemed the least prone to hurrying. Their lives seemed to be the human equivalent of taking very long baths. When they did move, it was a performance of beauty and grace, of great weight moved with minimum effort. And there can surely be no better final bow than the languid, quietly powerful rise, flick and fall of the fluke. I like to think that those aboard *Erebus* drew similar comfort from the whales' company on the long and increasingly hazardous journey south.

The year of 1841 arrived in dramatic fashion. As the midnight sun climbed over the horizon, the main brace was spliced and double rum rations were issued, to celebrate not just the New Year, but the crossing of the Antarctic Circle. They had reached 66°S 30'E, 'farther south than either "French" or "Yankies",' noted Cunningham, with some satisfaction. Conditions were changing fast. The ships were now on the edge of pack-ice, and the temperature by day barely rose above freezing. Extra provisions were available to celebrate the New Year, and extra-cold weather gear was handed out to the crew, consisting of a box-cloth jacket and trousers, two pairs of hose, two comforters (scarves worn around the throat to protect it from cold), a pair of water boots and a woollen cap known as a 'Welsh wig', the Royal Navy's equivalent of a beanie.

Captain Ross seemed to enjoy the excitement of those who had never been in the ice before. He hadn't expected to see so much of it so soon, and looked out over the freezing ocean with satisfaction: 'for it presented none of those evidences of impenetrability we had been led to expect'.

It was not until 5 January that a change in wind direction offered an opportunity to test his assessment. As they ran along the edge of the pack-ice, Ross, relying on word from the masthead, judged there to be enough leads, or ice-free channels, to risk an attempt to get through. It was a crucial moment, the first big test of the ability of these former bomb ships to push their way through close-packed ice, with no engines of any kind to help them. *Erebus* led the way in, slowly but surely slicing her way through, despite some heavy resistance as they went. After about 'an hour's hard thumping' they broke through to much lighter ice and were able to make faster progress, albeit 'at times sustaining violent shocks, which nothing but ships so strengthened could have withstood'. The ships had passed their first examination.

Over the next few days, as they made good progress to the south-east, Ross's aim of reaching the South Magnetic Pole was looking increasingly attainable. The ships' reinforced bows were having little trouble carving through ice some 6–8 inches thick, though the helmsman and the lookouts had to be constantly on alert to find the channels and avoid the occasional icebergs. These took McCormick's fancy: one, he noted, resembled a village church. On 7 January he shot a penguin, and later in the day four more: 'two with one shot'. This brought him satisfaction in more ways than one: 'I had thus an opportunity afforded me of landing on a piece of Antarctic ice for the first time, to pick up a penguin.'

Gradually the ice thickened and progress slowed. On 8 January a violent storm brought them to a standstill. But before the storm broke, Ross had worked out – from the darkening colour reflected in the sky – that there must be open water ahead. Sure enough, by noon on the 9th they found themselves once again in open sea, making four knots in a strong breeze.

Erebus and *Terror* had achieved something remarkable. Under sail alone, the two ships had successfully negotiated 134 miles of pack-ice and come out the other side.

Ross was not a gambler, but in this case he had taken a calculated risk. He had led his ships into the unknown. The ice could have trapped them or crushed them. And there was no Plan B. Once committed, turning back would have been virtually impossible. Judicious, understated, ever pragmatic as he was, Ross could not disguise his elation as he set course for the Magnetic Pole: 'Our hopes and expectations of attaining that interesting point were now raised to the highest pitch.'

McCormick, by contrast, seemed less concerned about the heavy hand of history and more concerned about Billy, the ship's goat and a great pet of the sailors, who had spent the day in his barrel, after having been given port wine in the gun-room. 'Paying the penance for his debauchery,' joked McCormick, only to add a poignant coda: 'Very unexpectedly during the first watch I found our poor young goat "Billy" dying.'

Ross and his helmsman had for a while been observing a polar phenomenon known as 'ice-blink', by which, owing to the refraction of light, clouds and sky can appear as solid physical features. It had manifested itself most famously in 1818, when John Ross had, embarrassingly, confused clouds for mountains on his expedition to discover the Northwest Passage. Given the furore that had ensued, it's not surprising that Sir John's nephew should now be rather more curious, assuming that what appeared to be a long, white coastline on the horizon might well be another instance of a polar mirage. That was until, at two in the morning, Lieutenant Wood, the officer on watch, roused the captain to report the unmistakable presence of a solid land mass.

With a cry of 'Land Ahoy!', Lieutenant Wood confirmed that not only had *Erebus* and *Terror* become the first sailing ships to break through the ice-pack, but they were now the first ships to come face-to-face with irrefutable proof that an Antarctic continent existed.

Surprisingly, Ross's first reaction was less than ecstatic. All he could see was that this 'coastline' had effectively blocked the way to his most coveted goal, the South Magnetic Pole. Nevertheless he was, like everyone else, humbled and overawed by what he saw as they drew closer to land. 'We had a most enchanting view of ... two magnificent ranges of mountains ... The glaciers that filled their intervening valleys, and which descended from near the mountain summits, projected in many places several miles into the sea ...The sky was a clear azure blue, with the most brilliant sunshine ... all that could be desired for giving effect to such a magnificent panorama.'

For Joseph Hooker, it was simply 'one of the most gorgeous sights I have ever witnessed'.

And there was another cause for celebration. Measurements showed that *Erebus* and *Terror* had reached latitude 71°14'S, passing Captain Cook's furthest south. 'We have now but Weddell's track to get beyond,' wrote Captain Ross, referring to the whaling captain's 74°15'S, a record that had stood since 1823.

Ross's first gesture of gratitude was not to the boat-builders, or even the crew who'd brought him here, but to those who had commissioned the expedition. He named the highest mountain of the range ahead of him Mount Sabine, after Edward Sabine, his childhood friend and most vocal supporter of the expedition, and then christened the majestic sweep of mountains to his north-west the Admiralty Range, in honour of his paymasters. In so doing, he was following a long-standing tradition. The giving of names to physical features seems to have been in the captain's remit and was done very much on the spot, without formal consultation or official approval – hence the reason Dumont d'Urville, for example, should have named his corner of the Antarctic after his wife.

As the expedition entered an unmapped world, a positive frenzy of namings was unleashed. Individual peaks along the range were given the names of the Admiralty Council: Mount Minto, after the First Lord; Mount Adam and Mount Parker, after senior naval lords. A long list of junior lords became mountains, too. At Captain Crozier's request, a nearby cape was called Cape Downshire, after the Marquis of Downshire, a wealthy Irish landowner and friend of the Crozier family. 'A remarkable projection of high, dark, probably volcanic cliffs' became Cape Adare, after Ross's friend Viscount Adare; and yet another became Cape Barrow, in tribute, as Ross put it, to 'the father of modern arctic discovery'.

When in West Antarctica filming *Pole to Pole* for the BBC, I remember being intrigued by the nearby presence of the Executive

Committee Range, named by the Americans in the 1940s. What next, I wondered: Chief Accountant Plateau, Water-Cooler Peak? Now I know they were just following an honourable tradition. Dull, but honourable.

The next thing to do was to formally annex this newly discovered land, which required more than head-scratching for names: it demanded positive footfall. On the morning of 12 January 1841, boats were therefore made ready to go ashore, but because there was such heavy surf crashing onto the ice, it was decided to detour to one of the small offshore islands. Thomas Abernethy skilfully steered one of the cutters through strong currents and they were finally able to scramble ashore on what turned out to be a guano-bed. McCormick described the peculiar sensation of making landfall on a pile of penguin droppings, which had been there a very long time. 'It had attained such a depth,' he wrote, 'as to give an elastic sensation under the feet, resembling a dried up peat-bog.' The Union Flag was duly planted, and glasses of sherry were raised to Queen Victoria and Prince Albert and their newest acquisition, Possession Island.

Ross records that the ceremony was witnessed by vast numbers of penguins, which showed their resistance to colonisation by 'attacking us vigorously as we waded through their ranks, and pecking at us with their sharp beaks'. Those ashore also had to cope with the stench of decades of ordure. While aware of the foul smell, the ever-practical Ross also noted that the guano 'may at some time be valuable to the agriculturalists of our Australian colonies'.

Confirming that 'the perfume arising from this colony was certainly not of an Arabian sweetness', McCormick observed the activity of the penguins more sympathetically than his captain did, describing their way of emerging from the water with a fine sense of wonder. 'I observed one bird make a most extraordinary leap upwards from the sea to the top of a perpendicular piece of ice ... alighting on its feet like a cat.' I was glad to read that, because on my own excursion to the Antarctic I found their gravity-defying leaps *out* of the sea a similarly extraordinary trick of evolution. But whereas, for me, the penguins were charming entertainment, for McCormick they were specimens: 'Knocked down an old penguin with my geological hammer and put him in my haversack ... with a few hastily-collected specimens of the black lava rock.' And for the appreciative Cunningham, they were dinner: 'very fine [penguin] it was,' he noted; 'it was cooked in a Sea Pie [and] had no taste whatever of fish as some of them had I have eat'.

Weather conditions ruled out any possibility of their making landfall on the continent itself, or Victoria Land as they had named it. Indeed, their main focus for the next few days was avoiding being blown against the shore by ever more violent gales. They progressed gingerly south. Ross noted the great number of whales they passed – thirty in one day. Observing them 'blowing or spouting', he wrote prophetically, and ominously, 'Hitherto ... they have here enjoyed a life of tranquillity and security; but will now, no doubt, be made to contribute to the wealth of our country, in exact proportion to the energy and perseverance of our merchants; and these, we well know, are by no means inconsiderable.'

An apparent trick of the light turned out to be another island, which, because it was discovered on his fiancée's birthday, Ross, ever the pragmatist, named Coulman Island, after his prospective father-in-law. Anne Coulman herself was allotted a cape at the southern tip of her father's island.

By now, everyone aboard must have realised this was why they had set out. This was exploration. Every nautical mile, every break in the clouds brought with it something no one on earth had ever seen before. At the same time the conditions were becoming harsher. The temperatures had dropped away further and an unhelpful southerly wind had strengthened. To ride it out, *Erebus* had to reef her sails, which must have been bitterly uncomfortable work for the crew. 'Freezing very sharp,' wrote Cunningham, 'every Rope frozen and Icicles hanging from all the Rigging and Gear.' By tradition, the men who had to trim the sails wore no gloves, for these were felt to impede a secure grip.

Fortunately, a brief spell of better weather followed, which, with a breeze behind them and every possible sail set, helped them make steady progress. Ross was encouraged as they headed towards their next goal: 'The adverse winds and weather were forgotten in the full expectation we now enjoyed of soon passing into a higher latitude than had ever before been attained.'

On Saturday 23 January 1841 he reached his goal. Weddell's record had been 74°15'S. Now *Erebus* and *Terror* were at 74°23'S or, as Sergeant Cunningham put it in his diary, 'farther south than any (Known) human being has been'. He added, with a nice touch of understatement, 'which is a feather in our Caps'.

The double rum ration with which they celebrated this momentous feat can rarely have seemed sweeter, nor the traditional toast 'Wives and lovers, may they never meet!' have been shouted more lustily. No matter that the weather had turned again, with persistent snow and gale-force winds. McCormick recorded that that night Captain Ross dined with his officers in the gun-room and raised the toast: 'Better luck still!'

Ross's hope now was that there might be a point at which the wind and the current would shift the surrounding pack-ice sufficiently to create a gap and give them their first chance to explore the Antarctic mainland. And on 27 January he saw just such an opportunity. He and a number of officers therefore embarked in one of *Erebus*'s cutters, whilst Crozier and his men from *Terror* followed in one of their whale-boats. The whale-boat proved to be the more stable of the two, and Ross transferred to join Crozier. When they were near enough to the shore, the boat crested a wave and Ross leapt onto the rocks. Using a rope that he had secured, several of the officers followed, 'but not without getting thoroughly wetted'. Joseph Hooker, missing his footing, fell between the stern and the rock face and was yanked out just as he was about to be crushed.

Ross stayed long enough to take possession of what proved to be another island, which he named after Sir John Franklin. With one of the men on the verge of freezing to death, there was only time to grab a few rock-samples, reboard the whale-boat and row hard for the ship. They arrived on board 'thoroughly drenched to the skin and painfully cold'. Few of Her Majesty's possessions would be as hard-won as Franklin Island.

The wonders kept on coming. Heading yet further south before a favourable breeze they made out, on the starboard bow, the shape of another spectacular peak. But this one was very different. As the skies cleared, a column of smoke could be seen drifting from its summit. And it was no trick of the light. They were looking not at spindrift from an exposed mountain top, but at a 12,500-foot active volcano. Joseph Hooker, who had clearly recovered from his near-death experience, breathlessly recorded: 'a sight so surpassing every thing that can be imagined ... that it really caused a feeling of awe to steal over us, at the consideration of our own comparative insignificance and helplessness, and at the same time an indescribable feeling of the greatness of the Creator in the works of his hand'.

Cunningham, in equal wonderment, watched the volcano's activity from the deck of the *Terror*. 'It would Shew first with a volume of Smoke, as dark as Pitch which would gradually become of a lighter hue and then the Flame would burst forth with great fury for some time, after which it would Subside for a few minutes and then reappear again.' He called it the Burning Mountain. Another witness to this astonishing sight was the blacksmith on *Erebus*, an Irishman called Cornelius Sullivan, who wrote down some memories of the voyage for a friend who served on *Erebus* later. For Sullivan, it was the

Splendid Burning Mountain. 'We did not land here nor did we deem it Safe to land either. Our nearest approach to this Phenomena of nature was eight miles.'

It fell to James Ross to give it a name. Setting aside all his friends and bigwigs back home, he chose to call it after the tough little ship that had brought them so safely, so far: Mount Erebus. The smaller, extinct volcano beside it he called Mount Terror. Erebus's hellish name seemed genuinely appropriate when, in November 1979, Air New Zealand flight 901 crashed into the mountain; 250 lives were lost.

Both ships were now making rapid headway south, past 76°. As they swung round a small island, briskly christened after Sir Francis Beaufort, the Hydrographer of the Navy, they found, ahead of them, a natural phenomenon every bit as impressive as the volcano they had just passed. 'We perceived,' wrote Ross, 'a low white line extending from its eastern extreme point as far as the eye could discern.' It was a sheer-sided cliff of ice, flat on top and towering above the ships to a height of 200 feet.

The sight brought everyone to the gunwales. On *Erebus*, McCormick clambered up to the crow's nest, 'but could see no termination to the great ice-wall, which we have named the Great Southern Barrier'. Sullivan the blacksmith was overwhelmed: 'no imaginative Power can convey an adequate idea of the Resplendant Sublimity of the Antarctic Ice Wall ... this noble battery of Ice that fortifyd. The Land two hundred feet high ... The bold masses of Ice that walld. In the Land Rendered this Scene Quite Enchanting.' It was the length of the barrier that he found most astonishing: 'As far and as fast as we run the Barrier appeared the Same Shape and form.'

The discovery of such a massive obstacle effectively decided one outstanding issue. Further progress towards the South Magnetic Pole could be finally ruled out. 'We might with equal chance of success try to sail through the Cliffs of Dover,' admitted Ross. But they had come close. It would not be until the next century, and Shackleton's *Nimrod* expedition, that anyone came closer.

Not that the expedition had been short of achievements. They had discovered and named a new land mass and new islands. They had found two volcanoes. And there were still further landmarks to be marked up on Ross's charts. Having acknowledged his bosses back in London, Ross turned his attention to those closest to him, to name two significant promontories that he could see. One of them he named Cape Bird, after his First Lieutenant. Another, the cape at the foot of Mount Terror, he named after his second-in-command, Francis Crozier, 'a friend of now more than twenty years standing ... to whose zeal and cordial cooperation is mainly to be ascribed, under God's blessing, the happiness as well as success of this expedition'.

What Ross had discovered was to play a vital part in the future exploration of Antarctica. The Great Southern Barrier proved to be colossal, the leading edge of an unbroken sheet of ice 300 feet thick and the same size as France. First seen as an insurmountable obstacle, it was to prove a gateway to the interior of the continent, a flat and stable access that was vital to both Amundsen and Scott on their journeys to the Pole. As for Cape Crozier, an outcrop of black basalt plunging 800 feet into the sea, this was to garner a fearsome reputation among future explorers. Apsley Cherry-Garrard in *The Worst Journey in the World*, his account more than seventy years later of Scott's polar expedition, left a powerful description: 'It is at Cape Crozier that the Barrier edge, which runs for four hundred miles as an ice-cliff up to 200 feet high, meets the land. The Barrier is moving against this land at a rate which is sometimes not less than a mile in a year. Perhaps you can imagine the chaos it piles up: there are pressure ridges compared to which the waves of the sea are like a ploughed field.'

Erebus and *Terror* sailed west beside the Barrier for some 100 miles in clear, smooth blue seas, with whales spouting and huge blocks calving off the cliffs of ice. McCormick was so taken with the stupendous scale of this ice-wall that he stayed on deck throughout the night, 'so as to see all I could of it; and well was I rewarded for the ... sacrifice of a night's rest and sleep by the grand and sublime panorama ... which arrested my gaze like some striking shifting scene on the stage'.

On 2 February, Ross recorded his position at latitude 78.4°S. The next day he put a cask overboard, containing a note of their position and their recent activities, and a request that anyone who found it should pass the paper on to the Secretary of the Admiralty. The note was signed by Ross and his officers.

Now a build-up of pack-ice and a change in wind direction caused Ross to decide, in consultation with Crozier, to turn east again and try to study the Barrier at closer range. On the pack-ice they passed seals, white petrels and Emperor penguins. Three of the latter, the largest of the species, were brought on board. But not as pets. 'They were very powerful birds, and we had some difficulty in killing them,' wrote Ross, adding a culinary note, 'their flesh is very dark, and of a rank fishy flavour.' As they were added to the larder, the process of living off the land went on. Two seals were captured and killed to provide oil for the winter. The ships' fresh-water supplies were replenished by hacking bits off a passing ice-floe.

The bird life, was, as ever, of great interest to ship's surgeon McCormick. On seeing hovering over the ship what he believed to be a new species of *Lestris*, or Arctic Yager, described by Audubon, the great American bird illustrator, as an 'indefatigable teaser of the smaller gulls', he took a pot-shot at it. His shot failed to despatch the bird cleanly and, after descending near the deck, it recovered and flew away with one leg broken. McCormick, unusually, felt compelled to justify himself: 'For notwithstanding that my duties as ornithologist compel me to take the lives of these most beautiful and interesting creatures ... I never do so without a sharp sting of pain and qualm of conscience, so fond am I of all the feathered race.'

So fond, indeed, that on the same night he recorded that 'Between midnight and one a.m. I succeeded in adding two more of the elegant white petrel to my collection, one falling dead on the quarter-deck and the other on the gun-room skylight ... a third I shot ... fell overboard into the sea.'

On 9 February, with the ice-pack to the north closing in behind the ships and threatening to trap them against the Barrier, Ross detected 'a remarkable looking bay', the only indentation he'd seen in the so-far-unbroken face of the ice. He decided to take the ships in. A quarter of a mile from the entrance he paused, tacking to determine the depth. It was 330 fathoms – 1,000 feet. Approaching further, it was clear that a spur of ice projecting into the water had created this deceptively protective inlet. It was a time to hold their breath. They were now closer to the base of the Great Southern Barrier than they had ever been. Looking up, they could see gigantic icicles hanging from the summit of the cliff. Cornelius Sullivan, like others, was agog. 'All hands when they came on Deck to view this most rare and magnificent Sight that Ever the human eye witnessed Since the world was created actually Stood Motionless for Several Seconds before he Could Speak to the man next to him ... Then I wishd. I was an artist or a draughtsman instead of a blacksmith and Armourer.'

The beauty and the spectacle were, however, perilous, for the sea here, sheltered from the winds, was freezing fast and piling up in layers around the ships. Suddenly clear water could not be seen, even from the top of the mast. Ross confessed later that he had feared they might be driven to destruction against the Barrier. Fortunately, a wind blew up in the nick of time and, with the help of their crews out on the ice with picks and shovels, *Erebus* and *Terror* were shepherded to safety. When Ross looked back, their channel could no longer be seen. They had had a very narrow escape.

For three more days the two ships probed the edge of the pack-ice, looking for an opening. Masts and spars and rigging became encased in ice, which, as McCormick remembered, 'rattled down on the decks from aloft, hanging about ... in long beads or bracelets ... giving the ship a very hoary aspect indeed'. They failed to find a way through. Ross therefore gave the order to turn round, and before long they found themselves within sight of Mount Erebus again. Even after all they had seen, their sense of wonder was far from dulled. Mount Erebus performed obligingly, shooting plumes of smoke and flame high into the air. 'The Landscape this first watch was the most Splendid I ever Saw,' William Cunningham wrote, '– it is beyond my power of description. Between the Land and the Volcanoe the Ice and the horizon with the Sun Shining brightly above all.'

A bay was discovered off the land, connecting Mount Erebus to the mainland, and was named McMurdo Bay after the senior lieutenant of the *Terror*. Later it was discovered that Ross had made one of his rare miscalculations, and that Mount Erebus and Mount Terror were both on an offshore island. McMurdo Bay was renamed McMurdo Sound, and the island that Ross had misdiagnosed as mainland was eventually named after him. Few names occur so frequently as his, on the map of Antarctica. The sea he sailed into after breaking through the pack became the Ross Sea, now the world's largest Marine Protection Area, with a fishing ban covering an area of 432,000 square miles. The massive Southern Barrier, after much argument over the definition of a barrier, is today known as the Ross Ice Shelf.

As the two small ships turned their backs on Antarctica, Ross recorded his disappointment: 'few can understand the deep feelings of regret with which I felt compelled to abandon the ... hope I had so long cherished of being permitted to plant the flag of my country on both the magnetic poles of our globe,' he wrote. But for his crew, there was surely nothing but relief. They had been away from Hobart for more than three months, six weeks of which had been spent in the ice. Much had been demanded of them – not only furling and unfurling sails in sub-zero temperatures, but clearing, cutting and heaving their ship through the ice pack.

And they had achieved all this without loss of life – indeed, seemingly in the best of health. D'Urville's expedition, only months earlier, had had to be abandoned after outbreaks of frostbite and scurvy. But as *Erebus* and *Terror* turned away from a world where, as Cunningham noted, they had never seen the sun dip below the horizon, he was able to write, 'Both Ships companies in the best of health – thanks be to God'. Not only were the men healthy, but it was clear there was no shortage of food, if McCormick's description of a Sunday lunch – after months in the Antarctic – is to be believed. 'We had some fresh beef roasted for dinner today,' he records, 'which had been killed in December last, and suspended under the mizzen-top in a bread-bag ever since. It turned out most excellent, being more tender and juicy than when first slaughtered. I opened a jar of Tasmania honey which had been given me by my kind friends the Gregsons . . . I also broached a bottle of whisky.'

Not that the run back to Hobart was ever easy. In the midst of one gale, Ross and Crozier found their ships being driven perilously close to a mountainous coastline that Wilkes had very recently charted. It was touch and go as to whether Ross would be able both to dodge the icebergs and clear the north-eastern point of the land mass towards which he was sure he was being remorselessly driven. The next morning, however, as the skies cleared and the wind abated, they could see no land at all. By the evening they were a few miles from where Wilkes had marked the eastern point of a mountain range, but as far as the eye could see there was only open water.

On Sunday 7 March McCormick confirmed that all he could see from the deck of *Erebus* was a procession of icebergs on the port side. 'We have passed over the spot where the American Arctic Expedition have laid down land, but we found only an open sea,' he wrote. Clearly Wilkes Land had been an illusion.

The realisation must have come as a relief to Ross, but it must also have been the cause for some quiet self-satisfaction. When he came to write about it, he generously surmised that Lieutenant Wilkes must have 'mistaken for land some of the dense well-defined clouds which so continually hang over extensive packs of ice – a mistake which we had ourselves, on many occasions, to guard against'. But even the phlegmatic Ross must surely have had the hint of a smile as he wrote about their next move: 'Before midnight [we] gained the position of the eastern point of the supposed land, and shaped our course ... under moderate sail, along the mountain range.'

The weather proved erratic. In the ever-changing conditions no two days were the same, as entries from Cunningham's diary for the first days of April reveal.

1st Thursday: Fine: a rattling breeze going right before it ... Ship going very steady 7 Knots

2nd Friday: A calm ... both ships lowered boats down ... got Soundings in 1500 fathoms [9,000 feet]: washed decks and Scrubbed paintwork

3rd Saturday: Stiff gale: going before it: rolling heavily: close-reefed topsails: averaging 7 knots ... Fine clear night

4th Sunday ... Set topgallant sails going 7 knots: both ships rolling very heavily. In the morning watch the *Erebus* had her port Quarter Boat washed away which came floating past us apparently not injured with her mast and oars in all nicely scraped.

Cunningham foresaw trouble here: 'Should she be picked up by any Ship it will be inferred that the *Erebus* is lost – but she's not.'

She certainly wasn't. Even now, Ross continued with his magnetic observations. Edward Sabine had told him that the regions in which they were now sailing would contain a focus of maximum magnetic intensity. Ross therefore duly took the measurements, only to find that, as at Wilkes Land, the strong magnetic forces that had been predicted didn't exist (they were actually much further south). McCormick, meanwhile, continued to prepare his collections for their storage boxes. The least happy of the 'scientists' on board was Joseph Hooker, who complained at being confined on the ship for so long, and finding so little of botanical interest south of the Antarctic Circle. 'The utter desolation of 70 South could never have been expected.'

This first Antarctic foray had been a voyage into the unknown for all 128 men, and the fact that they had achieved so much and returned, as Ross put it, 'unattended by casualty, calamity, or sickness of any kind' is a remarkable tribute to the men and their leaders. For *Erebus*, which for the first thirteen years of her life had seen no more of the world than the clear blue waters of the Bay of Naples and the Tyrrhenian Sea, it was a triumph. She and her sister ship had, with only the loss of a few spars and a quarter-boat, overcome conditions that no ship in history had had to contend with. It's not recorded whether Rice and his team at Chatham Dockyard were kept informed of her successes, but they should have been deservedly proud of what they had achieved in turning bomb ships into polar pioneers.

On 6 April 1841, a week before Easter, they had their first sight of the coast of Van Diemen's Land, and at midnight the Iron Pot light shone out, guiding them up Storm Bay to the mouth of the Derwent. The pilot came aboard at half-past nine next morning. It was an unsettled day, with strong squally cross-winds, but that didn't stop Sir John Franklin turning out to meet them, and three cheers rang out from *Erebus* as he clambered aboard from the *Eliza*, which had brought him down the river to welcome them. It was late in the afternoon by the time they reached Ross Cove and sent the anchors tumbling. Cornelius Sullivan greeted their safe arrival with an equally tumbling rush of relief and joy: 'All hands were in good health and Spirits Fresh grub and Liberty on Shore with a drop of the Creator – soon made our jolly tars forget the Cold fingers in the Frozen Regions, for very Little they thought of 78 South while Regealing themselves at Charley Probins the Sign of the Gordon Castle Hobart Town.'

The people of Hobart reacted ecstatically to *Erebus*'s return, throwing a celebratory ball and – as this theatre poster advertises – even a dramatic re-enactment of her first Antarctic voyage.

CHAPTER 7

DANCING WITH THE CAPTAINS

No sooner had *Erebus* dropped anchor in Ross Cove in April 1841 than the gregarious McCormick set about putting 146 days at sea behind him. The day after their arrival he dined at the Anglesea Barracks, renewing his old friendships with the officers of the 51st Infantry. Next morning he borrowed one of their horses and rode over to Risdon to see his friends the Gregsons. He was especially pleased to find his parrot not only still alive, but 'greatly improved in his vocal powers'.

William Cunningham also took up with his contacts at the 51st, particularly his old friend, the Bugle Major. He was glad to be safely returned, though his diary also sounds a note of dejection: 'I felt much disappointed in not having any letters from my friends.'

While the likes of McCormick and Cunningham socialised, Ross was busy. He knew that his Admiralty instructions required him to spend a second summer in the Antarctic, if necessary. His ships would need to be cleaned and repainted throughout, the rigging stripped and refitted and their hulls re-caulked. Then there were promotions to be made. Ross recommended Commander Crozier, whom he described in a letter to Beaufort as 'a regular trump', along with the First Lieutenant of *Erebus*, Edward Bird, whom he could hardly have commended more highly: 'I have frequently been obliged for many hours, to relinquish the entire conduct of the expedition to his well-tried ability and discretion.'

Finally, Ross sat down to compose his account of the voyage for the Admiralty. It was late summer before it reached England and, despite all the achievements he could claim, it received a mixed reaction. Beaufort, the Hydrographer of the Navy, and Edward Sabine were greatly impressed, Beaufort calling it 'one of the few modern voyages that will go down in history'. The top dogs at the Admiralty in White-hall, however, were less than enthusiastic. Quite bizarrely, the report, dedicated to Lord Minto, the First Lord, was also censored by him. It was never published in the Admiralty *Gazette* because, as Sabine informed Ross in a letter, 'of Lord Minto's extraordinary crotchet [notion] that because there had been no bloodshed your despatch ought not to be in the Gazette'. Such astonishing disregard of Ross's achievement was followed by less than open-handed generosity of recognition. Although there was agreement that Ross should be rewarded, there was argument as to what form his reward should take. Barrow and Lord Haddington – soon to be Minto's successor as First Lord – wanted him knighted by patent, but that would cost Ross £400. If he waited until his return and accepted the knighthood by personal confer, it would only cost £100. Beaufort advised him to wait. Ross's report was presented to the House of Commons on 7 September 1841. Sabine purchased thirty copies.

The international reaction to the report was far less restrained. Ross's exploits delighted von Humboldt and went down well in France. McCormick and Hooker would have been pleased to know that a leading French scientist thought the expedition's natural-history collections compared favourably with those of d'Urville, which he called 'very meagre and uninteresting'.

Of course the Antarctic explorers were always going to be heroes in Hobart, and the town that Ross referred to as 'our southern home' welcomed their return with unabashed enthusiasm. The Royal

Victoria Theatre in Campbell Street, a dockside music hall that the cream of Hobart society would not be seen dead in, lost no time in marking their achievement by putting on 'a grand nautical drama founded on the glorious discoveries of Captains Ross and Crozier'. Called, catchily, *The South Polar Expedition or The Discoveries of Captains Ross and Crozier*, it shared a double-bill with *Robber of the Rhine*. First night was barely a month after they arrived back, and the haste seemed to show. McCormick, the only senior member of the expedition to go and see it, watched it from 'a front box, curtained round, to ourselves'. He felt it 'rather indifferently got up, and not much better acted', and the *Hobart Town Advertiser* felt that the impersonations of the two captains 'cast a damp upon the energies of those who represented the distinguished personages'.

Sir John Franklin's daughter, Eleanor, was not allowed to go to the performance – 'papa does not encourage the theatre' – but had heard all about it. 'It was said to have been ridiculous in the extreme ... Sir John Franklin, for instance, had a head full of hair,' she giggled to a friend.

Meanwhile, a much bigger, grander and altogether smarter event was being planned. Something on a scale Hobart had never seen before: a celebratory ball to be held on board the ships, as a way of celebrating their achievement and thanking the people of Hobart for their hospitality. The date was set for 1 June, and the planning moved into gear with the formation of a committee, on which Surgeon McCormick served as honorary secretary for HMS *Erebus*. It was a role that gave him an opportunity to combine the scientific and the social. On Tuesday 18 May he wrote: '[I] attended the ball committee, and received a specimen of the *ornithorhynchus* [the duck-billed platypus, found only in eastern Australia] ... unfortunately it died in the transit, and I preserved its skin.'

On Friday 21st, with not much more than a week to go, the two ships were warped in as close to the shore as possible and lashed together. On Sunday 23rd, the Ball committee met in Ross's cabin and invitation cards were sent out, some to the dignitaries of the town and others to the officers of both ships, 'to enable them to pay a compliment to friends from whom they may have individually received attention during their stay'.

On the evening of 1 June the weather held, cool and fresh. The 'Erebus and Terror Ball' kicked off at eight o'clock. Carriages arrived at Government House and were directed to Ross Cove down a specially laid track, which wound through the trees to the waterside. Here Sir John had cleared the ground for a paddock, where guests could be dropped off. The two ships, bedecked with Chinese lanterns, stood a little way off the shore, joined to the bank by a bridge of boats – Erebus designated as the ballroom and Terror as the dining room and bar. Tarpaulins had been raised over the decks to provide cover. Passing between a pair of tall lamp-posts, guests approached, two abreast, through a canvas-covered arcade, decorated with flags and with branches of yellow wattle and other native plants 'as to resemble the mouth of a grotto', as McCormick described it in his journal, 'so that after wending along a gloomy narrow passage for some sixty or seventy yards, a flood of light all at once burst upon them on stepping from the gangway upon the quarter deck'.

The two captains and their officers, in full dress uniform, welcomed every guest as they stepped aboard. Someone had had the bright idea of hanging the ships with all the mirrors that the expedition had brought along, as gifts for any benighted natives they might meet. There were 700 mirrors in all, which, according to a letter from a breathless seventeen-year-old guest, 'reflected the lights beautifully'.

Captain Ross's cabin and the gun-room – male bastions, if ever there were any – had been turned into the ladies' dressing rooms for the evening, complete with mirrors, hair-pins and bottles of eau-de-cologne. The steps down to the lower deck, up which men normally raced on their way to the rigging, had been covered in red baize and the hatchway entrance hung with rosettes of red bunting.

The 'ballroom' was lined with flags, and contained two bandstands. On one, a cloth-covered rostrum garlanded with flowers, the band of the 51st Regiment played beneath a portrait of the young Queen Victoria. The other bandstand, just aft of the mainmast, was occupied by the Hobart Town Quadrille Band.

At eleven o'clock supper was served on HMS *Terror*. It took a little time for the 300 guests to negotiate the gangway from one ship to the other, but once aboard, a fine display awaited them. The sides of the ship were lined with black and scarlet cloth, with candles placed in front of the mirrors. McCormick felt that '[Lieutenant] McMurdo ... with his customary good taste, left nothing to be desired in its decoration and certainly threw us in the *Erebus* into the shade.' The chandeliers particularly caught McCormick's envious eye: 'tastefully formed of bright steel bayonets, which had a far more ship-shape appearance than our hired commonplace glass ones'.

A supper of chicken, pies, pastries, cakes and jellies with fruit was already set on the tables, and wine, port, sherry and champagne were all available. Ross and Crozier sat on either side of Sir John Franklin. 'Many toasts were drunk and speeches perpetrated, accompanied by loud cheering and emptying of wine glasses,' noted McCormick. They danced on the deck of the *Erebus* until six in the morning.

The whole night was viewed as a great success. Cunningham wrote in his diary that 'everything went off with the greatest éclat and hilarity'. This was in marked contrast to his much briefer entry the next day: 'clearing away the Wreck; Heads bad'. The newspapers could hardly restrain themselves and were already calling it 'the Glorious First of June'. The seventeen-year-old 'lady of fashion' gave her verdict in a letter to a friend: 'the Ball at Government House ... was considered the best that has ever taken place there. I had the honour of dancing with both Captain Ross and Captain Crozier.' Two nights later she was at a quadrille party, revelling in the attentions of other members of the expedition, which sound to have been generous, if not winningly romantic: 'Scarcely a day passes without some of the officers calling and bringing us specimens of granite, albatross's eggs and different things from the South.'

One conspicuous absentee was Lady Franklin, who had been travelling in New Zealand for the past four months and was doubtless regretting the timing of her trip. She returned to Hobart on the sloop *Favourite* nearly three weeks after the ball, to be met on her arrival by Sir John and Captain Ross. In a letter to her sister Mary, she told of her great joy at finding the two captains still in Hobart, and of how much she would miss them when they left.

Leaving Crozier to coordinate all the activities at the Rossbank Observatory, Ross made a journey to the south of the island, collecting specimens, gathering information about the geology and botany of the Tasman Peninsula and surveying the natural harbours and grand banks off the coast. Even when not officially on duty, he was noting, calculating and evaluating all that he saw around him. His earnest commitment to understanding and improving the world led him to another of his unashamedly interventionist recommendations. His later account of the voyage records his frustration that 'so charming a country should remain a useless desolate wilderness, although capable of producing an abundance of food for a large population, whilst so many thousands in England have hardly sufficient to subsist on from day to day'.

So far as nature was concerned, Ross was like McCormick and so many other of his contemporaries, inquisitive but unsentimental. At that time the world's population was less than one billion and resources were abundant. Today, with the population heading towards eight billion, the destruction of our habitat is seen as a threat rather than an obligation. For Ross, the rich seas and forests of Tasmania were not there to be conserved, they were there to be exploited.

To make the world a better place, one had to make it more productive. If there were fish, then they should be caught; if there were forests, they should be cut down. He couldn't see the wood for the price of timber. Woodland should become farmland, and quiet coves with good harbours should become productive ports.

Of the original inhabitants of the island, neither Ross nor anybody else had much to say. Almost all had now been killed or removed to Flinders Island. Hooker has a particularly poignant entry in his journal. 'Of the numbers that once inhabited this island, only three remain, all males, and they consist of an old, a middle aged man, and a child. They are very savage, but seldom seen.'

Ross was a successful, strong-willed and strong-minded individual who saw the world as being at the service of man. And from there it was a small step to seeing the British as those best suited to be the world's caretaker.

Erebus and *Terror* spent Christmas 1841 in the ice. John Davis aboard *Terror* depicts the scene.

CHAPTER 8

'PILGRIMS OF THE OCEAN'

'Early on the morning of the 7th of July [1841],' Ross wrote, 'we weighed, and stood down the river; his Excellency Sir John Franklin and many of our friends, came on board for the purpose of seeing us fairly off, and bidding us a long farewell.'

Ross and the men of *Erebus* and *Terror* were leaving Tasmania for the last time. Nearly two years had passed since they had left England, and at least one more Antarctic season lay ahead. It was a chance to build on the successes they had already achieved; to find a way to the South Magnetic Pole; to learn more about the ice barrier and the mountainous land that lay beyond it; to be able to confirm, once and for all, that a new continent lay beneath the ice.

It must have been a difficult leave-taking. The island had been good to them, comfortable and friendly. Now they were to exchange it once again for the risks of ice and snow. 'I experienced Great Kindness in Tasmania,' Cunningham wrote in his diary. McCormick confided to his journal how much he would miss the convivial company of the Gregson family in Risdon, where he spent his last day. Hooker had made a good friend of a Lieutenant Breton, whose house he described as 'perfectly English ... the drawing room table covered with as many new periodicals and knick-knacks as we are accustomed to see at home ... a pleasing change after four months of our narrow cabins'.

Crozier would have mixed feelings on leaving. Although Sophy Cracroft had turned him down, his infatuation with her remained – an infatuation that he would now have to keep to himself through another long Antarctic journey.

Lady Franklin said her farewells the night before they left, confessing later that 'Our last evening I found a very melancholy one.' She was to try and keep up a correspondence with Ross, though from a letter she sent to him two months after he'd left, it's clear that he was to be the less active participant. 'My dear Captn Ross,' she chided him, 'let me have the nice, long, gossiping letter you have promised – I have been writing to Captn Crozier ... Assure all my friends of the *Erebus* that I hold them in very kind remembrance ... May heaven bless you, dear Captn Ross – your very affect and sincere friend, Jane Franklin.'

Her husband's hospitality had made a universally favourable impression. Ross was particularly appreciative of his hands-on support for the observatory, and Hooker was gushing in his praise. 'Were I to devote a whole letter to the subject,' he wrote to his sister, 'I could not say too much of Sir John Franklin ... He is in all respects a good man and an ornament to his profession as a Christian and a sailor.' Hooker went on to recall the warmth of Franklin's greetings and farewells, especially on their return from the first Antarctic voyage. 'You would have smiled to see with what alacrity he came up the ship's side and welcomed us all, hat in hand, with the heartiest (to use a vulgar expression) pump-handle shake.'

Perhaps the greatest regrets at the expedition's departure would have been those of Franklin himself. That final party had been a triumph, but now he had to face up to increasingly bitter opposition to his governorship, both from disaffected locals and from an unsympathetic Colonial Office; this was to end in his dismissal from the post, and his own final departure from Tasmania, within two years. It was something that he, and his wife, would never come to accept. And something that would ultimately ensure that, although HMS *Erebus* was now sailing away, Franklin had not seen the last of her.

As instructed by the Admiralty, Ross first set course north-east, for Sydney, where he had orders to set up a station 'eminently fitted for the determination of all the magnetic elements'. The two ships reached Botany Bay and a week later were passing through the Heads into what Ross called 'one of the most magnificent harbours in the world'. The wind had dropped completely, and *Erebus* and *Terror* had to be towed into this magnificent harbour by their own boats.

Cunningham liked the activity in Sydney harbour: 'Every one Seems on the Move'. He noted the regular arrivals of new settlers on ships that had come from Britain. 'An Emigrant Vessel came in the afternoon from Scotland with a great many emigrants in her of both sexes.' A few days later, on 26 July: 'a large emigrant ship came in from England'. That night a grand dinner was given for all the Commissioned Officers at the Australian Club. Cunningham, though not invited, ferried some of the officers to the event: 'went up to the Town in the Dinghy at night: likes the appearance of the place very much'.

Hooker thought Sydney compared unfavourably with Hobart. He found the streets badly maintained, and the shops poorly stocked compared to those in the Tasmanian capital. He was very happy, however, to be introduced to Alexander MacLeay, an ex-Colonial Secretary who was not only full of interest in Hooker's collections, but gave him the run of his 25-acre garden, which proved to be a botanist's paradise. Through him, Hooker met some interesting and unusual men of science, including a Dr Buckland, 'who could tell the age of a skull by the taste'.

They completed their business in Sydney within three weeks and set sail for the Bay of Islands in New Zealand on 5 August 1841. *Erebus* was never one of the swiftest ships afloat, and Ross complained that even under full sail she could not make much more than eight knots across the Tasman Sea – and *Terror* even less. However, there was much to see and do. Flying fish landed on the deck, albatrosses and sperm whales were constant companions, and on 9 August a meteor was seen to burst in the south-western sky. It was a prelude to a shower of shooting stars that was expected in the middle of the month. Ross made sure he had instructed all the men on watch what to look out for. So zealously did they throw themselves into their task that one of the men was reluctant to be relieved from his post, saying he was sure two or three stars were about to fall, as 'he'd been watching them and could see they were shaking!'

Whilst taking measurements of depth and water temperature, they discovered a coral reef growing out of the seabed, of such an extent that Ross estimated it might 'in future ages form an island between New South Wales and New Zealand'. It is almost heart-breaking to read of coral growing, when now it seems almost everywhere to be shrinking.

Twenty-one days after leaving Sydney they reached the Bay of Islands, on the northern tip of New Zealand. The first British settle-ment in the country, it was principally used by whalers. As they turned into the bay, Cunningham was impressed by a large American whaling ship with nine whale-boats around it, and almost equally impressed by the unusual sight of a vessel fitted up as a grog shop. 'I thought at first she was a chapel.'

The whalers had lived in relative harmony with the local Maoris, but lately the British government had moved to formalise its claim to the whole of New Zealand. Eighteen months before the Ross exped-ition arrived in the Bay of Islands, Captain William Hobson had concluded a treaty with the Maori chiefs, guaranteeing them protec-tion and secure possession of their lands in exchange for British sovereignty. Implementation of the Treaty of Waitangi, as it was known, led to tensions, particularly over the definition of property and the pressure on Maoris to sell their lands. By the time Ross and his men arrived, these tensions had boiled over into violence between the Maoris and the colonial settlers.

Ross, aware of the volatile situation, ordered his men not to stray far from the ships and to be armed at all times. This didn't cramp McCormick's style, and the day after they arrived he was up and about: 'called at Colenso's printing office,' he noted, 'walked over the hills ... which are clothed with what is here called the tea-scrub, a fragrant aromatic plant bearing a pretty white bloom'. In the afternoon, 'I again landed by the Observatory ... and shot two of the tui or parson bird, a beautiful bird about the size of our starling.' He fell in with an ex-Royal Navy lieutenant-turned-missionary called Williams – 'a fine dignified-looking man, inclined to be stout' – who held Sunday services in Maori and claimed remarkable success in converting the indigenous population to Christianity. McCormick invited Williams and his wife on board and gave them some of his Antarctic specimens, whilst Ross showed them the magnetic instruments in the observatory. McCormick's collection had grown so extensive that he (and perhaps his fellow officers) must have been relieved that a few days later he was able to offload several boxes of specimens onto HMS *Jupiter*, recently arrived from Auckland and bound for London.

Meanwhile Hooker, having taken on supplies of bottles and jars at Sydney, was busy with a collection of his own, mainly fish and insect specimens. Captain Ross offered him every encouragement. His captain was, as Hooker put it, 'indefatigable in walking along the beach collecting everything and sending it to me to stow away', whilst ensuring that there was space in his cabin for Hooker to work. He had the use of a large drawing table under the starboard-side window, 'where no-one is allowed to interrupt me'. He also had drawers, a locker and a bookshelf in the cabin, so that 'no excuse is left for my not working. Captain Ross never permits even his own meal hours to disturb me, and at night I have one end of his table and may keep the light burning as long as ever I choose.'

The second anniversary of their departure, duly noted by Cunningham ('Two years from England this Day'), was marked by tragedy. Two Marines were returning to the *Erebus* when their dinghy capsized. One of them, George Barker, was drowned and the other was saved only by the providential intervention of soldiers who had witnessed the accident from the shore. Cunningham, a Marine himself, mourned a man 'much regretted by his Shipmates, as he was a merry lively fellow and one of the strongest men in the expedition'. John Davis, the twenty-five-year-old Second Master on *Terror*, concurred. In a letter home to his sister Emily he described Barker as 'one of those jovial characters that by his jokes kept the mess continually laughing round him'.

Further tragedy struck a few days later. The home of an English woman, Mrs Robertson, was set on fire by natives, and she, her manservant and three children were all murdered. Fearing an escalation in violence, the expedition, escorted by HMS *Favourite*, set sail from the Bay of Islands just before five o'clock on the morning of 23 November 1841. 'Our decks had all the appearance of a farm-yard,' wrote McCormick, '... consisting of oxen, sheep, goats, pigs, and poultry, and each quarter was festooned with a line of pumpkins.'

Once out of the bay, HMS *Favourite* raised the traditional three cheers, before heading off to Auckland. *Erebus* and *Terror* continued south and west towards Chatham Island, which Ross was keen to visit for magnetic observations and to explore its potential as a whaling station.

Two stop-offs in quick succession seem briefly to have undermined Second Master Davis's constitution. 'I was of course very seasick,' he recalled; 'we had been with little intermission six months in harbour, and I expected it. I shall never entirely get over it; I am very unfortunate that way.' The time ashore also seems to have undermined discipline on board – understandable perhaps, given the challenge of readjusting to the daily grind after quite long periods of relative freedom. At any rate, on their second day at sea James Rogers, one of the quartermasters on *Erebus*, who had been recently demoted and given thirty-six lashes for 'mutinous conduct', was being hauled on deck for more punishment, when he threw off his guards and hurled himself off the stern of the ship. He was rescued and brought back, but the whole incident caused John Davis to draw invidious comparisons between his own ship, *Terror*, and *Erebus*: 'that ship is not nearly in such good order as this ship,' he argued. 'There is too much familiarity between the men and the officers to please me.'

In fact, this seems to have been the only time Ross felt it necessary to punish one of his sailors (his great-grandson, Rear-Admiral M.J. Ross, said that he was not a fan of public punishments, though he was a firm disciplinarian). Ironically enough, a week later came the first instance of corporal punishment on HMS *Terror*. Crozier's log records: 'Punished Jn Irvine with 48 lashes for theft'. Cunningham mentions it in his diary as 'a very unusual thing with us but the individual richly deserved it, his crime being <u>Theft</u> Robbing his comrade, dirtiness and general irregular conduct'.

Cunningham's disgust at Irvine's dirtiness underlines the importance of personal hygiene aboard ship. The crew were usually split into 'divisions', supervised by an officer who made sure that healthy standards were maintained, and with different days of the week set aside for washing, shaving and mending. Some of the officers had washbasins in their cabins, but the men would usually bathe in basins or tubs on the forecastle, if it was warm enough. The colder it became, the more the men were confined, and the more necessary it was to keep checks on cleanliness. Parry, in his first over-wintering voyage in 1821, put in place a regular system. As he described it in his journal: 'Three quarters of an hour being allowed after breakfast for the men to prepare themselves for muster, we then beat to divisions punctually at quarter past nine when ... a strict inspection of the men took place, as to their personal cleanliness and good condition as well as sufficient warmth of their clothing.'

So influential was Parry that Ross and Crozier would almost certainly have taken similar precautions.

Three weeks out of New Zealand, they had their first taste of things to come as they emerged from dense fog to find themselves confronted by three massive flat-topped tabular icebergs. The largest of them, dead ahead of the ship, contained deep caverns carved by the sea water, and it was shedding columns of ice. Passing within a half-mile of it, Ross estimated its height at 130 feet, with a circumference of three-quarters of a mile. Temperatures fell and they woke on 18 December to find themselves surrounded by pack-ice. Light and easily dispersed at first, it became heavier as they ploughed on, sufficiently so to force Ross westwards on an avoiding course.

The ships slowly picked their way through, guided from patch to patch of open water by the shouts from the crow's nest. Tern, cape pigeon and white petrel flew around the ship. Seals on the ice were so slow to take fright that they were easily bludgeoned on the head and brought on board for food. In the stomach of one of them they found 9 lb of granite stones, which puzzled Ross, as they were a thousand miles from the nearest land.

The temperature was now sinking below freezing. Davis wrote to his sister complaining of chilblains, 'which were very troublesome and annoying'. 'I tried to keep them away by soaking my feet in rum every night,' he went on, 'but to no purpose. If you had met me at this time you would not have known your brother: my hair was very long and I had allowed my beard to grow all round under my chin for warmth: thick boots and Jim Crow hat, with a check shirt ... we all cut very pretty figures, like a masquerade.' He went on to complain that the ship's cat got into his drawer and tore up six of his charts, but the cat was soon forgiven, for on the 19th she presented them with three kittens. 'Such an event as that you may think nothing of, but to us it is a great deal, for a kitten tends to relieve the monotony of such a cruise as this.' The next day 'they were shown on a warmed clean plate to Captain Ross'.

Christmas Day, described by Cunningham as 'anything but a pleasant one', was spent negotiating tightly packed ice, close to a line of eleven icebergs, with much of the day in thick fog. Captain Ross joined some of the officers and midshipmen for a lunch of roast goose in the gun-room, but it was a muted celebration, with grey skies and the decks particularly cold and chilly from the ice-blocks stored there to provide them with drinking water. It was already much colder than it had been the same time the previous year. When a couple of days later McCormick and Ross set to work skinning and preserving three large penguins they had caught, their hands were so clumsy with cold that it took about four hours to process each bird. McCormick noted finding pebbles and half-digested fish in the birds' stomachs. Thanks in part to the specimens Ross and others brought home, people soon learned that small stones play an important part in penguins' nest-building, and the half-digested fish would have been food intended for their young.

Progress slowed to a trickle. The ships had run into pack-ice much earlier than during the previous summer and although they had now negotiated 250 miles through it, only thirty of those had been in the past week. They were still short of the Antarctic Circle as the old year came to an end. And things were getting worse.

'Friday 31st December. New Year's Eve ... ice closed entirely around us,' wrote Cunningham in his memorandum book. They were caught in a hard, barely moving pack, with slabs of ice squeezed together, occasionally cracking like gun-shots as they erupted into jagged pyramids on the surface. Nevertheless, Ross was bullish. They would find their way out soon, and morale was holding: 'The New Year was hailed by us all with ... feelings of confident hope and cheerfulness.'

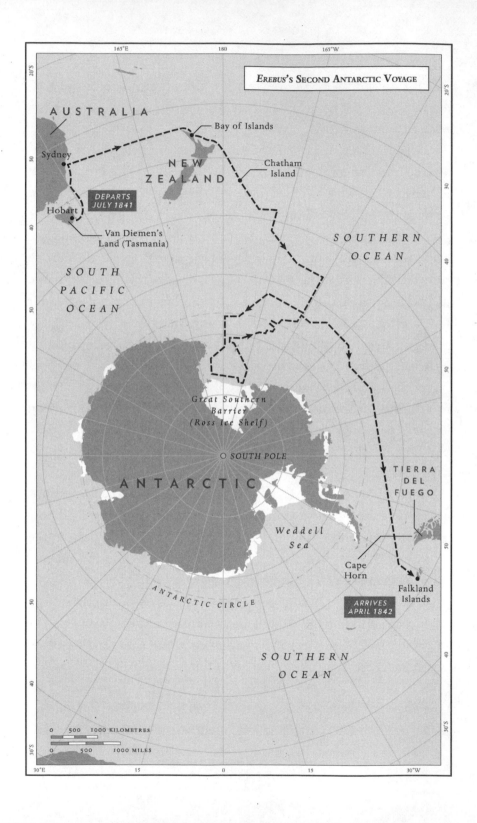

EREBUS'S SECOND ANTARCTIC VOYAGE

165°E   180   165°W

20°S

30

40

50

AUSTRALIA

Sydney

Bay of Islands

NEW ZEALAND

Chatham Island

DEPARTS JULY 1841

Hobart

Van Diemen's Land (Tasmania)

SOUTHERN OCEAN

SOUTH PACIFIC OCEAN

Great Southern Barrier (Ross Ice Shelf)

O SOUTH POLE

ANTARCTIC

Weddell Sea

ANTARCTIC CIRCLE

TIERRA DEL FUEGO

Cape Horn

ARRIVES APRIL 1842

Falkland Islands

SOUTHERN OCEAN

0   500   1000 KILOMETRES

0   500   1000 MILES

30°E   15   0   15   30°W

Second Master Davis shared this upbeat mood. Revelling in the fact that he could actually walk between the two ships, he dined on *Erebus* and afterwards went out with Joseph Hooker to 'cut out in the hard snow the figure of a woman, which we called our "Venus de Medici". She was made sitting down and about eight feet long.' They then dug down into the ice and carved out a room with an ice-table and an ice-sofa in it. The celebrations that followed were unconfined. A passing penguin would have observed sailors blowing horns, beating gongs, holding pigs under their arms to make them squeal, as each ship tried to outdo the other in sheer volume of noise. High spirits, but also a resounding affirmation of their existence in a silent, stationary world. The penguin, and any other living creature nearby, would have fled long before the cacophony climaxed with both ships sounding forty-two bells to see in the New Year.

As midnight struck, Captain Ross joined the two crews in the newly dug ice-room to shake hands all round and raise a toast to the health of all the men. Uniquely, as Davis noted, they were 'all up': no one was asleep, and no one was on duty, either – the enforced confinement on the ice meant there was no need to climb rigging, or furl sails, or man the ship's wheel, or keep lookout. The Clark Ross Expedition thus entered 1842 as a tableau in the ice, with everyone of whatever rank or station playing a part. According to Cornelius Sullivan, some of the *Terror*'s crew came across to *Erebus* and danced on the deck until five in the morning, after which there were one or two 'Pugialistic matches in the forecastle which peaceably ended'. As Sergeant Cunningham put it, 'Saturday Jan 1st. Was ushered in with joviality and hilarity. I hope it will go out so.'

After breakfast on New Year's Day all the men were issued with a new set of cold-weather clothing – a jacket, a pair of trousers, two pairs of boot hose, two comforters, two pairs of mittens, a Welsh wig, a knife and some thread and a red shirt. Second Master Davis was particularly pleased with the red shirt: 'very handy as they last a fort-night'. Between washes, I assume that means.

The crews had been out on the ice first thing, clearing away the snow to create an ice-ballroom, and building a pub to go with it. A sign, hanging from a boat hook and an ice-axe, and illustrated with Bacchus in one corner and Britannia in the other, proclaimed the pub's name as 'The Pilgrims of the Ocean'. On the other side it was called 'The Pioneers of Science', which, according to Davis, greatly amused Captain Ross.

For once, the leader of the expedition was happy to let down his luxurious hair. 'Captain Crozier and Miss Ross opened the ball with a quadrille,' wrote Davis to his sister. Ross, despite his Presbyterian earnestness, was not unfamiliar with drag. On the first Parry expedition, while still a midshipman, he had taken two female roles in plays put on during the Arctic winter, playing Mrs Bruin in *The Mayor of Garratt* and Poll in *The North-West Passage, or The Voyage Finished*. Once he had stepped out with Crozier, the floor was opened. Reels and country dances followed and, appropriately, ice-creams were handed round.

Thanks to the graphic talents of Second Master Davis, we have not only a written but also a visual reminder that exploration is not just about what is in the official reports. His watercolour 'New Year's Day on the Ice 1842. Lat. 66.32.S Long. 156.28. W' is, considering the circumstances, one of the most heart-warming paintings I know, with the flags flying, musicians playing and a Marine landing on his backside. Davis's letter to his sister Emily captures a spirit of sheer delight: 'you would have laughed to see the whole of us, with thick overall boots on, dancing, waltzing and slipping about ... and the best of it was there was not an ill word the whole time'.

What I remember most from my own travels in the Antarctic is the stupendous scale of the whitened landscape, and the huge overarching silence – a silence broken only by the creaking, cracking and groaning of the shifting ice. As I picture the sailors capering about, dancing waltzes and eightsome reels, the only human beings in the whole southern end of the earth, it seems a stunningly surreal image: ice, so often portrayed as a grim adversary, transformed briefly into a shining white dance-floor.

For this night, at least, all were equals. 'At about one o'clock as the captains left we first pelted them with snowballs and then cheered them, both of which honours they took with equally good humour,' wrote Davis. Even Ross, who airbrushed most frivolity from his later account of the expedition, was caught by the mood. 'If our friends in England could have witnessed the scene, they would have thought, what I am sure truly was the case, that we were a very happy party.' The festivities continued the next day, with a sort of slapstick Antarctic Olympics. There were greasy poles to climb and greased pigs to catch, and all to the raucous accompaniment of gongs (otherwise used in thick fog to keep contact with other ships) and cow-horns for trumpets.

The ice-pack showed no sign of releasing them. On 3 January, McCormick noted that he could walk from *Erebus* for at least half a mile in all directions. And, not being a man to stay on board if there were opportunities elsewhere, that's exactly what he did. Taking care always to keep a gun to hand, it is hardly surprising that when a white petrel flew past him he took a pot-shot at it. But this time something was different. The petrel fell onto an inaccessible part of the floe:

> but its mate, flying in company with it at the time, instantly alighted near the wounded bird, and placing its own beak in juxtaposition with the dying creature's, began a painful lamentation over its dying companion, curving its own neck over the prostrate form, and giving expression to a plaintive, murmuring, cackling note ... then as if acted upon by some impulse or instinctive feeling ... that this was death, and it could be of no further use, it took wing and flew straight away. Whilst I was endeavouring to get round the sludge-ice to pick the other up ... the poor thing feebly raised its head, after slowly staggering along the ice for a few paces, apparently its last effort.

What follows sounds something like a Damascene conversion. 'How little do we know of animal life and mind! For mind they have unquestionably, call it instinct or what you will. They are constructed on a very similar type to their lordly master, man ... The same brain and nerves, which in common with him render them sentient beings, must also endow them with the power of thought.'

For a trigger-happy bird slayer, this was quite an admission, and there was more to come as McCormick laid into people like himself: 'Many of these much-wronged and under-estimated beings should make him blush, exhibiting, as they often do, moral attributes of a high order.'

It was another three days before the wind changed to the east and they were able to find sufficient open water to cast off from the floe, leaving Venus de Medici and the ice-ballroom to float away, a tiny, tenuous reminder of the rarest of New Year celebrations.

In the days that followed, those happy memories must have seemed like fickle fantasies as the ships were dragged back into the ice-pack. They made slow progress. Sometimes they were reduced to tacking about in small pools of open water, like specimens trapped in one of McCormick's jars. The one positive thing – as they found themselves drifting all the way back to the point they had reached on Christmas Day – was that the ships were able to keep together. There was regular traffic across the ice between *Erebus* and *Terror*. Seals were hunted wherever possible, most successfully by Mr Oakley and Mr Abernethy. One of them weighed 850 lb and yielded more than 16 gallons of oil. Another, when opened up, was found to have 28 lb of fish in its stomach.

On 12 January 1842 the ice broke up sufficiently for the ships to make progress southwards. *Erebus* made 20 miles in one night, but by morning the ice was offering more resistance, and men were deployed with poles and boat hooks to try to push it aside. Both ships were now confined to a half-mile of open water and, to reduce any chance of collision, Ross ordered the ships to be made fast on either side of the same ice-floe. Which is how they were on the 17th when a heavy swell and a rapidly descending barometer warned of the approach of a strong north-easterly gale. It was preceded by an eerie calm. The temperature rose above freezing, dense fog enveloped the ships and snow began to fall. A huge iceberg loomed out of the mist, so close that all Ross could do was order all sails to be set on both ships and hope for the best. They avoided being crushed by only a few feet, the tip of *Erebus*'s spanker boom actually grazing the ice as it swept past.

Next morning the swell grew so strong that two of the 8-inch hawsers holding *Erebus* snapped under the strain and carried away two of the ice-anchors. Twelve hours later the gale finally struck, whipping up towering seas that sent waves smashing over the tops of the highest icebergs: 'little short of a West India hurricane in its force,' wrote McCormick.

Cornelius Sullivan was below decks on *Erebus* when the storm hit: 'Every crash threatening to Shake her timbers to pieces we Expected to see the masts fall overboard Every moment.' On *Terror*, John Davis recorded equally apocalyptic fears. 'Sometimes,' he wrote, 'we thought that the pieces we came against would grind us to powder.' This was the man who had so joyfully described the frolics on the ice less than three weeks earlier. 'Here we were then, two unmanageable ships drifting about in an unknown sea . . . and no possibility of helping ourselves.'

Ross was understandably worried. 'Soon after midnight,' he later wrote, 'our ships were involved in an ocean of rolling fragments of ice, hard as floating rocks of granite . . . and the destruction of the ships seemed inevitable.' For twenty-eight hours the fate of the two ships hung in the balance. Ross could only pray as he watched 'our ships still rolling and groaning amidst the heavy fragments of crushing bergs, over which the ocean rolled . . . dashing and grinding them together with fearful violence'. 'Each of us secured our hold,' he recalled, 'waiting the issue with resignation to the will of Him who alone could preserve us and bring us safely through this extreme danger.'

By the morning of 21 January, the tempest had subsided a little. *Erebus*'s stern had been badly damaged as she ducked and dived, and signals from *Terror* indicated that her rudder had been shattered beyond repair. A boat was therefore lowered to take Captain Ross over to examine the damage. It certainly seemed more serious than on his own ship. *Terror*'s rudder was in pieces and her sternpost so wrenched and twisted that it would be difficult to fit the spare. Apart from that, he was surprised and relieved to see how little serious damage either ship had sustained, considering their ordeal, and he was impressed with the way Crozier had kept his ship steady during the storm, carefully re-stowing the hold to give her maximum stability. They had, of course, survived wild weather in the South Atlantic before. But this was the first time that blocks of ice had bombarded the ships day and night, whilst frozen splinters, as hard as granite, waited to spear them from beneath.

Most of the crew were exhausted. They had been at emergency stations throughout the night and the previous day. Ross, too, was tired out. Davis recorded how 'The usual smile had gone from Captain Ross's countenance and he looked anxious and careworn.' Ross sent as many as could be spared below decks to rest. The others were put to work to repair the ships.

The broken rudder was hoisted aboard and the carpenters set to work stripping away splintered wood and replacing sections, whilst the armourers and Cornelius Sullivan, the blacksmith, forged new parts to hold it all together. They finished the work that same day, but there was still much to do. Some of the copper sheeting on both ships had simply been peeled away by the action of the ice and needed to be replaced. The carpenters on *Terror* were fashioning a completely new rudder.

The following days were calmer, but no less frustrating. The expedition remained at the mercy of the ice and the winds, unable to make much progress. Concentrated vigilance was required, twenty-four hours a day, to keep on the lookout for leads – those cracks in the ice that provided pathways for the ships – and for any heavy icebergs driven towards the ships by the swell. As if this wasn't enough, *Terror* nearly caught fire. The Sylvester's Patent Heating Apparatus, which had been in use around the clock to dry out the damp below decks, became so hot that parts of the ship were rendered untouchable and some blocks of wood ignited. Smoke billowed out, and water had to be poured into the hold to prevent it from catching fire. Nothing they had experienced on the first voyage had prepared them for anything like this.

It wasn't until the first day of February that there were signs of change. By the evening they could tell they were close to the edge of the ice-pack. Perimeter ice was always heavier, and *Erebus* took a few hard knocks before she at last broke through into open water at two o'clock the next morning.

Cornelius Sullivan expressed the general feeling of relief: 'Thank God and British Built Ships we See Ourselves Once more in the boosom [*sic*] of the open Sea after being closed up in the center of our Enemy for the space of 47 days.' For his part, Davis wrote of his inexpressible delight, but also his despair at their paltry progress. They had gained only 100 miles since Christmas Eve.

The cold was intense. A 1½-inch rope swelled with ice to at least 1 foot in circumference. When the sea broke over the decks, the men on watch, or the helmsmen at the wheel (there was no covered wheelhouse on either ship), were transformed into moving lumps of ice. One morning, as ice was being chipped away from the bows, a fish was found perfectly frozen to the side of the ship. It was removed with great care, thawed out and, as a sketch was about to be made to record this phenomenon, the ship's cat leapt forward and ate it.

Just after midnight on 22 February they came through another gale, to hear a cry from the lookout announcing that the Great Barrier was in sight. But they still could not find a way through it. Ross persevered for a while, in the forlorn hope that he might find access, but the ice was thickening fast and he realised that the Barrier seemed to have no end. On 23 February, standing 1½ miles out from the ice-wall, *Erebus* waited for *Terror* to catch up, so that the two ships could record their position at the same time. They were at 161°W and 78°9'30"S – 6 miles further south than their previous record. Second Master Davis, aboard *Terror*, recounted his feelings in his letter to his sister. 'The *Erebus* sounded, and we tacked in the spot she did, so that neither ship could say she was beyond the other. No one will ever beat that in this longitude, that I may safely say.' To an extent, he was right. No other sailing ship would ever get as far south as *Erebus* and *Terror* did that day. In fact no ship of any kind reached that far south for almost sixty years. Ross, who had already reached a record 82.43°N in 1827, could now claim to have achieved a feat shared only by his shipmates Edward Bird and Thomas Abernethy: to have been further north and further south than anyone else on earth.

Nevertheless, the second expedition had not lived up to the expectations of the first. The South Magnetic Pole remained tantalisingly out of reach; ice had trapped the ships for too long; and at one point they had come closer to disaster than at any time since leaving England. It was now time to extract themselves from the risk of further damage and head to a safe haven to refit and resupply. The season was over. Ross signalled to Crozier that he planned to make for the Falkland Islands.

Later that day, as they were taking soundings, the ever-curious Surgeon McCormick took one last look at the implacable ice barrier that had been beside them for so long and that had, at every turn, thwarted their chances of landing on the Antarctic continent. It provoked one of the finest descriptive passages in his journal:

> The day was cloudless, a bright sun in a clear blue sky, the rays of which, falling on the barrier, gave a beautiful effect to its steep, indented sides, the various angles and abutments of which stood boldly out in relief, alternately in light and shade forming a long, zigzag perpendicular wall of ice upwards of 100 feet in height ... Along its base numerous fragments of ice, of every form and size were scattered or piled together in the wildest confusion ... leaving recesses in these stupendous cliffs, hollowed out by the terrific power of these heavy seas which gales of wind have set in motion when sweeping over the vast and mighty surface of the southern ocean.

The brief Antarctic summer was over and the size and frequency of the icebergs were increasing. On the last day of February, as Davis recalled, 'we got amongst a great number ... some of them were several miles in extent, and at one time we counted ninety'. It was a highly dangerous time. They avoided one iceberg by less than 30 yards. 'I hardly breathed while we were passing it,' Davis wrote. 'The hands were on deck to tack, but she would not have gone round.' *Erebus* had already got past and her crew could only watch as *Terror* battled with the cauldron of water between her and the iceberg: 'They said in the *Erebus* that it was a very pretty sight, but more interesting to those safe than to those present.'

It's tempting to assume that as the ships made their progress north in the early days of March, the dangers lessened. In fact, the opposite was the case. There were fewer icebergs, but it was becoming harder to spot them, particularly as the nights lengthened to eight hours. Nevertheless Sergeant Cunningham felt confident enough to conclude his diary entry for 12 March: 'Making a beautiful passage so far for the Falkland Islands.' That reassuring entry was followed by a very different one: '13th Sunday: Such a one as I hope I may never spend again.'

With a strengthening wind, *Erebus* was still making seven knots when, just before 1 a.m., James Angelly, the man at the foretop, shouted a warning from 100 feet above them. 'All hands on deck!' was sounded. Men asleep in their hammocks were roused, and turned out half-naked and utterly confused. Among them was John Davis. 'I was in bed and on the sick list with my hand,' he later wrote. 'I had been awoken by the noise of reefing topsails, and lay awake listening. I knew something must be wrong, by the constant commands to the helmsman. At last someone regularly screamed down the fore hatchway, "All hands bear a hand on deck, every one!" – and immediately after came a crash. "Good God", cried I, "we are foul of an iceberg."'

Things now happened very fast. Ross heaved his ship over to port to avoid being crushed, only to find that HMS *Terror*, under topsail and foresails, had heaved to starboard and was bearing down on them. There was no chance of her avoiding both the iceberg and *Erebus*. A collision was inevitable. On board *Terror*, John Davis recalled what happened next. 'I opened my door to prevent it being jammed, and hurriedly put on two or three articles of dress and jumped up the hatchway, fully expecting to see the cliff of an iceberg over our heads, instead of which just abreast the gangway were the bows of the *Erebus* ... as far as the copper above our gunwhale, her fore topmast and bowsprit gone. Down we came crash, with a shock that nearly knocked me down.'

Captain Ross described the moment of impact:

The concussion when she struck us was such as to throw almost everyone off his feet; our bowsprit, fore-topmast, and other small spars, were carried away; and the ships hanging together, entangled by their rigging, and dashing against each other with fearful violence, were falling down upon the weather face of the lofty berg ... against which the waves were breaking and foaming to near the summit of its perpendicular cliffs. Sometimes she rose high above us, almost exposing her keel to view, and again descended as we in our turn rose to the top of the wave, threatening to bring her beneath us, whilst the crashing of the breaking upperworks and boats increased the horror of the scene.

In trying to avoid the iceberg, the ships had been put on a collision course and these two stout vessels, which had survived everything nature could throw at them, were now being repeatedly smashed against each other by the waves. On *Erebus*, Cornelius Sullivan watched in horror as *Terror* met his ship with sufficient force to drive her anchor deep into the 8-inch planking of the hull. *Erebus*'s bowsprit 'snapped to atoms', her foretopmast and all the booms, stays and rigging were torn away. 'At this moment,' Sullivan recalled, 'we poor pilgrims of the Ocean thought it was our last in this Life.'

From the vantage of *Terror*, Sergeant Cunningham described what happened next. 'They then recoiled from one another for a moment (which was one of awfull Suspense to the poor half-naked beings that crowded these decks). She took us again then on our main beam with a most terrible crash ... nearly Staving our side in, breaking our rubbing pieces right up and tearing the iron Sheathing into ribbons.' The two ships hung together for a few moments, before tearing apart again, cracking the masts and bringing spars crashing onto the deck. Then, in the midst of the chaos and disorder, Captain Crozier seized the moment to take *Terror* towards a frighteningly narrow gap in the advancing wall of ice. Recalling that agonising moment for his sister, Davis described the thoughts that had run through his mind: 'Emily, what were my fears? I was afraid to stand before a severe though merciful and just God; I was not fit to die. What would I not have given at that time for a single day to prepare myself for such an awful change! What thoughts passed in rapid succession through my brain! The events of a life passed in review before me in a few moments, and what had I to trust to except mercy?'

Terror slipped through the gap by a hair's breadth. It wasn't apparent, though, whether *Erebus* would be as fortunate. Indeed, as Marine Sergeant Cunningham strained his eyes into the darkness behind him, it looked to be all over: 'we could see nothing of the poor "Erebus" and in fact we could see no means how she could be safed'.

Erebus was in critical danger. The collision had almost completely disabled her, bringing down spars that had become entangled in the lower yards, preventing the crew from hoisting sail. Like Crozier a few moments before, Ross had to think fast, and in his subsequent account of the expedition, he described in detail what happened next:

> The only way left to us to extricate ourselves from this awful and appalling situation was by resorting to the hazardous expedient of the sternboard [the equivalent of putting the ship into reverse] … The heavy rolling of the vessel, and the probability of the masts giving way each time the lower yard-arms struck against the cliffs which were towering high above our mastheads, rendered it a service of extreme danger to loose the main-sail; but no sooner was the order given, than the daring spirit of the British seaman manifested itself – the men ran up the rigging with as much alacrity as on any ordinary occasion; and although more than once driven off the yard, they after a short time succeeded in loosing the sail. Amidst the roar of the wind and sea, it was difficult both to hear and to execute the orders that were given, so that it was three quarters of an hour before we could get the yards braced bye, and the maintack hauled onboard sharp aback – an expedient that perhaps had never before been resorted to by seamen in such weather: but it had the desired effect; the ship gathered stern-way, plunging her stern into the sea, washing away the gig and quarter boats, and with her lower yard-arms

scraping the rugged face of the berg ... No sooner had we cleared it, than another was seen directly astern of us, against which we were running; and the difficulty now was to get the ship's head turned round and pointed fairly through between the two bergs the breadth of the intervening space not exceeding three times her own breadth; this, however, we happily accomplished; and in a few minutes after getting before the wind, she dashed through a narrow channel, between two perpendicular walls of ice ... and the next moment we were in smooth water under its lee.

Terror burned a blue light to indicate that she was safe. When he saw a similar blue light shining not far away, Cunningham knew his worst fears had proved unfounded and that *Erebus* had made it, too ('which made every heart bound again with joy'). Staring back into the darkness, they could see just how lucky an escape it had been for both ships. The iceberg was not a lone drifter, but part of a long and continuous chain, with no way through other than the narrow slit that had saved them from destruction.

Sullivan had no doubt who was responsible for their survival: 'God Almighty, My friends, alone that Saved us from a miserable death 3000 miles from any land.' Cunningham concurred: 'I must here say that it was a most wonderful interposition of Divine providence that we were not all Sent into the presence of our Maker.' And Davis too: 'After daylight and we had signalized the *Erebus*, I went to my cabin; and never did a sinner offer up to the throne of the Almighty more sincere thanks.'

When McCormick came to write up his account of this narrowest of escapes, his praise was directed closer to home:

At such a perilous crisis a captain's responsibility is assuredly not one to be envied ... However, Captain Ross was quite equal to the emergency, and, folding his arms across his breast, as he stood like a statue on the afterpart of the quarter-deck, calmly gave the order to loose the main-sail. His whole bearing, while lacking nothing in firmness, yet betrayed ... the all-but despair with which he anxiously watched the result of this last and only expedient left to us.

The sternboard manoeuvre that Ross and his crew executed in the most dire and dangerous situation would have been a great gamble at any time. It was this almighty risk, rather than the Almighty himself, that saved the lives of his men.

Crozier had been equally cool on *Terror*. 'The Captain, when it was all over, said that he had not the slightest idea what he did during the hour and how we got through,' wrote Davis. But he went on to give a hint of what a terrifying experience it had been for those on board: 'only one was running out of his senses, but two or three were crying'.

Signals exchanged between the two ships confirmed that *Terror* was not seriously damaged, and *Erebus*, safe now in the lee of the icebergs, already had men on deck clearing the broken spars and the shredded rigging, whilst others waited to replace them.

A meteor shot across the sky.

Throughout the next day, despite it being the normally sacrosanct Sabbath, the crew worked on repairs. Whilst some set to work refitting the rigging, the carpenters were fashioning a replacement bowsprit and others were looking for the cause of a leak on the starboard bow. It was traced to the anchor that had rammed into her side during the collision. In the end they decided it was safer not to remove it and the anchor stayed embedded in *Erebus*, a defiant symbol of their near-death experience. Both ships had damaged their rudders, *Terror*'s so severely that a spare one had to be created out of oak planks, held together with ice-saws. The copper on both ships had, as Davis described it, 'curled up like brown paper'.

Within two days *Erebus* had her foretopmast up again and sails set on the topsail yard, ready to take advantage of the strong westerlies, which pushed her along at a brisk seven to eight knots. She might be bruised and battered, but she was making up to 160 miles a day.

As they approached Cape Horn, with its fearsome reputation, they expected the weather to worsen, but instead found clear skies and gentle breezes. 'Nearing the Horn fast,' noted Cunningham. 'Going 7 knots.' On 29 March, as Captains Ross and Crozier and the officers took measurements of the depth and temperature of the sea, Cunningham seized the opportunity for some household maintenance. 'Aired bedding. Slung clean hammocks and scrubbed the dirty ones. All of which I am very well pleased is done.'

If the weather continued fair, the safe haven of the Falkland Islands was now only a week away, and with it the chance to rest, recuperate and repair the damage from the last four turbulent months. They could be forgiven for thinking the worst was over.

But then, as dawn broke on 2 April, a gale blew in. They were familiar enough with gales by now and the men, accordingly, were up in the main yard shortening the sails as they'd done a thousand times before. This time, however, something went wrong. James Angelly, one of the quartermasters on *Erebus* and the man who had first spotted the icebergs that near-catastrophic night just a few weeks before, was high up on the rigging when the unthinkable happened. Despite his experience as one of the elite 'top men', he missed his grip, slipped and fell like a stone into the water. A lifebuoy was tossed out to him and at first it seemed that he had found it and was clinging on. *Erebus* tacked as fast as she could and turned towards Angelly – the sea was running too high for them to launch a cutter safely. They were 200 yards away from him when the wind swung round and forced them to manoeuvre again. As they turned, Ross saw Angelly 'seated firmly on the buoy', but noted in some alarm that 'he had not lashed himself to it with the cords provided for that purpose'. By the time the ship closed in once more, there was no one clinging to the buoy: 'to our inexpressible grief,' Ross recorded, 'our unfortunate shipmate had disappeared from it'.

Cunningham, on board the *Terror*, could not help observing that the *Erebus* had had more than her share of misfortune, 'having lost three men by drowning and one by suffocation and one seriously injured'. Marine George Barker, Boatswain Roberts, Edward Bradley, Captain of the Hold, and now Quartermaster James Angelly had all perished. 'Thanks be to God we as yet met no accident of any Kind.'

Two days later they sighted Beauchene Island, the most southerly of the 700 or so that make up the Falklands archipelago. Spirits should have risen, but any celebration on the *Erebus* was muted by the loss of one of their own. John Davis's words, written aboard HMS *Terror*, though a touch melodramatic, must have reflected the feelings of many, as the two tired ships approached the first human settlement they had seen since November. 'We have had a disastrous though successful cruise, and have had one of the most apparently miraculous escapes that the annals of any naval history in the world can record. It is that that has thrown us all into such low spirits.' The rain and thick fog that greeted them as they sought out an anchorage cannot have lightened the mood. There was no welcoming fanfare, the visibility being so bad that no one on the shore could see them.

A sketch, thought to be by *Terror*'s John Davis, of Port Louis, where Ross's expedition dropped anchor on 6 April 1842.

CHAPTER 9

'SUCH A WRETCHED PLACE AS THIS YOU NEVER SAW'

With the help of detailed charts compiled by Captain Fitzroy, who had brought HMS *Beagle* into the Falklands nine years earlier, *Erebus* dropped anchor at Port Louis, at the head of the long inlet known as Berkeley Sound, on 6 April 1842. The mist and rain were compounded by the bitterly disappointing news that no letters from home had arrived and by the knowledge that, owing to a delay in the delivery of supplies from Buenos Aires, the food on board ship was probably more interesting and varied than that available on land. As Joseph Hooker put it dispiritedly in a letter to his father: 'Such a wretched place as this you never saw. Kerguelen's Land is a paradise to it ... there are no letters, no newspapers, no society, male or female, no nothing, but plenty of Beef ... wild geese, Rabbits and Foxes'. Only Commander Crozier of the *Terror* and Lieutenant Bird of the *Erebus* had real cause for celebration: one piece of news that had made its way to the Falklands was that their promotions, recommended by Ross many months ago, had been confirmed.

The colony was a threadbare place. Richard Moody, the Lieutenant-Governor, a twenty-eight-year-old officer in the Royal Engineers, had only been in place two months and was quite likely overawed by the arrival of such an eminent explorer as James Clark Ross, not to mention the 126 men he brought with him. At a stroke, the population of the islands had doubled. Hooker, who was sometimes critical of Ross's reticence in informing the British public of their exploits, was pleased to report that 'The Governor says that our late success caused an immense sensation of triumph in England.' He was less charitable about the governor himself. 'The Purser has just been on shore. It was dark when he went and found his Excellency (the Lieutenant Governor) in a room without a candle and with a pompous secretary, but though drenched with rain, he had not the offer of glass of wine or grog.' There was no bread or flour in the settlement, and the governor found himself in the invidious position of having to beg and borrow some from ships that had been at sea for four and a half months.

When I arrived in the Falklands I found that, 175 years on, the population had grown from sixty to just over 3,000. Nearly half of those were born Falkland Islanders. Of the rest, 740 were described in the latest census as British, 241 St Helenians, 142 Chileans and 469 as 'Other'. The Other included three Georgians, one Sri Lankan and seventy-four Zimbabweans, who were part of a mine-clearing operation. I saw them working away, slowly and methodically clearing land-mines left over from the war of 1982 by the side of the rough old road that connects Mount Pleasant military airport to the capital, Stanley. The war or, as some prefer to call it, the conflict (for war was never officially declared) ended thirty-five years ago. It was a victory for Britain, seen by many as a great boost to national morale – a sign that we could still hack it. When James Clark Ross and *Erebus* arrived here in 1842, their memories of British military success would have been more recent. It had been less than thirty years since Napoleon was seen off at the Battle of Waterloo, and there were plenty of people alive who would have remembered hearing the news of Nelson's victory at Trafalgar.

The Falklands were born in conflict. By the time the Seven Years War ended in 1763, the French had lost most of their North American, Indian and West Indian colonies and were looking desperately for ways to re-establish their global influence. Louis-Antoine de Bougainville, a soldier and sailor – better known as the man who gave his name to that vibrant adornment of tropical walls and gardens, rather than for being the first Frenchman to circumnavigate the globe – conceived a plan. It was, in the words of historian Barry Gough, 'to plant the fleur-de-lys on the Falklands'. Louis XV offered royal support but no royal cash, so Bougainville financed the expedition himself. He enlisted ships and men from the port of Saint-Malo in Brittany and reached the islands in February 1764, christening them (after the city of his sailors and shipbuilders) les Îles Malouines, later rendered into Spanish as Las Islas Malvinas. The capital he named Port Louis, after his royal patron. Quite why he chose the Falklands isn't clear. His first impressions were unpromising: 'a country lifeless for want of inhabitants ... a vast silence broken only by the cry of a sea-monster; everywhere a weird and melancholy uniformity.'

But France was not the only country to stake a claim. Having landed elsewhere in the islands, the British registered their interest, whilst the Spanish claimed ownership of the whole lot through the terms of the Treaty of Tordesillas, which in 1494 had divided up the New World between Spain and Portugal. For the next fifty years the Falklands were claimed at various times by the French, the British, the Spanish and, with the growth of the southern Atlantic whaling industry, by the Americans as well. And then in 1820 a new country, Argentina, born from the wreckage of the Spanish Empire, announced a formal claim.

As I sit down to my first evening meal on the waterfront at Stanley (a deliciously served Patagonian toothfish), I hear a group at the table next door talking in Spanish. They are a party of Argentines who had taken part in the Falklands marathon less than a week earlier. The winner and runner-up were both Argentines, which hadn't gone down so well with the locals. Neither had the recent visit of the Argentine Swimmers for Peace, who had worn T-shirts showing the Falklands as part of Argentina.

First thing next morning, on my way to meet the editor of *Penguin News*, the Falklands' main paper, I notice handwritten signs stuck up in the windows of the Marine Exploration Centre: 'Drop Your Sovereignty Claim', 'Recognise Our Right to Self-Determination', 'No Dialogue is Possible Until Argentina Gives Up the Claims to Our Islands'. To be fair to all sides, foreign interest in the Falkland islands for much of their history has been more about where they are, rather than what they are. And the visit of Ross's expedition in 1842 was no different.

A priority for the newly arrived expedition was to draw up charts of their journey so far, and Ross delegated responsibility for this to the Second Master of *Terror*, John Davis. Towards the end of his long letter to his sister Emily, he admitted that the pressure was getting to him. 'I am really nearly blind, for I have been working night and day to get some charts ready for England which *must* go.' The next day he wrote in relief, 'I have finished my chart and Captain Ross said it could not be better.' As Davis drew his long and revealing letter to a close, one feels how intensely this young man, and many others on the voyage, must have been missing family and loved ones, after being away from home for two and a half years. 'Kiss my dear, dear mother for me,' he asks as he signs off; 'as for Ellen you may kiss her – and yourself too – and with love and remembrances to all the girls and friends, I am, as ever I shall remain, Your affectionate brother Jack.'

With winter approaching, the most immediate need was to secure a regular food source for the crews, and parties were sent out to slaughter anything edible, primarily geese, rabbits and the local wild cattle, descendants of the livestock that the French had brought to the island when they first came here in 1764. Hooker described them as 'possessed of indomitable courage and untameable ferocity', and went on to report a dramatic confrontation between hunter and hunted: 'the brave gunner of *Erebus* was struck down and the turf torn up in furrows on each side of his body by the diverging horns of a wounded and maddened bull'.

Ross was doubtless relieved when the Royal Navy ketch *Arrow*, which had been surveying the islands, put into Port Louis, and was able to give the hunting parties some local advice on the best way to deal with these meaty but dangerous beasts. They recommended using dogs.

Dr McCormick's first shooting excursion, as he called it, was on 11 April. His appetite for hunting seems to have been well and truly restored. He found rabbits on the low sandbanks skirting the beach and shot nine of them, and 'a few birds on my way back', including a hawk, four thrushes and, from the boat, a male upland goose. On 9 May he took out three oystercatchers, a rabbit, two black hawks and an ash- and white-backed hawk. Ten days later he added four more upland geese to his game-bag – 'their bodies when roasted supplied a delicious variety of food for our mess' – alongside 'four kelp geese, a steamer duck, a brown hawk, three ducks, three cormorants and two of the beautiful chionis'. Along with Thomas Abernethy, he also went out to hunt wild cattle. There was a touch of the Hemingways in one of these excursions. A shot passed through the mouth of an old bull, which charged at them and was only brought down with a second shot when the beast was almost upon him. 'It was an anxious moment though, as the infuriated beast, tossing his horns, and snorting blood from his nostrils, tore down upon me,' McCormick recalled. '... He gave a spring upwards as I fired, and came down with such ... force within a few feet of me as to make the earth tremble beneath my feet.'

The need to keep boredom at bay was always there, especially, it seems, on Sundays. After an entry for 17 April recording Divine Service, Sergeant Cunningham described the dangers of a day off. 'They all got insensibly drunk with some deleterious drug bearing the name Rum. At 8 p.m. went ashore with a boat's crew to endeavour to bring them off: found them lying about the Turf. One man nearly died in the first watch: had the Stomach pump applied to him.'

On 3 May, *Arrow* sailed for Rio de Janeiro, taking letters home and a request from Ross to have a new bowsprit sent out as soon as possible. The crew raised three cheers as they passed the *Erebus*'s stern and headed east, down the sound and out into the Atlantic.

As the southern winter approached, the days were spent taking magnetic observations, sending out hunting parties for bulls, striking the topmast and rigging a temporary bowsprit. A jetty was built to carry men and goods across from the boats to the shore. To keep the men further occupied, Captain Ross put them to work building observatories to check magnetic calculations, and what Cunningham refers to as 'Turf Houses', in which the cargo could be temporarily housed whilst the ships were hauled out of the water, laid on their sides and repaired and re-caulked. An astronomical and meteorological observatory was constructed near the fort built by Bougainville.

The day after my arrival I'm driven out from Stanley to the old capital of Port Louis to see what, if anything, remains of the presence of *Erebus* and *Terror*. I walk round the higher ground, where there is still some evidence of the observatories, then on down to the shore off which the ships were moored, and onto which they were hauled for their refit. The land that Hooker described as 'low and tolerably green' can barely have changed. A shallow valley runs to the sea. A line of stones, the remains of the pier they built, still runs out into the bay. A solid stone farmhouse, built as a barracks in 1843, dominates the gentle slope, with wide views down Berkeley Sound and the low headlands beyond. To the crew of *Erebus*, who had not seen family or friends for two and a half years, the featureless landscape must have driven many to frustration, and some to despair; but for me, only two days out of

London, the spaciousness of the Falklands is refreshing, even liberating. I draw simple pleasure from taking big, deep breaths of unpolluted air and being able to walk right up to the birds on the shore – shags, cormorants, night herons, oystercatchers – without any of them giving a damn.

There has always been a sense of the pristine in the Falklands. Apparently there were no flies on the island until after 1870. When they arrived they were seen as rare and exotic. Old ladies in Port Stanley kept bluebottles in cages. Charles Darwin, who spent longer in the Falklands than he did in the Galapagos, took rides out from Port Louis with some of the gauchos who made a living from hunting, and also went on walks where he found fossils that were 400 million years old. These were later to form a crucial part of the evidence for the existence of tectonic plates. 'The whole aspect of the Falkland Islands were ... changed to my eyes from that walk,' he later wrote.

Hooker, who had been depressed by his first sight of the Falklands, was also to change his mind when he began to explore beyond Port Louis. He noted sixty-five species of flowering plant and was particularly excited by the local tussock grass, which grew wherever there was standing water, and often to great height.

My own exploration of the Falklands is from above, on one of the regular flights run by FIGAS, the Falkland Islands Government Air Service. It seems the perfect way to get out of Stanley and avoid the last big cruise ship of the season, which will disgorge a thousand of her passengers onto the island for the next few hours. So I pay £50 for a Round Robin trip on one of the twin-prop Britten-Norman Islander aircraft that fly around the islands to deliver mail, and to drop off goods and passengers to the isolated communities outside Stanley.

It proves to be an exhilarating ride. The southern end of East Falkland Island is a wide expanse of low grassland they call Lafonia. It's a heavily indented landscape marked by meandering inlets and surface lakes and ponds. Then, as if in a movie, the land runs out below us, the clouds part and we're over open ocean, heading towards the rugged, sun-sharpened coastline of West Falkland. Soon we're over rock arches and sheer cliffs. Inlets have become fiords. We bank down to the tiny settlement of Port Stephens, whose airstrip is a sloping, bumpy meadow, and whose terminal is a shed into which half a car will just about fit.

Greeting the plane are the wife and family of the farmer on board and a curious group of Johnny rooks, big, inquisitive and completely fearless crows that sniff around for anything bright and shiny. They've been known to strip the accessories off cars, and camera crews are a favourite target. The pilot warns against leaving my smartphone unguarded. The crows don't need a password, he says, they just peck it to pieces. Having delivered the farmer, we hop 15 miles to another field, to pick up someone from the impressively tiny Port Albemarle, before returning across the Falkland Sound and running low over the islands – these, to the men of *Erebus* and *Terror*, would have offered their first sight of the Falklands. Two of these islands, Sealion and Bleaker, are home to tourist lodges surrounded by prodigious numbers of sea-birds, seals and penguins.

Tourism, along with oil reserves and a flourishing fishing industry, is one of the green shoots of recovery in the Falklands economy. As we bank and descend over Stanley, I can see the 57,000-ton cruise liner *Veendam* disgorging most of her 1,350 passengers into the welcoming arms of the shops, bars, cafés and restaurants of Port Stanley.

On board the 372-ton *Erebus*, Queen Victoria's twenty-third birthday was being celebrated. 'A dirty wet day,' according to Cunningham, it was marked by a gun salute and the serving of a double ration of beef and rum. That night the officers gathered aboard for a grand meal. The next morning at six o'clock the entire crew assembled to catch the high tide and haul their ship onto the beach, lie it on its side and inspect closely the damage sustained in the Antarctic. Carpenters then worked all day and night to replace timbers and restore some of the copper sheeting. Within thirty-six hours she was ready to be refloated. The same now had to be done for *Terror*, but that proved to be a much tougher job. As the Falklands winter tightened its grip, the work had to be carried out in wind, sleet and snow.

It was in these wretched conditions that an equally wretched incident occurred. A Boy (one of the young trainee seamen, usually aged between fifteen and seventeen) from *Erebus* accused one of the gauchos on the island of committing 'an unnatural crime' against him. Governor Moody duly ordered an inquiry, which found the charge to be false. The Boy's punishment was drastic. He was sentenced 'to receive three dozen lashes over the breech at three different parts of the settlement'. In his diary, Cunningham managed to sound both judgemental and dismissive. 'I consider it a very just and mild punishment . . . If it had been an adult I certainly think he deserved hanging. Continuous rain all night.' Maybe there's a hint here of the vehement attitude to public exhibitions of homosexuality, which surely must have been part of life on board, albeit privately. There is no reference to it in any of the contemporary documents.

Towards the end of June, a new arrival was spotted working her way up Berkeley Sound. It proved to be HMS *Carysfort*, a man-of-war out of Rio de Janeiro, commanded by Lord George Paulet and bringing not only news from home, but much-needed provisions and a new bowsprit for *Erebus*. Cunningham, for one, was overjoyed to receive letters and some old newspapers from England, but he was less happy with the behaviour of the crew of *Carysfort* on shore leave the next day, 'all of which got very Drunk,' he wrote – adding, 'and one man Drank to that excess that he was suffocated as the Stomach pump could not work in consequence of the piece of beef sticking in his throat in heaving up'; he was buried two days later. On another occasion, some of the men from *Carysfort* were reported to have broken at night into a store owned by an Irishman named John Scully and stolen some liquor. The ship itself seems to have been unlucky, too: an attempt to take on water resulted in one of her boats running onto the rocks and having to be abandoned, until men from *Erebus* could extricate her the next morning.

But whatever *Erebus* may have thought of *Carysfort*, *Carysfort* clearly enjoyed being in the company of *Erebus*. A letter from her second-in-command, John Tarleton, to his sister Charlotte described a number of very convivial get-togethers: 'there came a series of dinners, so that we were almost every day engaged at home and abroad, the Captains first and then ourselves. We made room for twenty in the gunroom and gave them a grand champagne turnout.' He found Captain Ross 'a very superior man, with whom it was a great pleasure to be in company'. Of Ross's recently promoted second-in-command, Tarleton made the observation, oddly borne out by many others: 'Captain Crozier of the *Terror* is I should imagine, a devoted follower and better suited for a second than a first.'

Where men from *Carysfort* and *Erebus* seem to have been in full agreement was in their low opinion of the governor. Hooker had noted that 'his Excellency' had not had the common courtesy to offer the ship's purser a drink. Tarleton thought Moody 'a great prig. He had me to a miserable dinner in his miserable house one day, when he coined more absurdity than you would have supposed possible.' Perhaps this coloured Lieutenant Tarleton's view of the Falklands. Although he enjoyed the social life, and the hunting and shooting and the many wardroom dinners, he wasn't able to raise much enthusiasm for the region for which Governor Moody was responsible: 'There is not a shrub higher than one's knee ... a small colony might find subsistence in East Falkland, but there is nothing at present to repay the capitalist.'

On this note, and after a farewell dinner aboard *Erebus*, HMS *Carysfort* gave three hearty cheers and sailed away down Berkeley Sound.

★★★

Although *Erebus* and *Terror* had been refitted by the end of July, Ross had to stay in these bleak and stormy surroundings until the next magnetic-term day, which wasn't until September. Always on the lookout for ways to keep the men busy and to stem the increasing number of incidents of fighting and drunkenness, he turned his attention to the small cemetery above the harbour.

'In order to give our people healthful exercise and useful occupation,' he wrote, 'I directed them to be employed building a wall seven feet thick and as many high round the spot which had been hitherto used as a burial ground but which was at present without any enclosure.' There weren't many graves to enclose. One, though, belonged to a key figure in Antarctic exploration: Captain Matthew Brisbane, who had accompanied the Scots whaling captain James Weddell when he had achieved the furthest south in 1823. Brisbane had been a resourceful, if unlucky, ship's master, who had survived three shipwrecks, each time building himself an escape vessel out of the wreckage. Whilst in charge of the British settlement at Port Louis in 1833, however, he and a number of others had been murdered and dragged out of their homes by a group of renegade Argentines and rebellious native convicts. His body had then been roughly buried. Nine years on, Ross, doubtless feeling some kind of kinship with a fellow explorer, ordered the bones to be given a proper burial in the newly walled cemetery, complete with a brand-new headstone. The inscription read 'To the Memory of Matthew Brisbane who was barbarously murdered on the 26th August 1833. His remains were removed to this spot by the crews of H.B.M. [Her Britannic Majesty's] ships "Erebus" and "Terror" on the 25th August 1842.'

The headstone still exists. As does the cemetery, now unused and overgrown. The turf wall erected by the men of *Erebus* and *Terror* has mostly been weathered away, and it's easy to scramble through the makeshift fencing that now encloses the old graveyard. There, in the north-west corner, beneath one of the Falklands' very few trees, is a replica of Brisbane's gravestone. The original, removed from this exposed site on the side of the hill, is now kept in the fine Dockyard Museum at Stanley.

While walking back from the museum some days later, I run into a modern-day explorer, one of the crew of the *Ernest Shackleton*, a British Antarctic Survey ship, which has just arrived in port from South Georgia, bringing home scientists and observers from various remote Antarctic destinations. They invite me on board, where I can see that they are still readjusting to 'normal' life after many solitary months collecting extraordinarily detailed data on the fringes of the Southern Continent. These latter-day Hookers and McCormicks nod appreciatively when they hear of my interest in their counterparts of the 1840s. The *Ernest Shackleton*'s sister ship is called *James Clark Ross*.

After my visit, I walk back to Stanley along the shore path. Out to sea, silhouetted against the evening sky, is an assortment of wrecked vessels in various stages of disintegration, emblems of the perils of these South Atlantic waters. The path leads onto Stanley's main street, which is called Ross Road, so I feel quite at home. And Captain Crozier, whom Tarleton judged 'better suited for a second than a first'? He's immortalised in Crozier Place, Stanley's only shopping mall.

Feuerländer-Typen.
Originalzeichnung von J. Bungart.

On her third Antarctic voyage, *Erebus* stopped off in Tierra del Fuego so that a magnetic observatory could be built there. 'The Fuegians,' Ross wrote later, 'are truly described as the most abject and miserable race of human beings', although he also admitted that they were good company. This German engraving dates from 1881.

CHAPTER 10

'THREE YEARS FROM GILLINGHAM'

Once the magnetic measurements had been completed on the appointed term day, the ships were prepared for a short expedition to undertake a survey of magnetic activity around Cape Horn. Surgeon McCormick, in one of the rare calls on his medical services, gave a final round of treatment to the sick daughter of one of the Falklands residents, forty-six-year-old Captain Allen Gardiner, a naval man and an 'ardent' missionary. His daughter survived, but Gardiner and six others, including his young second wife, later starved to death whilst trying to spread the word of God to the natives of Tierra del Fuego.

On 8 September 1842, with a fair wind and all sails set, *Erebus* cleared Berkeley Sound in a morning. Her senior lieutenant, Mr Sibbald, had been left behind with a team of six other officers to maintain the observatory at Port Louis. HMS *Terror* left without its much-respected First Lieutenant, Archibald McMurdo, who had been diagnosed with a long-standing stomach condition and was to be invalided back to England for treatment. Ross had written a letter to the Admiralty explaining the situation and recommending McMurdo for promotion. As it turned out, being sent home was not a bad career move for McMurdo. He rose to the rank of Vice-Admiral and died thirty-two years later, having left his mark firmly on the map of

Antarctica in the shape of a McMurdo Sound, an ice-shelf, an ice station, a system of dry valleys and a polar 'highway'.

It took the two ships some ten days to cover the 425 miles to Cape Horn. It was not an easy journey. Only two days out of the Falklands, Cunningham recorded his ship as 'labouring very heavily and Shipping heavy Seas over all'. On the night of Saturday 10 September, the wind was 'blowing harder than I think I ever saw it'. By the 12th it was 'a complete hurricane. Ship at times nearly on her beam ends.' Nor did the weather let up. On the 15th there was 'a Tremendous Sea on'. They spent most of this punishing week below decks, with storm sails rigged and the hatches battened down. By contrast, when they reached Cape Horn, where bad weather was generally expected, the seas were calm and the skies had cleared. 'It is probable we saw this cape of Terror and tempests under some disadvantage,' wrote Ross, with a hint of regret.

I now understand his disappointment, for I had a similar experience rounding the Horn whilst filming for the BBC on board a Chilean naval patrol boat, the *Isaza*. All set for storm-tossed seas, and given drastic warnings of what to expect and how to strap ourselves into our bunks, we were plunged into anticlimax. The ferocious ocean was millpond-calm. Ross, unsure of his ship's safety on the surrounding rocks, felt it was enough to watch and marvel, but our Chilean hosts lowered a Zodiac and landed us on Cape Horn itself. It was not just the soft and gentle weather that tamed the Cape's reputation that day, but the presence of a big, soppy dog called Bobby, who leapt down the cliff at the end of America to welcome us, effusively attaching himself to our cameraman, as if he hadn't seen a human leg for weeks.

I remember thinking how privileged we were to be there in the expert company of the Chilean Navy. I apologised to the captain of the *Isaza* for taking up so much of their time, and their space. There were, after all, six of us and twenty of them on a ship 150 feet long.

Now that I know that on *Erebus* there were sixty-three people on a ship 105 feet long, I don't feel quite so bad.

The Cape stands on the southernmost of the Wollaston Islands and it was on one of these, Hermite Island, that Ross spotted a haven, St Martin's Cove, where *Erebus* and *Terror* could moor up. For Darwin, who had visited the Wollaston Islands thirteen years earlier, this was 'one of the most inhospitable countries within the limits of the globe'. Ross's expedition was greeted by hail, snow and freezing wind. Amid all this, they could make out an encampment at the head of the inlet where fires were burning and native Fuegians gathered. A group of them came out in a canoe and indicated the best place to drop anchor, and they were duly followed by others. Cunningham described one canoe in which there were '4 men 1 woman and 1 child all completely naked except their shoulders ... The woman stood up quite unconscious of the delicate Situation she was in, exposed to the impertinent gase and remarks of the Ships company.' The sight of her evoked a sense of pity. 'Poor creature,' Cunningham went on; 'hers must be a miserable existence to drag out, for in addition to having a young child she had to paddle the "Canoe" and apparently do all the work.'

Ross took a boat to the shore and chose a site for an observatory. Clearing it was a difficult job. A large party of men, under Captain Crozier's direction, worked for several days stripping away trees and undergrowth, only to reveal a swamp beneath. Not to be defeated, they drove piles through it till they reached the clay base. Sand-filled barrels made a reasonably firm platform and the observatory was duly erected.

For Hooker, the Wollaston Islands were a source of endless fascination. In some ways, they were like the Western Isles of Scotland: with similar narrow arms of the sea pushing into the land, and deep, enclosed bays protected by low mountain ranges. He found more plant species on Hermite Island identical to those back in Britain than he had done anywhere else in the southern hemisphere. He was also intrigued that so many plant species in the islands of Tierra del Fuego were the same as those he had observed in remote places in the Kerguelens and Van Diemen's Land. Since the prevailing winds and ocean currents of the South Atlantic move from west to east, he could only assume that plant life on the Kerguelens and in Tasmania actually originated on Tierra del Fuego, with seeds from this inhospitable region being carried by wind and waves across thousands of miles of the stormiest ocean.

Ross, on the other hand, saw only the bleakness of the island on which they were now encamped: 'these wild scenes,' he recorded, 'are rendered gloomy ... and positively forbidding by the almost total absence of animated nature, and by the clouded sky, constant storms and vexed ocean, added to the silence which is only broken by the hollow voice of the torrent and the cry of the savage'.

On Sunday 25 September, Cunningham noted, gloomily, 'Three years from Gillingham.' The next day the gun-room steward from *Terror* was laid across a cannon and given twenty-four lashes for 'neglect'.

As Ross and his officers set to work in the observatory, increasing numbers of curious natives would congregate at the shelter – part hut, part wigwam – to watch what was going on. Ross was not much impressed by them. 'The Fuegians are truly described as the most abject and miserable race of human beings,' he tutted, comparing them unfavourably with what he called 'their northern prototypes, the Esquimaux'. The menfolk, he noted, were small, with an average height of no more than five feet, and they were indolent, leaving the women not only to propel the canoes but also to dive for the sea eggs and limpets that were their main source of food. But even the stern Captain Ross had to admit that they were good company. They had a notable talent for mimicry, which fascinated the ships' crew, and they were always ready to join in a dance or a song. One morning Ross came across some of his men teaching the Fuegians how to wash their faces. They didn't like the sting of the soap, however, so they washed their hands and feet instead. Before the expedition left, a suit of clothes had been found for each of them.

At the beginning of November they sailed out of St Martin's Cove, having found room on board for 800 young beech trees to take back to the treeless Falklands.

Once there, some of the crew immediately set to work unloading and planting the trees. Others were pressed into repair work on an English whaler, *Governor Halkett*, which had made an emergency detour to the Falklands after springing a leak in her cargo of whale oil. It took them a week to strip out the ship, plug the hole in her bows and re-stow her, leaving little time for hunting parties to go out and restock supplies. McCormick, however, did his best, procuring eggs, geese, rabbits and steamer ducks. And it wasn't just the shotgun that he used this time. A particularly grisly journal entry for 17 November reveals that he was experimenting with other methods of despatch. 'This evening I tried the effects of hydrocyanic acid on three penguins, to ascertain the speediest and most humane method of ending their existence. One dram of the diluted acid destroyed a bird in one minute and fifty seconds.'

By the time they were ready to leave, a positive menagerie had been assembled on board. 'Our decks formed quite a farmyard,' McCormick wrote. 'In the boat amidships five sheep were stowed away, the same number of wild pigs, with a litter of young ones. In the port waist were three calves ... In the quarter-boat two turkeys and a goose ... each quarter was festooned with dead rabbits, geese, seal, and snipe, with a quarter of beef and veal, and dried fish in every direction.' He drew the line, however, at horse-flesh, and was horrified to discover that a recent breakfast had consisted not of beef-steak, as he had assumed, but of 'a young colt' that had been 'thoughtlessly, to use a mild expression, shot, on the previous day by a party from the midshipmen's berth'. For Surgeon McCormick, who, since they left England, had taken aim at almost every kind of living creature he encountered, killing a horse was a step too far: 'there was nothing whatever that could in any way justify the taking the lives of these harmless, inoffensive creatures, and it is very sad ... that the happy life of freedom led by these noble animals ... should have been closed by so wanton an act of cruelty'.

With final provisions safely stowed on board, *Erebus* and *Terror* set out on their third Antarctic voyage on Saturday 17 December 1842, hoping once again to break their own record of furthest south. But something had changed; the mood had shifted. Previous legs of the journey had been embarked upon with general enthusiasm. This time there were dissenting voices. Up until now, Ross had been widely admired. Now Hooker, writing to his father a few months later, sounded his first note of criticism of the expedition's leader. 'I believe we should have gone to some better place than the Falklands during [the] last dreary winter,' he wrote. 'Honor, empty honor retained the officers.' He also suggested that there had been little appetite for a third season of Antarctic exploration. 'You can hardly conceive how earnestly we hoped at the Falklands that the Admiralty would have recalled us and sent us anywhere else.'

This was not a feeling shared by the expedition's leader. Ross was in agreement with the first part of the sentiment – no one, he noted, felt 'the smallest regret' on leaving the Falkland Islands – but when he came to write his account of the voyage, he claimed that the mood aboard was bullish, 'every one rather rejoicing in the prospect before us, of again resuming the more important business of our voyage'. These were fine words. But the fact remained that a turning point had nevertheless been reached. Over the next few months the captain was to sound increasingly out of touch with his crew. Post-Falklands, it was never the same expedition.

★★★

It didn't get off to the most auspicious of starts, either. As the ships slipped out of harbour, the Port Louis garrison, which had gathered to bid them farewell, fired a rather messy salute, in the course of which the captain of a merchant brig had his hand fractured and, according to Cunningham, 'a Man belonging to the Settlement had his right arm broke and both hands nearly blown off'. 'We hove to,' he went on, 'and both came on board of us to get dressed.'

Once away, the weather was deceptively benign, but no sooner had they rounded Cape Pembroke and were out on the unprotected ocean than the storm systems powered in, and a relentless succession of westerly gales lashed their starboard beam. The hatches were battened down and three of their pigs drowned.

On Christmas Eve the first iceberg was spotted at 61°S. The night was very rough and the ship rolled fiercely. It was all too much for one of McCormick's avian companions: 'I found a little pet of mine, a young oyster-catcher I had brought from the Falklands with me, unable to stand up on his legs, and panting and gasping for breath. Up to this time he had appeared lively, and ate readily; but now he took only a very small bit or two of food. He lingered through the day, his eyes gradually becoming dimmer, and on my turning in at night, I found him out of his basket, dead on the deck.'

Despite this bereavement, the sociable McCormick was at the heart of the Christmas celebrations, presiding over a lunch that was 'really a sumptuous one for these regions' – these regions being the waters off Elephant Island, where, seventy-four years later, Ernest Shackleton was to leave his shipwrecked crew while he set off for South Georgia on one of the greatest rescue journeys in maritime history. The captain and officers of HMS *Erebus* were rather more fortunate. They spent Christmas 1842 in the gun-room, feasting on veal, calf's head and champagne.

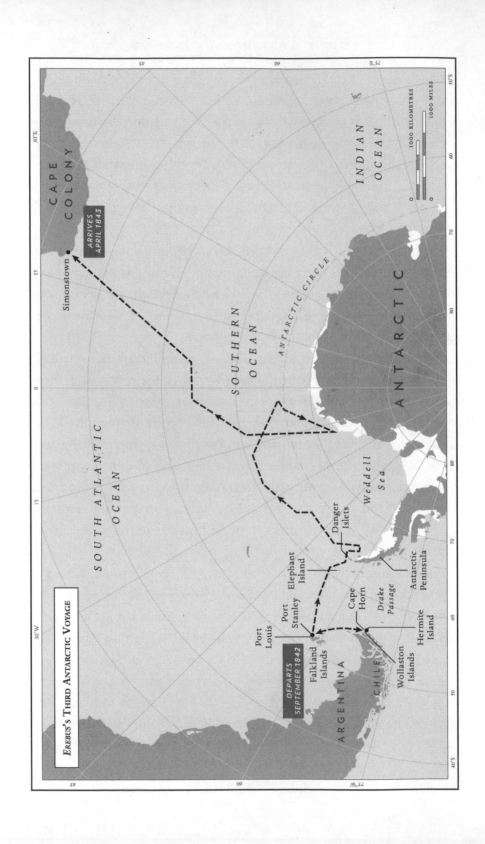

Erebus's Third Antarctic Voyage

Three days later, as the ships edged slowly southwards, land was spotted for the first time. It was the northern end of the Antarctic Peninsula, a long, thin strip of land curving out from the continental mainland like an upraised scorpion's claw.

Ross's aim was to sail due south in the direction James Weddell had taken twenty years earlier, when he had reached latitude 74°S. The current and tide were against them, however, and an added hazard was the sudden appearance of a cluster of previously uncharted rocky outcrops, which Ross christened the Danger Islets. Not dangerous for penguins apparently. In 2016 it was announced that a super-colony of 1.5 million Adélie penguins had been found on one of them. I was a little intrigued as to why a colony of this size had taken everybody by surprise. How do you not notice one and a half million penguins?

I was lucky enough to explore this part of the peninsula in 2015, and one thing that struck me was how many of the names given to physical features mirrored the mental states of those who named them. Apart from Danger Islets, there is Cape Longing, Cape Disappointment, Delusion Point and Exasperation Bay, only slightly compensated for by Useful Island, on the other side of the peninsula. It's a dramatic landscape that inspires strong emotions. Not only are there towering peaks on land, but there are equally impressive structures on the water. The narrow strait down which Ross sailed between Joinville Island and the tip of the peninsula is known as Iceberg Alley. One mega-slab of detached ice-shelf, known as B15-K, is 37 miles long and it took us two hours to pass it. In the summer of 2017 a trillion-ton iceberg the size of Delaware broke away from the Larsen Ice Shelf and drifted into the Weddell Sea. Rising 600 feet above the water and dropping 700 feet below, it was formed by ice-shelves cracking under pressure from their own weight.

It had been a while since the expedition had added to Britain's colonial possessions, but this was rectified on 6 January 1843 when Ross and Crozier, followed by a party of officers, took boats across to a small rocky outcrop, which they named Pyramidal Island. During a short ceremony a Union Flag was raised and it was annexed in the name of the Crown. Dr McCormick pleaded to be one of the shore party, but Ross resolutely respected the rule by which no ship was allowed to be left without a medical officer on board, and it was Hooker's turn to go ashore. A frustrated McCormick was left on the deck of the *Erebus* 'to glean all I could through the medium of the telescope'. I rather wish that he had been allowed to participate, because his observations were always original. Only a day later his journal contained this description of a penguin, 'walking away upright as a dart . . . looking like an old monk going to mass'.

By the beginning of February, Ross was reluctantly pulling his ships out of the thickening ice-pack, through which they had been threading their way for a mind-numbing six weeks. The assumption on board must have been that, as William Cunningham recorded in his diary, 'we are going to make our retreat to the cape of G Hope'. But Ross had no intention of making for the 'cape of G Hope' just yet. He was determined to find the clear water that Weddell had sailed through, and which Ross remained convinced would, if followed, take him and his expedition tantalisingly further south.

For ten more days they sailed east along the edge of the ice-pack, cautiously probing for a way through, but they were still 480 miles short of their previous record when Ross finally accepted defeat. It was early March and the winter ice was closing around them. In the teeth of an approaching gale, Ross ordered the red ensign to be flown, a signal to the *Terror* that this third and last Antarctic voyage had reached its limits.

For Robert McCormick, it was an emotional moment. 'I went on deck just as the ship tacked, to take a last look at the pack, which now appeared astern.' On that same day, William Cunningham wrote simply: 'Hurra!!'

Physically, the crews of *Erebus* and *Terror* were in surprisingly good shape, and they were on double pay, but one can't help feeling that the remorselessness of such prolonged exposure to the elements must have taken its toll. Life in the Navy meant long absences from home, and that was something everyone who went to sea accepted – indeed, that was why some of them went to sea in the first place – but few had ever had to endure such extreme conditions for so long as the men of *Erebus* and *Terror*. More than a year of their three and a half years away had been spent in or near the most inhospitable continent on earth, with no relief from the relentless cold and no human contact of any kind, other than those men squeezed together on the two ships that carried them into this wilderness. And here they were, for a third season, grasping frozen lines with frozen hands, soaked to the skin, clinging to the rigging as the ships pitched and tossed and icebergs three times higher than their masthead loomed out of the darkness. And Cape Town still 2,500 miles away.

Marine Sergeant Cunningham, who is the nearest we have to the voice of a working seaman, dutifully fills his diary with the practical detail of the day – how the sails are set, the speed, the course taken, the weather conditions – and only occasionally does he pass a personal opinion. As they laboured northwards in heavy seas, raked by searingly cold winds and viciously recurring squalls of sleet and snow, his few words speak of resignation rather than accusation: 'Ship very uncomfortable, but Can't be helped.' McCormick doesn't complain much, either: 'a heavy sea running, which with the thick weather rendered our situation by no means a desirable one' is about as alarmist as he gets.

For the expression of stronger feelings one must turn to the letters home, which, unlike journals, did not have to be turned over to the Admiralty. And it is from Joseph Hooker's long letter to his father, written on *Erebus* after they had reached quieter waters on 3 April, that we learn a darker side of the story. He writes bitterly of the stresses and strains that were beginning to show, even before they embarked on this last Antarctic voyage. 'When I told you in writing from the Falklands' how easy a cruize this was to be I only told you what was given out, most likely for the purpose of keeping the men together ... It was no secret amongst us officers that we all detested the prospect of the utter monotony and life of misery that awaited us, and there was not one, in either ship, that would not have given up his pay, could the sacrifice have ordered us anywhere else with honor.'

And he goes on, striking at the very heart of Ross's motivation for the voyage: 'few take the slightest interest in the science of this cruise,' he argues. 'I believe that one half of them did not expect to be out so long, and that they would have Bear and grouse shooting, smooth water and all agreeable recreations of a N. Polar voyage. They are indeed grievously mistaken; from the day we leave Port there is no enjoyment until we drop anchor again, except to such anomalous animals as myself who can be happy with a trumpey piece of moss or seaweed.' There's a sense here that the single-minded determination that drove Ross – whether he was courting Anne Coulman in the teeth of her father's opposition, or doggedly sailing along the Great Southern Barrier in the hope of being able to penetrate even further south – could become a stubbornness that his men found hard to endure.

Hooker is aware of the risk to his reputation, should such mutinous sentiments get out, and specifically warns his father not to pass on anything from the letter apart from scientific facts and observations. Officially, after all, the Antarctic expedition was a success. Unofficially, it extracted a traumatic toll. Hooker's farewell to the Antarctic – 'I cannot tell you how rejoiced we are to be leaving it for good and all!' – is in the same spirit as Cunningham's simple 'Hurra!!' Except that it's personal. What Hooker reveals is that, after three and a half years away, his admiration for his captain is no longer unqualified. 'Captain Ross says he would not conduct another expedition to the South for any money ... nor would any of us go if he did.'

On 26 March, Cunningham's diary records a good breeze, the ship averaging six knots a day and, most of all, 'No Icebergs Seen'. This is the only sentence in his diary that is underlined.

On 4 April 1843, Table Mountain came into sight and, after exchanging colours with the Admiral's flagship, HMS *Winchester*, a pilot boat escorted *Erebus* and *Terror* into Simon's Bay. Ross and Crozier presented themselves to Rear-Admiral Percy Josceline, the commander-in-chief, almost exactly three years after they had left South Africa for their Antarctic adventure.

On the credit side, they had achieved something remarkable and unprecedented. Without serious loss of life, and with neither vessel suffering any permanent damage, Ross and Crozier had safely brought back two small sailing ships and 128 men from the end of the earth. Whatever criticism there might have been of Ross's aloof and sometimes driven style of leadership, he had fulfilled the Admiralty's instructions almost to the letter, falling short only in his failure to reach the South Magnetic Pole. His second-in-command, too, had done everything required of him. In the older, smaller of the two ships, Captain Crozier had proved himself a skilful and resourceful navigator, utterly dedicated to his ship and his crew. During the fiercest of storms he set a fine example, riding out the worst of them on twenty-four hour call, napping in a chair or out in the open on deck.

But for both men there had been a price to pay. Crozier's hair had turned grey in the three years they had been away, and the considerable dangers that he and Ross had come through together had marked them. At a dinner with the two captains, Admiral Josceline's daughter, Sophia Bagot, made a telling observation. 'Their hands shook so much they could hardly hold a glass or a cup,' she wrote to a friend. 'Sir James Ross told me ... "You see how our hands shake? One night in the Antarctic did this for both of us."'

Ascension Island was one of *Erebus*'s last ports of call before her return to England in September 1843.

CHAPTER 11

HOMEWARD BOUND

If Ross's men assumed they would now be setting off straight for home, they didn't know their leader. As *Erebus* and *Terror* were towed out of Simon's Bay on 30 April 1843, Ross definitively recorded that 'we had now turned our backs on the Antarctic regions and had fairly begun our homeward way', but he then added, ominously, 'though we had one object yet to fulfil, which was to go to Rio de Janeiro for magnetic purposes'. Can we hear the distant gnashing of teeth in the officers' mess at this news?

Their roundabout route to Rio took them via one of Britain's loneliest outposts, Ascension, a volcanic peak rising from a mid-Atlantic seabed 4 miles deep. In 1815 it had been garrisoned on the orders of the British Admiralty because it was the nearest land to Napoleon's island prison of St Helena. The fact that St Helena was 800 miles away shows just how paranoid they were about possible rescue missions.

Even today, Ascension Island remains pretty inaccessible. When I make a visit, my only option is to fly on a twice-weekly RAF service that refuels there before going on to the Falklands. The onscreen map for the seventeen-hour flight is quite eccentric, showing initially only Brize Norton, Washington and Ankara, before giving up on names altogether, once over the Atlantic. For several hours the screen resembles an Yves Klein canvas, before a tiny dot appears in the top right-hand corner, followed, minutes later, by one of the more surreal in-flight announcements: 'We will soon be starting our descent into Ascension.'

To my surprise, the airfield at Ascension is huge, with a long runway and an enormous tarmacked apron. This, I later learn, dates from the days when the island was one of the designated landing strips for returning US Space Shuttles. During the Falklands War it was one of the busiest airfields in the world, a vital link in a round-the-clock shuttle of Vulcan bombers.

This morning there's one lone C-17 freighter squatting on the tarmac as we taxi towards a group of temporary-looking service buildings. One of these is the transit lounge, known, invitingly, as the Cage, where passengers are held whilst the plane is refuelled before the next eight-hour leg to the Falklands.

Instead of spending an hour in the Cage, I'm welcomed by a tanned, enthusiastic young man who introduces himself as the Administrator of Ascension. He indicates his car, registration A1, and whisks me off on a whistle-stop tour of the island. It begins with a visit to the elegant, well-appointed Government House, which is about halfway up the peak of the extinct volcano they call Green Mountain. From a lush garden there is a fine view out over the dry, brown-baked desert-like coastal plain below. Any higher ground bristles with masts, aerials, early-warning domes and satellite dishes. The war may be over and the American Space Shuttles a thing of the past, but Ascension's central position at the narrowest point between Africa and South America makes it a communications hot-spot. A tiny speck of Empire, but a speck worth having.

On 28 May 1843, *Erebus* would have stood out in the deep-blue sea below, and Surgeon McCormick would have been taking in this same view in reverse. He walked up Green Mountain, as did Charles Darwin, who had been here some ten years earlier. This steep volcanic slope, rising to nearly 3,000 feet, is a naturalist's paradise, with a whole chain of ecosystems, ranging from virtual desert to tropical rainforest.

The other great attractions of this tiny but bountiful island are its giant turtles. McCormick saw several hundred of them, and estimated the largest at over 400 lb. At dawn, on a return visit from the Falklands, I witnessed a score of these turtles, which had come ashore to lay their eggs under cover of darkness and were now dragging themselves back towards the ocean. Exhausted after digging in the sand and giving birth, they moved infinitely slowly, their heads drooping every now and then as they contemplated the distance ahead. With the approach of daylight and the growing heat, they had to redouble their efforts. Frigate birds circled overhead, waiting to pick off the young as they hatched. Apparently only one in a thousand survives to adulthood.

Surgeon McCormick dined on turtle soup the night before they left for their last port of call. Rio de Janeiro, to the south and west, was a bigger and better source of provisions than the islands and the only place where *Erebus* could have a new bowsprit fitted. McCormick took the opportunity to experience some city life, stopping to investigate Pharoux's, a 'capital large new hotel', before going on to Madame Finot's in Rua do Ouvidor to purchase a box of insects. As he passed one shop his attention was caught by the sight of thirty Creole girls making flower wreaths out of feathers. One can only imagine what the sight of thirty Creole girls might have meant to a young man who had been sailing the Antarctic for three years. But beyond noting them, McCormick tells us nothing more, other than that later that day he bought two parrots, one grey, one green.

Ross, for his part, recorded his deep frustration that all the letters for the two ships had been mistakenly sent to Montevideo, and could not be returned to Rio for a month. He decided this was too long to wait, and as soon as his magnetic observations were completed and the new bowsprit fitted, he wasted no time in hoisting sails and, taking advantage of some unusually strong southerly winds, they put Sugar Loaf mountain behind them and set course for London.

They were still more than 5,000 miles from home, but the winds were favourable and just over two months later, on 30 August, they were within sight of St Agnes Lighthouse on the Isles of Scilly. Ross's long account, almost at an end, records that at first light on 2 September 'the shores of Old England came into view'. McCormick, as ever, adds a little more colour to the moment: 'Very fine day, but with light, contrary airs. At nine a.m., upon going up on deck, I saw the land of old England again, after some four years' absence.' Two days later they were close to Beachy Head, and McCormick found the words to match the moment. It was a day to celebrate: 'the sea smooth as a lake, and studded with countless vessels; whilst the line of coast, displaying the rich, golden-yellow fields of corn, some in sheaf, some still standing, altogether gave animation to the scene'. At Folkestone, Ross left his ship and caught the train to London. He went straight from the station to Somerset House, overlooking the Thames, to report to the Admiralty. Here, as he later remembered it, he received 'the most gratifying reception from Lord Haddington, Sir William Gage and my highly valued friends Admiral Beaufort and Sir John Barrow'.

It was on the morning of Thursday 7 September 1843 that *Erebus* and *Terror* arrived at Woolwich, and in the early afternoon that they weighed anchor. Their long voyage was finally over. For four years *Erebus* had been home to sixty-three men: a cramped and crowded home that had been flung about in countless storms, lashed with breaking waves, bent by shrieking winds, bruised and buffeted by advancing ice, frozen stiff and smashed in collision. And, throughout the journey, no words but praise for her performance. In the obligatory Sailing Quality Report for the Admiralty, filled out by Charles Tucker, her master, and the ship's carpenter, and signed by Ross as captain, *Erebus* received a solid, if laconic end-of-term report. 'Does she roll easy or uneasy in the trough of the sea? *Easy.* Does she pitch easy? *Easy.* Is she, generally speaking, an easy or uneasy ship? *Very easy.*'

For most of those who had called *Erebus* and *Terror* home for the past four years, this was the moment to say goodbye. The leader of the expedition, though only forty-four, certainly had no intention of going to sea again – and was in no shape to travel anyway. The long voyage had exhausted him.

Ross was awarded a knighthood (which he accepted this time round) and a plethora of honours from various bodies, including medals from the Royal Geographical Societies of both London and Paris and an honorary doctorate from Oxford University. John Murray commissioned a book from him, for the sizeable advance of £500, but it took Ross four years to complete it. He wasted no time, however, in marrying his patient fiancée, Anne Coulman, having finally won her father round by promising that from now on he would stay at home. The marriage, more than anything, signalled his future intentions. Ross was hanging up his boots.

Francis Crozier, best man at Ross's wedding, was to have his own future much influenced by a woman, but in his case it didn't end as happily. Sophy Cracroft, with whom Crozier had been so smitten in Tasmania, returned to London with the Franklins in June 1844. Though she had rejected him once before, Crozier once again tried to win her favour, writing letters and arranging meetings with her throughout that summer. But nothing much had changed since Tasmania and she turned him down again, insisting that she would not want to marry a man who spent his life at sea. Was she just being polite? Crozier's biographer, Michael Smith, hints as much: 'Crozier in 1844 was not an attractive proposition. His grey hair and middle-aged spread hinted at someone carrying the burdens of an exacting life, and looking a little more than his 47 years.'

That he was a hugely capable, decent man was not in question. His ability was recognised by his election as a Fellow of the Royal Society. Nor is there any evidence of the equivocal niggles over his leadership that Hooker revealed about Ross. Crozier had a good relationship with all his men, exemplified by his gift of his silver watch, which he'd carried for fifteen years, to Sergeant William Cunningham, the Marine from Belfast whose daily diary remains one of the most honest accounts of the Antarctic expedition.

Whether or not Crozier's Irish origins counted against him in the medals and promotion stakes or whether he was simply not pushy enough, we shall never know, but the success of the expedition was not enough to overcome the failure of his pursuit of Sophy Cracroft. He became seriously depressed and, rather than sail again, took a year's leave from the Navy, on half-pay, and set off to travel in Europe.

The recipient of Crozier's watch never went to sea again. Sergeant Cunningham married two years after his return home. Promoted to Quartermaster Sergeant and later becoming a Yeoman of the Queen's Body Guard, he died of cirrhosis of the liver in 1884 at the age of seventy-five. His shipmate, the painter and lively correspondent John Davis, had an illustrious career, becoming Naval Assistant to the Hydrographer and inventing a new, improved sextant. He died in 1877 at the age of sixty-three.

The year after their return Robert McCormick was elected to the Royal College of Surgeons. His hopes for promotion in the Navy rested largely on his work as a naturalist, but the naval establishment decided that any advancement had to be on his medical qualifications, which, through no fault of his own, had hardly been tested. His persistence in pleading his case didn't help and, when he finally received promotion in May 1859, it was to the office of Deputy-Inspector of Hospitals, from which he was retired at the age of sixty-five. Ironically even his contribution as a naturalist was overshadowed by others – Hooker included – and his autobiography had to be self-published.

He nevertheless outlived many of his more successful contemporaries, dying in 1890 at the age of ninety.

The other great survivor was Joseph Hooker. In the last letter to his father he had sounded disillusioned. 'I have received a great deal of kindness from Captain Ross for which I thank you,' he wrote, acknowledging his father's help in securing him a place on the voyage; 'had others, who deserved it better, received the same, this Expedition would have been a very happy one. To conclude, I may and will honor and thank Captain Ross very much, but love him I never can or could.' But if there was now little trace of the youthful joy and enthusiasm with which he had left home, Hooker had at least discovered his calling. 'Botany alone has rendered many months tolerable which otherwise might have been to me, as they were to others, scarcely endurable.' Now the young assistant surgeon was set to become the most successful botanist of the Victorian era, producing *Flora Antarctica*, a handsome four-volume account of his researches on the voyage, and later succeeding his father as director of Kew Gardens, a position he held for twenty years. He was showered with honours and medals, including a knighthood and the Order of Merit. Hooker was twenty-two when *Erebus* set off for the Antarctic, and he was ninety-three when Captain Robert Falcon Scott, preparing to set off for the South Pole, asked him to raise the flag that marked the start of the expedition. Born in the reign of George III, Joseph Dalton Hooker died in the reign of George V, on 10 December 1911.

The reception of the returning expedition was respectful, but muted. They had been away a long time. Their greatest successes had been in the early stages of the voyage and, despite much good work after that, Ross had not been the sort of man to court public opinion with constant reports of progress. Hooker complained more than once of what he called 'Ross's foolish jealousy of not sending news'. Promotions were made and men commended, but no great interest was shown in mounting exhibitions or lecture tours and, apart from

Ross's own account of the voyage, precious little was written about it at the time.

It was to be almost twenty-five years after the ships returned before all the data they had gathered on terrestrial magnetism was analysed and published. By that time the Magnetic Crusade had lost its urgency. The whaling business shrank, as gas began to replace oil for lighting, and there was less reason to send so many ships so far south. The right whale, from which so many whalers made their livelihood, was ruthlessly exploited in northern waters and few made their way to the South Atlantic any more.

For the next sixty years the Antarctic remained virtually forgotten.

Most of those who served on the Ross expedition were long dead by the time a new generation of explorers revived public interest in Antarctica, but their successors were only too aware of the debt they owed to the efforts of Ross and Crozier and the men of *Erebus* and *Terror*. Roald Amundsen, the most accomplished polar traveller of them all, paid his own tribute in his book *The South Pole* nearly seventy years later.

> With two ponderous craft – regular 'tubs' according to our ideas – these men sailed right into the heart of the pack, which all previous explorers had regarded as certain death. It is not merely difficult to grasp this; it is simply impossible – to us, who with a motion of the hand can set the screw going and wriggle out of the first difficulty we encounter. These men were heroes – heroes in the highest sense of the word.

Captain Scott concurred, describing the Clark Ross expedition in his introduction to *The Voyage of the 'Discovery'* as one of 'the most brilliant and famous that have been made'. 'Few things,' he went on, 'could have looked more hopeless than an attack upon that great icebound region which lay within the Antarctic Circle; yet out of this desolate prospect Ross wrested an open sea, a vast mountain range, a smoking volcano and a hundred problems of great interest to the geographer.' His conclusion was generous: 'It might be said it was James Cook who defined the Antarctic Region, and James Ross who discovered it.'

HMS *Erebus*, with a token crew aboard, was towed downriver from Woolwich to Sheerness, where she had her copper repaired, before she was stripped down, cleaned out and her rigging and upper parts of the mast dismantled.

For four years she had resounded to shouted orders, thudding feet, slapping sails and the ship's bell sounding the half-hour. Now, as 1843 drew to a close, and Londoners rushed to buy their copies of *A Christmas Carol*, she lay silent, her broad beam and squat stocky lines rocking gently off the coast of Kent, where the Thames estuary becomes the North Sea. Just another ship waiting for work. Except for one thing that marked *Erebus* out. Never again in the annals of the sea would a ship, under sail alone, come close to matching what she and *Terror* had achieved.

Erebus and *Terror* set sail for the Northwest Passage.

CHAPTER 12

'SO LITTLE NOW REMAINS TO BE DONE'

One of the immediate, if seemingly paradoxical, consequences of the success of the Antarctic expedition was renewed interest in the Arctic. *Erebus* and *Terror* had barely docked before Captain Frederick Beechey, who had served with Sir John Franklin in the 1818 expedition to the North Pole, was using Ross's achievement to drum up interest in another naval foray to the frozen north. Nothing came of it until the tireless Second Secretary at the Admiralty, John Barrow, became involved. He had encouraged Ross's expedition to the south, but his heart – and his ambition – was always in the north. Now nearly eighty years old, he saw a last chance to achieve the goal to which so much of his life's work had been directed: the conquest of the Northwest Passage. Such progress had been made over the past twenty-five years that now only 100 or so miles between east and west were still unexplored. All that remained, now, was to join the dots. This had proved easier said than done.

I can understand why. I went through part of the Northwest Passage in August 2017, in an ice-strengthened Russian ship called *Akademik Sergey Vavilov*. My first impression was how much greater the distances were than they appeared on the map. What looked to be an intricate, almost cosy lacework of islands and narrow channels was, in reality, an enormous area of wide seas and massive treeless plateaux. Lancaster Sound is more than 60 miles wide at its eastern end, and never less than 40 miles of water lie between the islands on either side of it. Devon Island, to the north, is the largest uninhabited island on the planet, a tundra-covered land mass the size of Iowa. To the south is Baffin Island, the fifth-largest island in the world, twice the size of Great Britain. We had all the modern apparatus of precise maps and charts, GPS location-finding, sonar soundings designed to make navigation as simple as possible, and a ship many times bigger and stronger than anything that Barrow could muster. But in practice our captain was having to adapt our route hour by hour to avoid build-ups of ice. Not a lot seemed to have changed.

With Ross's safe return from the Antarctic showing what a well-planned, publicly funded expedition could achieve, Secretary Barrow marshalled his formidable powers of persuasion for one final attempt to achieve his lifetime's ambition. In December 1844 he submitted to Lord Haddington, the new First Lord of the Admiralty, 'A Proposal for an attempt to complete the discovery of a North West Passage'. It opened with a clear statement of his case: 'There is a feeling generally entertained in the several scientific societies, and individuals attached to scientific pursuits ... that the discovery, or rather the completion of a discovery, of a passage from the Atlantic to the Pacific, round the Northern coast of North America, ought not to be abandoned, after so much has been done, and so little now remains to be done.'

Barrow bolstered his case politically by raising the spectre of the Russians (who at that time owned Alaska) getting there first. A successful navigation of the Northwest Passage, he warned, 'if left to be performed by some other power, England, by her neglect of it, after having opened the East and West doors, would be laughed at by all the world for having hesitated to cross the threshold'. He strengthened his case scientifically by arguing that a fresh expedition could help complete the magnetic survey of the globe – still a potent motive. To butter up the Admiralty, he drew attention to the training that an expedition like this offered to the seamen of the future, at a time when the Royal Navy had no wars in which to apprentice young officers. And to butter up the accountants, he argued that the journey could be accomplished within a year, and at one-third the cost of the recently returned Antarctic expedition. And last but not least, he pointed out that two ice-tested ships were ready and waiting in the Thames estuary. It was an impressive case, and it drew impressive support.

Arctic heavyweights Sir John Franklin, Sir Edward Parry and Sir James Clark Ross gave full support to Barrow's proposal. All of them, apart from Ross, recommended that steam propulsion, despite having failed on John Ross's *Victory*, be considered an essential component for any future attempt. Colonel Sabine and the Council of the Royal Society endorsed the commercial potential of an expedition, arguing the case for its contribution to the cause of magnetic observation and navigational improvements. The cumulative effect of such overwhelming enthusiasm persuaded the Prime Minister, Sir Robert Peel, to give the proposal his full backing. Sir John Barrow heard of his decision the day before he retired from the Admiralty. He could scarcely have wished for a better leaving present.

But time was tight. If the momentum of the go-ahead was to be maintained, the expedition had to be made ready within a matter of months. If they were to reach Lancaster Sound, the gateway to the Northwest Passage, before it iced over, they had to be away by early May 1845.

The most pressing business was the selection of the new expedition's leader. James – now Sir James – Clark Ross, was top of the list. He had been a key member of seven expeditions already and had proved a safe pair of hands in the Antarctic. Knowing what we now know of the state of his hands in Cape Town, it is perhaps not surprising that he turned down the offer. His promise to his new wife and her father-in-law was cited as his reason for refusing, as was his claim that he was, at forty-four, too old for this sort of thing. This seems like special pleading, given that he then threw his support behind his fifty-nine-year-old friend Sir John Franklin. It seems more than likely that Ross had just had enough.

Franklin's candidacy had another strong advocate, too. Lady Jane Franklin, now back in Britain, was lobbying hard on behalf of her husband, after he had been summarily dismissed from his governorship of Van Diemen's Land by Lord Stanley, then Minister for the Colonies; and she proceeded to use her friendship with James Ross, which she had so assiduously cultivated in Tasmania, to call in a few favours. She spoke candidly about her husband: 'what weighs most upon my mind,' she wrote to Ross, 'is that at the present crisis of our affairs and after being treated so unworthily by the Col Office, I think he will be deeply sensitive if his own department should neglect him ... I dread exceedingly the effect on his mind of being without honourable and immediate employment.'

It's not clear whether this entreaty came before or after Ross wrote to Sir Francis Beaufort, the Hydrographer of the Navy, commending Franklin for 'being so pre-eminently qualified for the command of such an expedition', but her pleadings clearly had the desired effect. Not that everyone was convinced. Lord Haddington at the Admiralty, for example, interviewed Franklin and expressed some concern that, at sixty, he might be too old for such an arduous task. Franklin replied, indignantly, that he was not sixty. He was only fifty-nine. For his part, Sir John Barrow had a clearly expressed preference for a rising star, thirty-two-year-old Commander James Fitzjames. But in the end it may well have been Sir Edward Parry who had the last word. He told Haddington that, in his opinion, Franklin was 'a fitter man to go than any I know', adding, 'and if you don't let him go, he will die of disappointment'.

So despite the suspicion that he was chosen out of pity, Sir John Franklin was confirmed as leader of the latest Northwest Passage expedition, with James Fitzjames as his second-in-command on *Erebus*. The post of captain of HMS *Terror* and overall second-in-command was initially offered to a Captain John Lort Stokes, who had captained the *Beagle* on her third Pacific journey, but when he turned it down, the inevitable choice was Francis Crozier. Crozier had in fact been offered the leadership of the entire expedition by Lord Haddington, and had agonised over his decision whilst he was on his emotional recuperation tour of Europe. Interestingly, James Clark Ross hadn't supported Haddington: it's as if he knew the fragile state Crozier was in and was trying to protect him from taking on too much. What we know of Crozier's mood seems to support this. Writing from Florence late in 1844, he explained to Ross his decision to turn down the leadership role: 'I sincerely feel I am not equal to the hardship. I am, in truth, still of opinion as to my own unfitness to lead. You, on that subject as well as all others, know my whole mind.' Only a few months later Crozier felt sufficiently recovered to accept the role of second-in-command, and he was duly confirmed in his new post on 3 March 1845.

By comparison with the Antarctic voyage, the genesis of this latest expedition was full of doubts and compromises: about age, about mental and physical fitness and, in some cases, about the wisdom of such an expedition at all. Dr Richard King, an argumentative, opinionated character who had been on several overland Arctic expeditions, was adamant that the extent and thickness of the ice would doom to failure any maritime traverse of the Northwest Passage. He wrote to John Barrow warning him, quite graphically, that he was sending Franklin to the Arctic 'to form the nucleus of an iceberg'.

But there was no time for a debate. The ships were being prepared, and officers and men were falling over themselves to be taken on. Even Crozier caught the mood, assuring Ross that 'I feel quite satisfied in my own mind that I was right in volunteering to go second to Sir John, and also in not volunteering as leader, come of it what may.'

His happier state of mind might well have been influenced by the fact that whilst the preparations were going on at Woolwich Dockyard, Crozier stayed with James and Anne Ross at their house in nearby Blackheath.

One issue that was never in contention was the choice of vessels for the expedition. After their Antarctic success, *Erebus* and *Terror* had earned a formidable reputation as the toughest, most dependable ice-resistant ships in the British Navy. On 5 February orders were issued for *Erebus* to be brought out of temporary retirement at Sheerness and towed upriver to Woolwich Royal Dockyard, where master ship-wright Oliver Lang was put in charge of refitting her, and her sister ship *Terror*, for Arctic duty.

The London riverside has changed dramatically even in my lifetime. Into the 1940s the Port of London was the busiest in the world, extending along 11 miles of river bank; 60,000 ships were loaded and unloaded every year. Nowadays trade doesn't reach this far upriver. Britain's imports and exports come and go from Felixstowe and Tilbury and the London Gateway. Sentiment for the old days nevertheless lingers on, and this part of London is still dominated by the legacy of years gone by. Though there are no working docks any more, the modern railway that takes me to Woolwich is called the Docklands Light Railway. Its driverless trains pass through stations with names like Pontoon Dock, Canary Wharf and Heron Quays. From the train I can see the vast bulk of the Tate & Lyle sugar refinery, once the hub of a huge import business. Now the steam from its chimneys blows past a sign hanging from the walls: 'Save Our Sugar!' Then the railway line plunges under the Thames and I get off at the first station on the south side, Woolwich Arsenal. An eye-tighteningly icy wind sears off the river as I take my map out and make my way across General Gordon Square towards the old Arsenal buildings. Most of them have been pulled down and are being rebuilt as luxury apartments. A less luxurious development of seven tower blocks runs east alongside the river. They're accessed via a street called Erebus Drive, so I guess this must be where the wharves and workshops stood, and where the ship was prepared for her last voyage. The river looks cold and choppy and colourless.

At the entrance to the building site for the new residential development two of the original Arsenal buildings survive. One is now a pub called the Dial Arch. Its original purpose is evident from two mighty columns on either side of a sundial, topped with stacks of cannon-balls. Adjacent to it is a low-roofed, characterful red-brick building with a lead-capped tower at one corner and a cannon on the grass outside. This is the Royal Brass Foundry, now an outstation of the National Maritime Museum, and here, if my information is right, are stored the only copies of the plans to convert *Erebus* from bomb ship to ice explorer.

I ring a doorbell and am admitted to what is the most reassuring office environment I've seen in a long time. In a world where so many people sit in headsetted ranks at empty desks and full screens, the occupants of the Royal Brass Foundry potter about in a warm, friendly clutter, surrounded by kettles and jars of coffee on stained trays, box-files piled on copiers and pictures Sellotaped to the wall. Behind this laid-back ambience is an extraordinary archive of more than one million ships' plans and a huge photographic collection, which is currently being digitised. A number of plans of both *Erebus* and *Terror* have been ordered up for me, and they are captivating.

They are elegantly inscribed as the work of 'Mr. Oliver Lang, Woolwich Yard, March 17th 1845' (only two months before the expedition left), and I'm drawn in by the fine line of the detail, precisely ink-drawn on cartridge paper and still clearly legible, 170 years on.

I find out a lot about *Erebus*'s exterior and interior. Shipbuilders have a language all their own. By the end of the morning I've learned about orlops, knees, rabbets, riders, pintles, gudgeons and scuttles.

I know I won't remember them all, and I can imagine that's the way those who drew up these plans would like it to be. However much I want to know about *Erebus*, I'll always be a landlubber. But this visit has brought me much closer to her. I've a better sense of her frame and how it was toughened, and how everything inside her was so carefully thought out. Here at the Brass Foundry I can see how a strong ship was made even stronger. I can see for myself why she was able to achieve so much. On these stiff sheets of cartridge paper is the formula for her survival.

Much of the work Lang and his men did was superficial, adding strength to the hull and decks, waterproofing bulwarks and augmenting the iron reinforcement in the bow. Internally, not a lot was changed from what had worked so well in the Antarctic. The Fraser patent cooking and water-production system was retained in the galley. It was designed to use the steam produced during cooking to distil water from snow and ice.

Heating was provided by Mr Sylvester's system, an early form of central heating, which took warm air from a brick furnace through 'a square iron tube, above a foot in diameter, running all round the sides, and distributing a comfortable warmth to every berth in the ship', as it was described by the makers in 1839. This had already proved its worth and came with an enthusiastic personal endorsement from a Captain James Ross of London. 'The admirable performance of this most invaluable invention of Mr Sylvester cannot be mentioned in adequate terms of praise.'

The most drastic alteration to the two vessels was the controversial installation of a steam-driven screw-propeller system, one of the first ever applied to wood-hulled warships. Sir Edward Parry, who had been given overall charge of the preparations, justified it in a letter to the Admiralty in January 1845: 'I conceive that an advantage ... may now be gained from the adoption of a small steam-power (equal to the production of a speed of 3 or 4 knots) in each of the ships employed on this service,' he wrote, before going on to suggest 'perhaps a pair of small locomotive engines of 50 horsepower, with a moveable screw propeller, all of which might be placed in a very small space and completely secured from injury by the ice; and no fuel to be used except for pushing through the narrow and ever-varying channels between the masses of ice, where there is no means of doing so'.

This was the brief to which Oliver Lang and his team had to work. And they had just three months to get it right. With no time to build new equipment, Parry suggested that they use second-hand locomotive engines – lighter and much smaller than the marine steam engines of the time. The firm of Maudslay, Sons and Field, which was in charge of the work, procured two locomotives, though there are different opinions as to where they might have got them from. In a letter to Ross, Crozier names the Dover Line. The *Illustrated London News* at the time credited them to the Greenwich Railway. Respected Franklin scholars Peter Carney and William Battersby have plumped for the London and Croydon Railway. Their well-argued conclusion is that the two locomotives that gave up their engines in the cause of Arctic exploration were No. 2 'Croydon' and No. 6 'Archimedes'.

Whatever their source, the two engines arrived in Woolwich on 18 April and were taken to the quayside where the ships were moored. James Fitzjames noted the arrival of one of them from the window of his lodgings: 'The engine is down alongside drawn by 10 coal-black horses and weighs 15 tons.'

The engines were then lowered into the hold of each ship, into a double-height compartment just aft of the mainmast, and connected by a 32-foot-long shaft with a 7-foot-high gun-metal propeller. Lang had redesigned the sterns of the ships to allow space for the propeller to be retracted when not in use. The *Illustrated London News* reported their Lordships at the Admiralty being particularly impressed by this ingenious solution to fitting a steam-drive propeller to sailing ships, 'the objection and difficulty of shipping and unshipping it on the outside being completely obviated'.

Among those less excited about the installation of steam engines was Sir James Clark Ross, united for once with his uncle, Sir John. They took the view that the engines were heavy to carry and as yet unproven. Concerns were also expressed that the installation of the propeller lifting gear might weaken the sternposts and the security of the rudder. Then there was the question of the extra weight of coal required to drive the engines. This was partly solved by the creation of a lighter 'patent fuel', consisting of bricks made from compressed coal dust and coal tar.

Whatever the doubts, the chunky bomb vessel that had slid down the slipway at Pembroke nearly twenty years earlier was now one of the best-equipped ships in the Navy. *Erebus* and *Terror* were at the cutting edge of maritime technology, with a 25-horsepower capacity to help them through the ice. Not exactly a game-changer, though. A modern ice-breaker has a capacity of 40,000.

As work on the ships began, the selection of their officers and crew was also under way. Commander James Fitzjames, rather than Sir John Franklin himself, was charged with staffing, despite the fact that he had no Arctic experience. What he did have was the wholehearted support of Sir John Barrow, who had, of course, proposed him as leader of the expedition.

Sir John may have had a personal interest in doing so: there is evidence to suggest that Fitzjames had helped Barrow's son, George, out of some embarrassment whilst stationed out in the East: 'A matter of honour or maybe even a homosexual incident,' suggests Fitzjames's biographer William Battersby, who calls him 'The Mystery Man of the Franklin Expedition'. It's not even clear who Fitzjames's parents were. Battersby suggests that he was the illegitimate child of the diplomat and womaniser Sir James Gambier, who served as British Consul-General in Rio. Fitzjames joined the Navy in 1825, around the age of thirteen, serving on an expedition to survey the River Euphrates early in his career, and then as a gunnery lieutenant in the China War, less opaquely known as the First Opium War.

By all accounts, Fitzjames was popular, good company, a legendarily good mimic, a man who could be all things to all men. He was an entertainer, with a sharp eye and a way with words. When he was serving on HMS *Cornwallis* during the First Opium War he put his impressions of Shanghai into verse:

> *To the south of the town, where Chinese take their tea*
> *And with grottoes and bridges, most curious to see.*
> *Of a labyrinth form; in fact such a scene*
> *As appears on our English blue plates (when they're clean).*

He was brave, too. In 1835 he dived into the Mersey to save a man from drowning. A grateful City and Corporation of Liverpool awarded him the Fitzjames Cup.

As the expedition's departure day drew closer, Fitzjames moved to Woolwich and took rooms at 14 Francis Street. Colonel Sabine, the chief scientific advisor to the expedition, was nearby, at the Woolwich Academy, where he set up a facility to train the newly appointed officers in the use of instruments for magnetic observation. Meanwhile Fitzjames moved fast to fill the various positions. On 4 March, Charles Osmer, aged forty-six (one of the oldest members of the expedition, but recently married and with a one-year-old child), was appointed as paymaster and purser on HMS *Erebus*. He had previous Arctic experience with Beechey in the Bering Strait. Charles Frederick Des Voeux, who had sailed with Fitzjames before, was chosen as First Mate on *Erebus*, and Henry Le Vesconte, who had been second-in-command to Fitzjames on a ship called *Clio*, was appointed lieutenant. Dr Stephen Stanley, who had sailed with Fitzjames on the *Cornwallis*, became chief surgeon, with Dr Harry Goodsir as his junior. Like Joseph Hooker in the Antarctic, Goodsir was a keen naturalist as well as a surgeon.

Among others recruited in that breathless month of March were two whom Fitzjames knew well. James Fairholme, who had been with him on the Euphrates expedition, was chosen to be one of the three lieutenants on *Erebus*, and Edward Couch, who had served with him in the China War, was recruited as a mate. Fitzjames has been criticised for choosing old friends over old Arctic hands, but there was some logic in this. If you were going to spend many months, and possibly years, in close proximity, then it was as well to be surrounded by people you got on with. Not that those with polar experience were ignored. Apart from the captain himself and Charles Osmer, there was Second Master Henry Collins, who had served on whaling ships, and Lieutenant Graham Gore, who had sailed on George Back's Northwest Passage expedition.

The six years between the Ross expedition and the Franklin expedition had seen the invention of a photographic process, called – after its inventor Louis Daguerre – the daguerreotype. In 1839, around the same time the Ross expedition was setting out for Antarctica, the first full-face photograph of a human being was taken by Robert Cornelius in Philadelphia. By the time the expedition returned, in 1843, photography was part of everyday life.

Lady Franklin, always alert to the latest scientific advances, secured the services of a photographer, William Beard, to make three-quarter-length daguerreotype portraits of the leading officers on HMS *Erebus*, and these were later published in the *Illustrated London News* for September 1851. The collection is invaluable in being the first such portrait gallery of its kind, but it is also infinitely poignant, as it introduces us to a group of largely young men full of confidence and expectation. It offers us a chance to put faces to names – the names of those who were never to come back.

Franklin doesn't come out of it well. Despite the impressive cocked hat and medals, his jacket looks uncomfortably tight, his face jowly and pasty. According to Lady Franklin, he'd been plagued by influenza since coming back to Britain. He had also been preoccupied since his return with trying to put his side of the story of what had gone wrong in Van Diemen's Land and, urged on by his wife, was cooperating on a pamphlet of self-justification, the composition of which weighed heavily on his mind. In addition, he was on a rigorous schedule of personal appearances. Unlike the Antarctic expedition, this was a very public enterprise, and Sir John had to be available to greet a stream of prominent visitors to the dockyard and attend a host of official functions. On 20 March, with less than two months to go before departure, the Royal Artillery, anxious to assert its part in the magnetic work of the expedition, hosted more than a hundred officers and scientists at the Woolwich Officers' Mess, with Franklin as guest of honour. A month later he was alongside the First Lord, raising money for a sailors' church in Bishopsgate, and later that same day he dined at the Royal Geological Society. The camera, in this case, didn't lie. Here was a man with the weight of the world on his shoulders.

By contrast, thirty-two-year-old Fitzjames – bare-headed and curly-haired, his long side-whiskers mirrored by long epaulettes – looks comfortably unrestricted, his jacket open to reveal a smart waistcoat, telescope in the crook of his left arm. It's no surprise to learn that Fitzjames, amused, and amusing, composed short pen-portraits of his fellow officers, which help bring their formally posed photos to life.

Twenty-nine-year-old Henry Thomas Dundas Le Vesconte, holding Erebus's Signal Book in his left hand, is the only one photographed with a recognisable part of the ship in the background. It's a valuable image, this one, as we can see over his right shoulder the double wheel with which the ship was steered. It is, unbelievably, the only photograph of the Erebus in existence. Fitzjames noted that Le Vesconte was 'shy and reserved' and had bow-legs.

James Reid, the ice-master from Aberdeen, looks out, eyeglass raised as if already searching for distant obstacles. 'Rough, intelligent, unpolished with a broad north-country accent,' Fitzjames thought.

Lieutenant Des Voeux, cap in left hand, thumb of right hand tucked inside his jacket, looks as if he's trying to appear more mature than his nineteen-and-a-half years. 'A most unexceptionable, clever, agreeable, light-hearted obliging young fellow,' reckoned Fitzjames, adding that Des Voeux had one glass eye.

Stephen Stanley, the surgeon, leans back comfortably, open-faced, hair carefully dressed and brushed forward in a curl over his ear. 'He is rather inclined to be good-looking, but fat, with jet black hair, very white hands, which are always abominably clean, and the shirt sleeves tucked up; giving one unpleasant ideas that he would not mind cutting one's leg off immediately, if not sooner.'

Lieutenant Edward Couch defies the fashion for facial hair and shows us a quiet smile. 'A little, black-haired, smooth-faced fellow … Writes, reads, works, draws, all quietly. I can find no remarkable point in his character except, perhaps, that is, I should think, obstinate.'

The third of the young lieutenants who served as mates on *Erebus*, twenty-one-year-old Robert Orme Sargent, was described by Fitzjames as 'A nice, pleasant-looking lad. Very good-natured.'

Dr Harry Goodsir, sitting in profile, leaning on his right hand, was an extremely well-qualified assistant surgeon. Aged thirty-eight and from a gifted Scottish family, he had already been Conservator of the Museum of the Royal College of Surgeons in Edinburgh. He was also the naturalist of the expedition. Fitzjames clearly had time for him. 'He is long and straight, and walks upright on his toes, with his hands tucked up into each jacket pocket. He laughs delightfully.'

Lieutenant Graham Gore, also thirty-eight, sits for the camera with arms tightly folded, as if huddled against the cold, the peak of his hat pulled down low, eyes on the middle-distance. Fitzjames, affably puncturing any vanity the older man might have, wrote of Gore, 'he plays the flute dreadfully well, draws, sometimes very well, sometimes very badly, but is altogether a capital fellow.'

Captain Crozier is the only member of *Terror*'s crew to be photographed, which seems to confirm that, as far as Jane Franklin was concerned, this was Sir John Franklin's expedition and, *Erebus* being his flagship, that was where the interest lay. Fitzjames offered no pen-portrait of Francis Crozier.

Information on the expedition's officers is relatively easy to come by. To find out more about the crew, we have to rely on Muster Books and Description Books, kept by the paymaster and purser on every ship in the Navy. Though we shall never know what the rank-and-file seamen looked like, these records, painstakingly scrutinised by naval historian Ralph Lloyd-Jones, do help bring the often-ignored to life.

James W. Brown, listed as 'Caulker', was from Deptford, very close to Woolwich, and had been in the caulking trade for many years. The job involved keeping the ship's seams watertight, using strips of old rope called oakum coated with tar. John Cowie, an able seaman aboard *Erebus*, was thirty-two, married and had his name tattooed on his right arm. This was quite common in the Royal Navy, as Lloyd-Jones suggests, matter-of-factly, 'in case their mutilated body ever had to be identified'. Francis Pocock, another able seaman, was originally a fisherman on the mouth of the Medway. He was described as being 5 feet 4 inches, freckled, with hazel eyes, light-coloured hair and he had had smallpox. John Strickland from Portsmouth was twenty-one and had a 'florid' complexion, 'Marked lightly with Smallpox', whereas John Franklin's steward, Edmund Hoar, who had an anchor tattooed on his arm, had been vaccinated (a vaccine against smallpox had existed since it was discovered, by Edward Jenner, in 1796). Joseph Lloyd, a twenty-five-year-old from Greenwich, was discharged from *Erebus* about ten days before they sailed, possibly because he was married and had had second thoughts about going to the Arctic. Or perhaps he was clairvoyant.

Fourteen members of the crew of *Erebus* were 'First Entries' – men who had not served in the Royal Navy before, but many of whom had gained experience on whaling ships or might already have sailed in the Arctic as civilians. Most of the First Entry men were in their twenties, though the leading stoker on *Erebus*, James Hart, from Hampstead, was thirty-three.

Though the ships had been crowded enough before, there were eleven more men on *Erebus* and *Terror* than there had been in the Antarctic, the additional posts being three first-class stokers on each vessel (presumably required to man the steam engines), one extra engineer on each ship and, for the first time, ice-masters, men whose speciality was navigating through ice: James Reid on *Erebus* and Thomas Blanky on *Terror*. Both had previously worked on whaling ships. Blanky, whose real name was Blenkinhorn, had also for a time kept a pub in Whitby. To take part in the expedition, James Reid had given up the offer of a job on *Neptune*, bound for Quebec, explaining in a letter to his wife, 'A number of people think it strange of me going but they would go if they knew as much about ice as I know,' before adding, with not altogether convincing bravado, 'it will show that I am not frightened for my life like some men'.

In addition to a boatswain, an engineer and a carpenter, all of whom were warrant officers, there were twenty-two petty officers on *Erebus*, with self-descriptive jobs like Sailmaker, Caulker, Cook and Blacksmith, and there were twenty able seamen. There were no ordinary seamen, the more junior, lower-paid rank, on either ship – an indication of the selective status of the expedition.

Only nine men in the two crews had sailed with Ross in the Antarctic: five on *Terror* and four on *Erebus*. These included Richard Wall, aged forty-five, from Staffordshire, who retained the post of cook on *Erebus*. His conduct on the Antarctic voyage had been described as

'Very Good'. James Frederick Elgar Rigden, thirty-four, who had served on *Erebus* throughout her Antarctic journey, was appointed captain's coxswain. The Description Book noted him as being '5'7 and a half inch tall, with a fresh complexion, grey eyes, brown hair, with two sailors and his initials "JR", tattooed on his right arm'. He was one of fourteen men aboard *Erebus* who came from the seafaring county of Kent. In addition, *Erebus* had seven Royal Marines and two Boys (midshipmen) aboard. A total of sixty-eight men. Their average age was twenty-eight.

With the men putting in eleven-hour days, the main engineering work had been completed in time for a high-level visit from all the Lords of the Admiralty in the third week of April. They visited a test-ing room for anchors, admired Sylvester's heating apparatus and the Massey double-action brass bilge pumps, installed to deal with the inevitable intake of water leaking through wooden hulls. They also noted the 'strong sheet iron' reinforcing the bows and the removal of all copper sheathing around the hull, 'as no danger is to be appre-hended from the attacks of shellfish or barnacles'.

With the engines fitted, and the decks and bows strengthened, the emphasis now turned to taking on stores and provisions, for what the Admiralty calculated could be a three-year expedition. For lighting beneath the grey, overcast skies of the Arctic, 2,700 lb worth of candles made from whale or rapeseed oil were ordered, alongside hundreds of Argand lamps, oil lamps with wicks and glass funnels. To ensure the survival of sixty-eight men who would have no opportunity to restock on the way, *Erebus* alone was supplied with 18,355 lb of biscuits; 69,888 lb of flour; 612 lb of pemmican (a concentrate of fat and protein); 16,416 lb of beef in 8-lb pieces and 16,320 lb of pork in 4-lb pieces stored in casks full of brine; 11,928 lb of sugar; 4,822 lb of chocolate; and 10,920 pints of concentrated soup (in either vegetable or gravy form). And crucially, to help combat scurvy, there were 4,750 lb of lemon juice, cranberries, pickled walnuts, Normandy pippin apples and carrots stored in sand. In addition, nearly 8,000 tins of preserved meats were loaded on board. The formula for preserving food in tins had been discovered by a Frenchman, Nicolas Appert, in 1810, and they had proved their worth on two previous Arctic expeditions, as well as on the Ross expedition to Antarctica. Three tons of tobacco and 200 gallons of wine were also loaded and, to ensure the all-important grog rations could be maintained, the two ships between them carried 4,500 gallons of 130–140-proof West Indian rum.

Sir John Franklin was especially concerned with the educational and recreational well-being of his crews. There were state-of-the-art instruments for research into magnetism, geology, botany and zoology. Mr Beard the photographer gave them a daguerreotype camera. Evening schools were to be held for the men during the winter months for which 'Common Arithmetic' books, paper, pens, ink, slates and slate pencils were provided.

Both vessels had extensive libraries. Most ships were issued with the basic 'Seamen's Library', but on this expedition it was augmented to some 1,200 volumes per ship, with technical works on steam propulsion, accounts of previous Arctic expeditions, geographical and nautical magazines, the latest bestsellers, such as *The Pickwick Papers* and *Nicholas Nickleby*, and evergreen favourites like *The Ingoldsby Legends* and Oliver Goldsmith's *The Vicar of Wakefield*. They also had stacks of the humorous satirical magazine *Punch*, which had first appeared four years previously and ran until 2002. And of course, given Franklin's evangelical enthusiasm, there were religious works, too.

For entertainment there were two hand-organs, each with a repertoire of fifty different tunes. As on the Antarctic expedition, the officers would have had to contribute from their own funds towards personal supplies of food and drink, and little luxuries like dressing-up outfits for on-board theatricals, musical instruments and, in

Franklin's case, a monogrammed china service and specially designed wine rack. All the officers were required to buy a set of silver spoons and forks.

The *Illustrated London News* of 24 May 1845 carried wood engravings of some of the accommodation. Fitzjames's cabin looks cosy, despite the restricted space. It was about 6 feet wide, with a bed and book-shelves above, an oil lamp, a writing desk, a washbasin, and a porthole with additional light provided by a prism, known as a Preston Illuminator, set into the deck above. Sir John Franklin's cabin, with double windows set into the stern, is shown spread across the width of the ship, with a bed on one side, lockers on the other and cupboards for charts. A chess set is seen, laid out on one of the side-tables.

It all added up to as well-appointed and carefully thought-out an enterprise as had ever been assembled.

As the date of departure drew closer, so did a growing sense of hope and expectation. The era of peace and progress, which was to reach its apogee in the Great Exhibition six years later, had created a mood of confidence in the country. But national confidence is precarious and needs to be fed a constant diet of achievement. A successful discovery of the Northwest Passage would be just the right sort of dish for the Admiralty to serve up – a glorious advertisement for a climactic com-ing-together of Britain's naval, scientific and technological advances. It would confirm that Britain could be as great at peace as it had been in war. James Clark Ross's Antarctic expedition was appreciated but barely noticed. The Franklin expedition was expected to be heroic.

Not everyone was carried along by this growing mood of self-belief. There were some for whom 'the aura of invincibility', as Crozier's biographer Michael Smith calls it, masked serious and pos-sibly life-threatening misjudgements. Archibald McMurdo, Crozier's trusted second-in-command in the Antarctic, doubted Franklin would return. Dr Richard King, who coined the phrase 'nucleus of an iceberg' to warn of Franklin's fate, remained adamant that the expedition would be 'a lasting blot in the annals of our voyages of discovery'. Less easily dismissed were the very similar views of Sir John Ross, veteran of two Arctic missions, who felt strongly that a smaller, more flexible expedition was the only way to approach the challenge. In his experience, some of the Arctic waterways were both narrow and shallow; the bigger and heavier the ships, the more chance of their getting stuck. John Ross met Franklin shortly before they sailed and urged him at the very least to leave indications of their progress, and depots of food and spare boats, along the way in case he should need to retreat. Franklin, harried on all sides no doubt, would not consider failure. John Ross's last words to him reiterated his advice. 'I shall volunteer to look for you,' he promised him, 'if you are not heard of in February 1847; but pray put a notice in the cairn where you winter, if you do proceed, which of the routes you take.'

After the naval lords' inspection on 24 April, Franklin took up his quarters on *Erebus*. The publicity, thanks to such organs as the *Illustrated London News*, had made onboard visits a hot ticket. Sir John Richardson, who had been through hard times with Franklin on various Arctic adventures, brought his nephew, also called John, to see them off. Looking back on the visit many years later, John junior wrote to a friend, 'My chief recollection ... was that my uncle tipped me a golden half sovereign and that the ship smelt very nasty.'

Out on the Thames, *Terror* tested her new engine. She was able to reach a top speed of four knots, but according to John Irving, one of *Terror*'s lieutenants, the ship made 'dreadful puffings and screamings and will astonish the Esquimaux not a little'.

Equally likely to 'astonish the Esquimaux' was Lady Franklin's gift of a monkey to HMS *Erebus*. 'I can easily conceive that the dressing him up would be a source of great fun to them,' she wrote. '... I should like also to give something of the sort to the *Terror*, but not knowing whether Captain Crozier would approve of a monkey I think I had better get a cockatoo.'

On 5 May 1845 the Admiralty issued its sailing instructions to Sir John. There were twenty-three clauses. The majority of them dealt with the importance of scientific research, and in particular measure ments of terrestrial magnetism. There was also an instruction only to use the engines 'in circumstances of difficulty'. Their lordships were quite adamant as to the route Franklin was to take. He should head due west through Lancaster Sound and Barrow Strait to Cape Walker and on to the Bering Sea. He was expressly instructed not to examine any channels leading northwards or southwards. No specific orders were issued to erect cairns or leave any indications of their progress, although one clause, after stating that 'Any Eskimos or Indians whom he may meet are to be treated as friends and to be given presents', includes the afterthought: 'If possible he is to induce them by means of rewards to convey dispatches to the stations of the Hudson Bay Company.'

The normal practice of dropping overboard positional records in tin cylinders was to be maintained, although even this was judged to be less about rescue and more about 'ascertaining the set of currents in the Arctic Seas'. The Admiralty was not interested in things going wrong. That would be defeatist. Their instructions embodied confi- dence and certainty. 'When he has passed Bering Strait, he is to go to the Sandwich Islands [now Hawaii] ... after leaving the Sandwich Islands he is to go to Panama and is thence to send an officer to Eng- land, while he himself is to return home round Cape Horn.'

On 8 May, Lord Haddington, the First Sea Lord, hosted a reception in honour of Sir John Franklin, at which were gathered most of the great names of nineteenth-century polar exploration: Barrow, Parry, James Clark Ross, Sabine and Back all drank to the success of the expedition that would solve the puzzle of the Northwest Passage once and for all.

Four days later, amidst huge public interest, *Erebus* and *Terror* were towed downriver to Greenhithe, a village on the south bank of the Thames, now midway between the Dartford River Crossing and the Bluewater Shopping Centre. Here final supplies, including gunpowder for her three six-pounder cannons (which every ship of the Royal Navy took as a precaution), were loaded. The crew were paid four months' wages in advance, double pay for the Arctic – the balance to be given out to their families whilst they were away. There was then a delay of almost a week, owing to the late arrival of some food supplies. By now everyone was raring to go. Franklin, Fitzjames and Crozier knew that the earlier they could reach the mouth of Lancaster Sound, the better the weather conditions on the way into the Passage would be.

Despite the frustrating hold-up, Lieutenant Fairholme, in a letter home to his father, painted a rosy picture of life on board as they awaited departure: 'Lady Franklin has given us, among other presents, a capital monkey, which with old Neptune, a Newfoundland dog which is coming, and one cat will be all the pets allowed ... Saturday night seems to be kept up in due nautical form, around my cabin, a fiddle going as hard as it can and 2 or 3 different songs from the forecastle; in short, all seems quite happy.'

On Sunday 18 May, Sir John read Divine Service aboard *Erebus*. By all accounts he spoke well. 'He had the most beautiful and impressive manner I ever heard, even in a clergyman,' wrote Fairholme. It was a poignant occasion. Franklin's wife Jane, his daughter Eleanor from his first marriage, and Sophy Cracroft all attended, Eleanor and Sophy staying behind afterwards to help arrange the books on the shelves in his cabin.

Nothing much more remained to be done. James Fitzjames wrote his last letter to Sir John Barrow before leaving, thanking him for his help and support and promising him, very specifically, that 'I say we shall get through the North West Passage this year, and I shall land at

Petro-Paulovski [capital of the Russian peninsula of Kamchatka] and shake you by the hand, on the 22nd February 1846'. Sir Roderick Murchison, President of the Royal Geographical Society, added his own contribution to the prevailing mood of buoyant confidence: 'The name of Franklin alone is indeed, a national guarantee.'

At half-past ten in the morning of 19 May anchors were weighed, the ships swung through 360 degrees to make sure their compasses were working, and the Franklin expedition to the Northwest Passage finally got under way, with twenty-four officers and 110 men aboard. Crowds cheered from the dockside. Sir John waved vigorously to his family as they receded into the distance. The sight of HMS *Erebus*, fresh-painted black, with a distinctive white band around her hull, leading the best-supplied expedition ever to leave British shores must have given them all confidence that the best that could be done had been done.

To this day there is a pub by the river at Greenhithe called the Sir John Franklin, where you can have a pint of beer and steak and chips and stand at the spot where Franklin's family saw him for the last time.

A pencil sketch by Captain James Fitzjames of *Erebus* and *Terror* at anchor off the Whalefish Islands, near Disko, on 8 July 1845. An accompanying note states that it was 'sent home from Greenland, with his last letters, to Lady Franklin'.

CHAPTER 13

NORTH BY NORTH-WEST

The River Thames, from the Pool of London to the sea, has always been one of the world's great maritime thoroughfares, and yet it has remained resolutely un-triumphal. Despite the exalted status of their mission, no lanes were cleared for *Erebus* and *Terror*. The best-equipped Arctic expedition ever to leave these shores picked its way between ferries, lighters, cutters, luggers, barges bringing sea coal from the north-east, newly built warships out on trial runs, tall and powerful clippers on their way to and from the Far East: all servicing, in one way or another, the world's most prosperous city. And it was not just the surface of the Thames that was congested. All London's waste, human and industrial, spilled unchecked into her waters, and would continue to do so until Sir Joseph Bazalgette provided the capital's first effective sewage system twenty years later.

The Franklin expedition's launch onto this toxic highway in May 1845 was decidedly ungraceful. Because of the enforced delay in departure, the Admiralty decided to minimise the vagaries of the winds by having the two ships towed by steamers until they were clear of British waters. The vessel charged with hauling the Franklin expedition out of London was HMS *Rattler*, a brand-new 9-gun sloop, one-third longer than *Erebus*, with the distinction of being the first steam-driven screw-propelled warship in the world. Among the ragbag of accompanying vessels was the *Barretto Junior*, a transport ship carrying supplies that would be transferred to *Erebus* and *Terror* when they reached Greenland. She was towed out by HMS *Monkey*, a tugboat rather appropriately named, bearing in mind Lady Franklin's gift to the officers.

Once clear of the Thames estuary, the little armada turned north up the east coast, and was making fair progress until the approach of a severe storm forced them to drop anchor off the town of Aldeburgh in Suffolk. The deterioration of the weather all along the North Sea coast alarmed the Admiralty so much that word was sent to Franklin advising him to double back and take the more sheltered route along the English Channel, round Lizard Point and north through the Irish Sea. Franklin and Crozier were dead against any rerouting, being mindful of any further delay; and by the time the order was delivered to them, they were already on the move again.

The storm off Aldeburgh was Fitzjames's first experience of *Erebus* in rough weather. He referred to her in his journal as 'an old tub' and, at the height of the storm, likened her and *Terror* to 'little ships in musical clocks that bob up and down in a very solid green sea'. Sir John Franklin was more reassuring about his ship's performance. In a letter to Jane, he described how, when they became temporarily separated from their escort vessels in fog off the Northumberland coast, 'the old *Erebus* and *Terror* managed very well together'. They were never going to be the fastest ships on the water, but Franklin was respectful of the partnership. 'It is satisfactory to perceive,' he went on, 'that the *Erebus* and *Terror* sail so nearly together that they will be good company keepers.' The bad weather did, however, affect some of the other ships. As the conditions worsened and they battled on in the teeth of a persistent north-easterly, it was clear that *Monkey* would not be able to pull the bulky transport ship *Barretto Junior* all the way up to Scotland. She was sent back to Woolwich and was substituted by the paddle frigate HMS *Blazer*.

As the days went by, the officers and men acclimatised themselves to new surroundings and, in many cases, new colleagues. Fitzjames played chess with Charles Osmer, the forty-six-year-old purser. 'I was at first inclined to think he was a stupid old man,' he admitted, 'because he had a chin [nineteenth-century slang for someone who talked a lot] and took snuff, but he is as merry hearted as any young man, full of quaint, dry sayings, always good-humoured, always laughing, never a bore, takes his "pinch" after dinner, plays a "rubber", beats me at chess.'

Once they were at sea, Franklin was transformed from the pasty-faced, uncomfortable figure that he cut in the daguerreotype portraits. Lady Franklin reported back to James Clark Ross: 'You will be glad to hear that Sir John has entirely got rid of his cough ... and takes but one pinch of snuff a day with which the purser tempts him.' She quoted Dr Stanley's diagnosis: 'he has entirely thrown off every vestige of his influenza, was quite a different looking man from what he was at Greenhithe, and is in health and energy everything that could be desired.' He held open house in his cabin, allowing Goodsir, the naturalist, to make use of one of the tables, and giving permission to Dr Stanley to dry out his stuffed birds on another. Lieutenant Edward Couch, one of the mates on *Erebus*, wrote approvingly of Franklin, calling him 'an exceedingly good old chap. The captain leads church service morning and evening on Sundays. He is quite a bishop. They say we would sooner hear him than half the parsons in England.'

A week after setting out, as the ships were off the Farne Islands, Franklin reported to the Admiralty that the wind and sea had been so high that the hawsers keeping the ships apart were in danger of being carried away, creating a high risk of collision. He ordered the ships to uncouple from each other and make their own ways to Stromness in the Orkney Islands, their last assembly point before Greenland.

The wind dropped as they sailed north, and by the time they reached the Orkneys, Lieutenant Fairholme was waxing lyrical: 'I never saw anything more lovely than the scene last night, as we ran through the narrow passages among these little islands. In themselves there is nothing of the beautiful, as they are perfectly bare, but there was such a sky, and such a summit or such a glass-like sea that it was quite worthy of the Gulf of Smyrna.'

They put into Stromness harbour on Saturday, the last day of May 1845. There was a longer-than-expected delay here as they regrouped after the stormy passage from London. The *Barretto Junior* had been carrying ten live bullocks, which were intended to be slaughtered and their meat preserved. Four of them, however, had died on the way north and needed to be replaced. But the God-fearing people of Stromness would not trade cattle on the Sabbath, so replacements could not be found until after the weekend. Another reason for the delay is suggested in a letter from James Reid, the ice-master, to his wife. Noting that his captain 'allows no swearing on board', he added that 'Sir John Franklin will not start on a Sunday.'

Officers were allowed ashore, but Crozier would not allow any of the ordinary seamen from *Terror* off the ship, for fear of drunkenness. Aboard *Erebus*, on the other hand, when Robert Sinclair, Captain of the Foretop, and Able Seaman Thomas Work, both Orkney men, requested compassionate leave to visit, in one case, a wife not seen for four years, and in the other a mother not seen for seventeen years, Fitzjames acceded. They returned safely to the ship by Monday, but, because of unfavourable weather, departure was delayed by yet another day. That night the lights of Stromness proved too much of a temptation. Thomas Work unloosed one of the ship's cutters and took three other sailors ashore, returning later in the night clearly the worse for wear.

It is not recorded whether Franklin knew about this, but when Fitzjames discovered their misdemeanour he was lenient. Admitting that 'according to the rules of the service, these men should have been severely punished', he judged that, on this occasion, 'Men know very well when they are in the wrong.' At four in the morning he ordered David Bryant, the Sergeant of Marines, and Lieutenant Gore to scour the ship for any spirits and throw them overboard. It took two hours to rid the ship of illegal alcohol, but the offenders were allowed to stay with the expedition, for which they were duly grateful. In view of what lay ahead, a sterner disciplinarian than Fitzjames might have saved their lives.

Stromness is a sturdy little town with a long seafaring tradition. Situated on the western side of the largest of the Orkney Islands, the town is cradled in the arm of a south-east-curving promontory that protects it from the full force of the Atlantic. When I visited the islands, the winds on the low hills were strong, sending the turbines spinning and clearing the skies. Sharp, bright sunlight spread across the green and treeless fingers of land running down to the sea, and picked out complex patterns in the ancient rock on cliffs near the town. *Erebus, Terror* and their accompanying flotilla would have dropped anchor close to the tight network of streets at the centre of Stromness, where their masts would have towered above the gabled and chimneyed stone-walled houses that run down to the sea. They would have been aware of a plain stone-built warehouse with its own pier, standing end-on to the water. This was the headquarters of the Hudson's Bay Company, which had virtually run the Arctic trade since the end of the seventeenth century. The company recruited many men from the Orkneys, who were often happy to take on the privations of ice and snow rather than try and eke out a livelihood from the small farms on the island.

Though the officers remained resolutely positive about their mission, a hint that the ordinary seamen had a more realistic take on what was to come can be found in a last letter home from Alexander Wilson, the assistant carpenter on *Terror*, to his wife Sarah. It begins with the constant anxiety of men at sea – the unreceived letter:

Dear Wife I fully expected a letter here for when I arrived, but I hope I will get one tomorrow from you. I hoop the children is quite well and I hoop Sarah's face has got better and I hoop you send them to school regular. I hoop Dear Wife you will go to a place of worship as often as you can and put your trust in the Lord … If it is God's will that we should not meet again I hoop we will meet in heaven their to enjoy life everlasting. Dear Wife every night I lay down in my hammock I offer up a silent prayer for you and my Dear children. Dear Wife I know this voyage will be a severe trial for us all but there is everything here to make us comfortable.

As a frontier port for the North Atlantic, Stromness was used to arrivals and departures, but because the ocean beyond the red sandstone portals of Hoy Sound is so fierce, it was necessary to employ twenty-six pilots in Stromness and at various points around the Atlantic coast to help shepherd ships out to sea. The waves were often so rough that it was impossible for the pilots to get back safely, and they would therefore have to stay on board ship until the return journey, from Newfoundland or New York or wherever. The perils of the ocean nurtured superstitions. There was a lady called Bessie Miller who lived in a hovel on a hill above Stromness and 'sold' winds to sailors. If you wanted a favourable wind, it was worth paying Bessie to fix one for you. So strong was the tradition that even those who didn't believe a word of it still walked up the hill to see her. Just in case. There is no record of anyone from the Franklin expedition going to see Bessie.

On Tuesday 3 June 1845 the ships were at last ready to go. Alexander Wilson just had time to add a breathless postscript to his letter: 'Monday Night. My Dear Wife I have not received a letter from you yet and we are going to sail in the morning. So goodbye goodbye but if you have sent one perhaps it will follow us and if it does not return to you you may be sure I have got it goodbye and god bless you.'

***

At first light *Erebus, Terror* and *Barretto Junior* were towed out into Hoy Sound by *Blazer* and *Rattler*. On their starboard side were the last lights of Stromness, to port the dark, majestic silence of the hills and cliffs of the island of Hoy. Beneath them, the currents of the Atlantic and the North Sea swirled to meet each other. Beyond the headlands were white-caps and blustery, salty winds. There could scarcely be a more epic location for a last glimpse of Britain and it must have stirred mixed emotions, especially for those who had never been to the Far North before.

Fifty miles west of the island of North Rona, when they were judged to be clear of offshore rocks and contrary winds, the time came for *Rattler* and *Blazer* to take in their tow-lines and head back home. Everyone knew that this was more than a routine farewell. Owen Stanley, an officer on the *Blazer*, painted the ships rising and falling on the swell, a smudge of smoke emerging from *Rattler's* funnel, and an eyewitness described it:

> At the sound of the boatswain's pipe, the shrouds of the *Rattler* and *Blazer* were in one instant lined by their crews, all anxious to out vie each other in the pleasing task they were about to perform. The word was given, and three cheers, loud and hearty as ever escaped the lungs of British tars, saluted the ears of Sir J Franklin and his gallant colleagues.

The escort vessels took back with them an able seaman from HMS *Terror* who was feared to be suffering from tuberculosis, or consumption as it was commonly known. This was something to be seriously avoided on tightly packed ships embarking on a long voyage. In the officers' mess on *Erebus* they joked about the illness, passing around a rumour that the ship's monkey, Jacko, might be suffering from consumption, too. After examining the monkey, the ship's doctor reported to Fitzjames that 'he certainly has a very bad cough, but the only other symptom I see of it is the rapid consumption of everything eatable he can lay his paws on'.

Lieutenant Fitzjames watched the escorts go: 'in an hour or two they were out of sight, leaving us with an old gull or two and the rocky Rona to look at; and then was the time to see if anyone flinched from the undertaking. Every one's cry was, "Now we are off at last!" No lingering look was cast behind. We drank Lady Franklin's health at the old gentleman's table, and, it being his daughter's birthday, hers too.' The wind strengthened, turning to the north. *Erebus* led, with *Terror* following behind. They were not quick ships, and *Barretto Junior*, despite being heavily laden, had to keep as little sail as possible in order not to outrun her companions.

One can imagine James Fitzjames at the table in his narrow cabin, about a quarter the size of the great spread of the captain's cabin next door, but snug enough, with a bookshelf in an alcove above the bed, and on the bulkhead a picture of his closest friend and foster-father, William Coningham. He had promised Elizabeth, William's wife, that he would keep an account of the journey for her. This was the day he was going to start. He picked up a porcupine quill and dipped it in the inkwell:

Her Majesty's ship *Erebus*, at sea, June 8th 1845, Ten p.m.

You appeared very anxious that I should keep a journal for your especial perusal. Now, I do keep a journal, such as it is, which will be given to the Admiralty; but, to please you, I shall note down from time to time such things as may strike me, either in the form of a letter, or in any other form that may at the time suit my fancy.

We can only be thankful that Fitzjames wrote so attractively and so diligently, by his own account regularly staying up until two in the morning to record his thoughts and observations, before going on watch at five.

I commence to-night, because I am in a good humour. Every one is shaking hands with himself [presumably a metaphor for confidence and self-congratulation].

We have a fair wind, actually going seven knots, sea tolerably smooth, though we do roll a little; but this ship has the happy facility of being very steady below, while on deck she appears to be plunging and rolling greatly.

Now that the prolonged leave-takings were over, the work of the expedition began. Sir John Franklin called his officers together to talk through the instructions from the Admiralty, 'and the necessity of observing everything from a flea to a whale'. He also emphasised how important it was for every man to take notes, write journals and make sketches and paintings of what they observed.

His scientific zeal was matched only by his evangelical enthusiasm. Whatever the weather, he would preach a sermon on Sundays. As far as Fitzjames was concerned, Franklin was a more-than-impressive speaker. 'Sir John Franklin read the church service today and a sermon so very beautifully,' he recorded on one occasion, 'that I defy any man not to feel the force of what he would convey.' Franklin's openness, good nature and enthusiasm for what lay ahead, moreover, won over officers and crew alike. Fairholme wrote home approvingly: 'Sir John is a new man since we left ... looks 10 years younger and takes part in everything that goes on with as much interest as if he had not grown older since his first Expedition.' Franklin himself clearly basked in the goodwill on board, writing to Sir Edward Parry that 'It would do your heart good to see how zealously the officers and men, in both ships, are working, and how amicably we all pull together.'

Sir John enjoyed, and expected, company. He was always available in his cabin and every evening would invite three officers to dine with him. Captain Crozier was one of those regularly invited to these evenings, but, perhaps not surprisingly, as he had to be ferried over to dinner and back in a small boat across a frequently choppy North Atlantic, he found such relentless hospitality a bit of a trial. His reluctance might well also have had something to do with Franklin's propensity to buttonhole his diners with his mistreatment in Van

Diemen's land, and with the pamphlet that, once completed, was going to vindicate him. At any rate, while admitting to his old commander, James Clark Ross, that 'Sir John is very kind and would have me dining there every day if I would go', Crozier made it plain that 'I cannot bear going on board *Erebus*.' On several occasions he actually feigned illness.

The constant presence of Fitzjames at Sir John's side could well have been another reason for Crozier's reluctance. There was no open warfare between them, but the Admiralty's express wish that Fitzjames should be put in charge of the magnetic observations had put Crozier's nose out of joint. And understandably so. After four years on the Clark Ross expedition, he was a far more experienced seafarer than Fitzjames. He had been elected a Fellow of the Royal Society for his work on terrestrial magnetism.

Once the weather moderated, they were able to drop a net to a depth of 300 fathoms (1,800 feet). Harry Goodsir, the resident naturalist, was delighted, as the 'catch' revealed molluscs and plankton, whose role in the marine ecology he couldn't wait to reveal to his fellow officers. Fitzjames was less impressed, teasing Goodsir as being 'in ecstasies about a bag full of blubber-like stuff, which he has just hauled up in a net, and which turns out to be whales' food and other animals'.

It's hard to know how the wretched bullocks on board the *Barretto Junior* were faring as the ships rode the storms, but the domestic livestock on *Erebus* were, according to Fairholme, finding their sea legs. Neptune the dog, already known as Old Nep, was running up and down the ladders with ease: 'he is the most loveable dog I ever knew,' wrote Fairholme, 'and is a general favourite'. Jacko the monkey was 'a dreadful thief' and 'the annoyance and pest of the whole ship, and yet not a person in here would hurt him for the whole world'.

Over the next few days, as the ships navigated an uncomfortable combination of fog and foam, work went on below decks to prepare for the long days, months, even years ahead. The books selected for the voyage were taken out of storage and arranged on shelves in the mess. Reid, the bluff Scottish ice-master, continued to amuse the much younger officers with his knowledge of the lore and language of the sea – like how best to get the salt out of a very salty fish, and how to identify ice-blink, the polar mirage caused by light reflected off the ice-cap. Occasionally there would be a great event to celebrate: the thirtieth anniversary of the Battle of Waterloo, for example, was marked on 18 June by the drinking of the Duke of Wellington's health at the captain's table.

That day was a significant occasion for James Fitzjames, too. In a letter to William Coningham he spoke of a possible promotion. 'There was a talk before we left England of a brevet on this day [a brevet being a promotion without additional pay]; if this be true, I think it more than probable that I shall get the rank of captain. With this idea I took a glass of brandy and water at half-past ten and drank your health.' He added that his habit of late-night letter-writing had not gone unnoticed, 'for Reid has just said, scratching his head, "Why, Mr Jems, you never seem to sleep at arl; you're always writin!" I tell him that when I do sleep, I do twice as much as other people in the same time.'

Gradually they edged towards Greenland. Fitzjames, for one, was much taken by the clarity of northern waters: 'The sea is of the most perfect transparency – a beautiful, delicate, cold-looking green, or ultramarine. Long rollers, as if carved out of the essence of glass bottles, came rolling towards us; now and then topped with a beautiful pot-of-porter-looking head.' With the likelihood of ice approaching, a crow's nest, invented by William Scoresby, the whaler-turned-Arctic-explorer, in 1807, was installed on the main top-gallant masthead. It consisted of a hooped canvas cylinder, which, 100 feet above the deck, would be Ice-Master Reid's domain.

By the last week in June the winds turned to the south-west and blew them through rough seas round Cape Farewell at the southern tip of Greenland and on into Davis Strait. Franklin, it seemed, had been expecting the conditions, writing home that 'It would have been contrary to the long experience of the Greenland Seamen if we had gone round Cape Farewell unattended by a gale.'

At eleven o'clock on the 25th, and with the sun just setting, Fitzjames wrote excitedly to Elizabeth Coningham: 'I am very sleepy and tired but did not like to go to bed without writing on the first day on which we have seen Arctic land. The air is delightfully cool and bracing, and everybody is in good humour, either with himself or his neighbours. I have been on deck all day taking observations.' His fellow officers were fishing, after a fashion. 'Goodsir is catching the most extraordinary animals in a net … Gore and Des Voeux are over the side poking with nets and long poles, with cigars in their mouths and Osmer laughing.' He summed up a general mood of excited anticipation: 'We bounded along merrily, shaking hands with ourselves and making imaginary shortcuts through America to the Pacific.'

Even Captain Crozier seems to have been affected. Writing to his nephew as he guided *Terror* up the Davis Strait, he assured him that 'All is getting on as well as I could wish. Officers full of youth and zeal … If we can only do something worthy of this country which has so munificently fitted us out, I will be only too happy.' Being Crozier, though, he couldn't help qualifying his optimism: 'it will be an ample reward for all my anxieties,' he added, 'and believe me … there will be no lack of them'.

The warm weather passed. Thick fog came down, taking the daytime temperatures close to freezing. They passed a brig out of the Shetlands and hove-to, to allow the captain to come aboard. He was fishing for cod on the banks and for salmon in the fiords – 'a new scheme quite in these parts,' noted Fitzjames. It turned out that he had once sailed with Thomas Work, 'the little old man' who hadn't seen his wife for four years, and was very pleased to find him aboard.

The next day they crossed the Arctic Circle and entered a new world of icebergs and constant daylight. Fitzjames, like many others on board, had never seen such scenes before. 'I had fancied icebergs were large transparent lumps, or rocks of ice,' he wrote, before going on in some wonder: 'They look like huge masses of pure snow, furrowed with caverns and dark ravines.' As the Greenland coast came in sight, disappointingly indistinct under thick, low cloud and with the peaks of its mountains concealed, he could pick out glaciers and fiords. A little later they sailed through a shoal of some hundred walruses, 'diving and splashing with their fins and tails, and looking at us with their grim, solemn-looking countenances and small heads, bewiskered and betusked'.

Now that they were north of the sixty-fifth parallel, Franklin set about complying with the Admiralty's instructions to make regular drops of tin cylinders containing a record of their position. Crozier would have been familiar with the process from his days in the Antarctic. Reports were to be written on specially issued stiff blue paper. Directions, printed in six languages (English, French, Spanish, Dutch, Danish and German) asked the finder to send the canister to the Secretary of the Admiralty in London. Four years later one of Franklin's cylinders washed up on the Greenland coast, less than 200 miles from where it had been dropped. It was the only one ever to be found.

Fairholme, meanwhile, was spellbound by the ever-increasing number of icebergs, the likes of which he'd never seen before: 'While passing near one of these, which I had just remarked was about the size of the North Foreland, it suddenly fell to pieces with an awful crash, sending the spray up to a great height, and leaving a field of sharp and broken ice.'

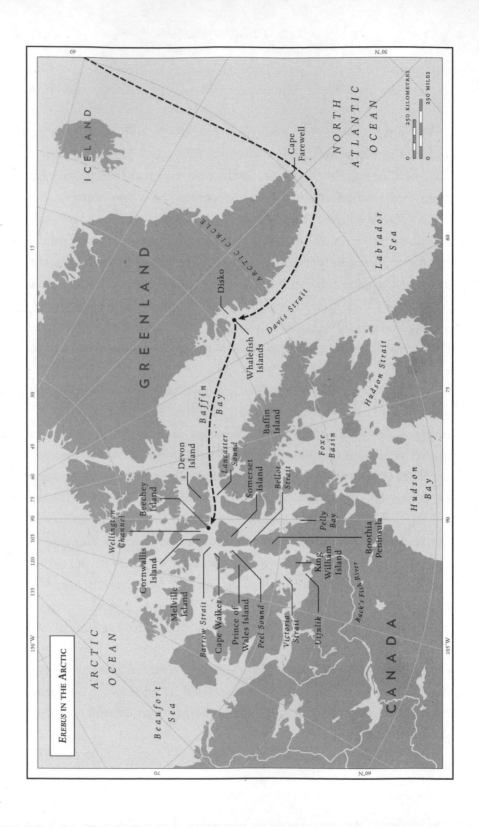

EREBUS IN THE ARCTIC

ARCTIC OCEAN

ICELAND

GREENLAND

Beaufort Sea

Melville Island

Barrow Strait

Cornwallis Island

Wellington Channel

Beechey Island

Devon Island

Cape Walker

Prince of Wales Island

Peel Sound

Somerset Island

Bellot Strait

Lancaster Sound

Baffin Island

Baffin Bay

ARCTIC CIRCLE

Disko

Whalefish Islands

Davis Strait

Cape Farewell

NORTH ATLANTIC OCEAN

Labrador Sea

Hudson Strait

Foxe Basin

Pelly Bay

Boothia Peninsula

King William Island

Victoria Strait

Utjulik

Back's Fish River

Hudson Bay

CANADA

60

50°N.

60°N.

50°W

135

120

105

90

75

60

45

30

15

60

70

75

90

105°W

250 KILOMETRES

250 MILES

Almost halfway up the west-Greenland coast is Disko, the largest of Greenland's offshore islands. In 1845 it was a Danish trading and seal-catching station supporting a native population of some 100 people. A few miles south, in Disko Bay, are the Whalefish Islands. Sir Edward Parry had been this way before and recommended them to Franklin as a safe and sheltered place in which to transfer materials from the *Barretto Junior*, for the building of an observatory and for the final stocking of the ships for the Arctic. The squadron weighed anchor in the bay, with the intention of proceeding on towards the Whalefish Islands the next morning.

This proved to be much easier said than done. Owing to an unusual error on the part of the experienced ice-master, James Reid, *Erebus* mistakenly started to lead the ships in the wrong direction towards the northern end of Disko Bay. Rather strangely, Captain Crozier, who had been here before, and who must have been aware that they were sailing in the wrong direction, made no signal, but merely followed on. He may simply have been doing what he did best: following the lead of others. But from what we know of his feelings about *Erebus*'s second-in-command, it's tempting to think that he wanted to leave it to Franklin and Fitzjames not only to work out their mistake for themselves, but to experience the embarrassment that acknowledging it would cause.

Once the error was spotted, they turned about, headed south and found the islands, but were unable to locate the anchorage. A cutter was lowered from *Erebus*, and Lieutenant Le Vesconte rowed out to take a closer look. He was met by five Inuit, paddling kayaks, two of whom led the ships into a narrow, well-protected, almost land-locked channel where they finally moored.

'The scenery is grand, but desolate,' wrote Fitzjames, adding that it was populated by very large mosquitoes. James Thompson, engineer on board *Terror*, bore this out, sending home a graphic description of mosquitoes that 'bite very bad my arms are very much bitten with them and they are more enormous than the English Bugg'. Ice-Master Reid complained to his wife that 'I have been sadly annoyed by them and my face and hands are all swollen with their bites.' All of which made the building of the observatory, and the repetitive tasks of measuring magnetic field, dip and variation uncomfortable as well as irksome.

The contact with the Inuit was put to good use. Goodsir and Fairholme spent time at the local settlement compiling a dictionary of Inuit words and phrases that might come in useful. Fitzjames and Fairholme tried out the kayaks. Fitzjames, in particular, found them a tight fit and tricky to navigate: 'They have the smallest possible canoes here, into one of which I was determined to get last night, so got my trousers off and paddled about for some time, but at last over I went, head downwards, where I remained till rescued.'

The work of transferring the *Barretto*'s cargo took nine days, with the men working from four in the morning until six in the evening. 'We are fully occupied in filling up every hole and corner of the ship with stores,' wrote Franklin. 'I have taken into my cabin ... potatoes which are packed in ten cases and store conveniently without interfering with either Mr. Goodsir's table or my own, or another at which I think Mr. Le Vesconte will take up his position and make the charts.' Seven of the bullocks taken on board at Stromness had perished by the time they reached Disko. Now the remaining three were slaughtered, each ship being given three or four quarters of beef to hang up in the rigging and provide fresh meat for the expedition's first Christmas.

Despite the work of loading and the daily routine of taking magnetic measurements, the young officers were having the time of their lives. 'You've no conception of how happy we are,' wrote Fitzjames. 'Osmer has just come from on deck (midnight) and is dancing with an imaginary skipping rope. I said to him "What a happy fellow you are, always in good humour." His answer is "Well sir, if I'm not happy here, I don't know where else I could be."'

***

But what was on the minds of the two captains, who were infinitely more experienced in the conditions that lay ahead?

Knowing that once they parted from their transport ship it might be months, even years, before they could get letters home again, Sir John Franklin spent much of his time in the Whalefish Islands in copious correspondence with friends, family, business associates and naval colleagues. The longest letter was to his wife Jane. It ran to some fourteen pages, and from it we can form a pretty good idea of the things that preoccupied him as he prepared to take his men through the Northwest Passage.

Sir John was clearly very concerned to do the best by his wife, and although she might not have been on *Erebus* in person, her spirit was there in almost everything he did. 'My dearest love,' the letter starts, 'I begin the month in your service.' He is aware that she wants to be viewed as very much a part of the whole enterprise, and likes to be seen as everyone's friend. 'Fitzjames has been making a sketch of the harbour of which he intends sending you a copy. Mr Gore has made a very faithful drawing for you of our parting with the Blazer and Rattler. I feel very much gratified by the kind feeling of the officers towards you.' 'I'm sure there is nothing they would not do to please you,' he assures her.

Much of the letter is taken up, not with things naval or explorational, but with the constant revisiting of his treatment in Van Diemen's Land or, more significantly, *her* treatment in Van Diemen's land. He had to hand a copy of the pamphlet they had written, stating their case against Montagu and Lord Stanley, and he tells her that he has canvassed the opinions of his colleagues about it. Fitzjames has read it, of course, as have Gore and Fairholme, 'and one and all of them exclaimed what a villain that Montagu must be'. He has also shared it with Crozier, who has been similarly sympathetic: 'we had a little conversation about the Pamphlet when alone together. He repeated that the conduct of Lord Stanley and Mr. Montagu was disgraceful. I think he intends writing a few lines to you.' It's hard to know how strongly Franklin himself felt about the pamphlet. His wife was the driving force behind it. At one moment he echoes her anger, and the next he seems to be humouring her.

His fitness for leadership is something else that Sir John dwells on. Even at this stage, with the enterprise well under way, one gets the impression that he constantly needs to reassure himself that he's the right man to lead the expedition. He's acutely aware that reservations about his age and lack of recent experience were voiced before he landed the commission, and clearly these still rankle. So, too, does the existence of a more suitable candidate – someone his wife and the world admire inordinately: James Clark Ross.

His feelings about Ross are ambivalent. On the one hand, Franklin is appreciative of the fact that Ross recommended him in the first place. 'His conduct towards me has been kind throughout as regards the Expedition,' he writes, 'and he has acted as a man ought to do who is convinced that I should have spurned taking the least advantage of him by proposing my own services had he the last desire to have gone.' On the other hand, knowing that Ross had been first choice is still proving quite a bitter pill to swallow. And it's made more unpalatable by Ross letting slip that he had turned down tempting inducements from the Admiralty and a promise to postpone the expedition for a year, if he agreed to lead it. Ross's observation that 'the navigation of the Arctic Sea is not near so full of danger as that of the Antarctic' had done nothing to boost Sir John's sense of self-worth.

To battle his various demons, Sir John turns to what he believes to be his own strengths: 'I think perhaps that I have the tact of keeping the officers and men happily together in a greater degree than Ross – and for this reason – he is evidently ambitious and wishes to do everything by himself – I possess not that feeling.'

And that, judges Franklin, is not the only difference: 'my officers are from a different class of society and better educated than those on any former Expedition – so says Parry – and certainly if we call to mind those officers who were with Ross – there was scarcely one with the exception of Hooker above the ordinary run of the service'. This revealing little glimpse of prejudice is so uncharacteristic of what we otherwise know of Franklin that one can only assume it was drawn out of him by some quite deeply felt need for self-justification.

Franklin's relationship with Francis Crozier, and Crozier's enigmatic behaviour, is another nagging concern. He has not been blind to the constant absence of his second-in-command from his dinner table. He is, after all, an inclusive, clubbable man who regards his get-togethers as a way of binding together what nowadays would be called his team, and the fact that Crozier has only made two appearances bothers him. 'Entre nous,' Sir John confides to his wife, 'I do not think he has had his former flow of spirits since we sailed, nor that he has been quite well.' Franklin suspects that Crozier's unrequited love for Sophy lies at the bottom of it, but he can't find a way of talking to him about it. 'He has never mentioned Sophy – nor made the slightest allusion to her and I sometimes question myself whether or not it would be agreeable or proper for me to speak of her to him.'

Crozier's aloofness has manifested itself in another way, too. Given how much time he spent with the Franklins in Hobart, Sir John has clearly been hoping that Crozier would send some sort of message to Lady Franklin. Yet when they were ashore collecting plant specimens, he reports Crozier telling him 'that he had last evening been writing to you but had torn his letter up for fear you should judge from it that he was not in good spirits'. He returns to what he prefers to think of as the reason for Crozier's coolness: 'I have no doubt if there be any cause for lowness of spirits on his part as connected with Sophy, that he will give me by and bye an opportunity of conversing with him on this subject.'

That Crozier was not happy is unquestionable, but given the range of his grouses, I wonder whether even he could have put his finger on precisely what was wrong. He clearly resented being passed over in favour of Fitzjames as officer in charge of magnetic observations. Equally clearly, he perceived slights that weren't there: 'My sugar and tea have not made their appearance,' he wrote on one occasion. 'I cannot at all accounts say much for Fortnum and Mason's punctuality – they directed my things to Captain Fitzjames's *Erebus*, but by some strange accident they discovered my name sufficiently accurately to send me the Bill.' He had not approved of Fitzjames granting shore leave to the men in Stromness, and he was critical of the way in which *Erebus* was run ('Look at the state our commander's ship is in,' he wrote on one occasion; 'everything in confusion'). Nor was he any friend of the auxiliary steam engines, which he saw as adding extra weight, with little return: 'how I do wish the engine was again on the Dover line and the Engineer sitting on top of it; he is a dead and alive wretch full of difficulties and is now quite dissatisfied because he has not the leading stoker to assist him in doing nothing'.

Crozier's general discontent and malaise come over most clearly in one of the last letters he wrote from the Whalefish Islands. It's addressed to his old friend and fellow explorer, James Clark Ross. Crozier and Franklin had recently heard news that although spring and the break-up of the ice had come at the right time, the last winter in the Arctic had been severe and the next one could be worse. Timing was essential. 'All things are going on well and quietly, but we are, I fear, sadly late …' he writes. 'What I fear from being so late is that we shall have no time to look around and judge for ourselves, but blunder into the ice and make a second 1824 of it [a reference to Parry's expedition, on which Crozier was serving as a midshipman, which took eight weeks to cross from Greenland to Lancaster Sound and remained trapped in the ice throughout the next bitter winter]. James, I wish you were here, I would then have no doubt as to our pursuing the proper course … I am not growling, mind. Indeed I never was less disposed to do so.'

He perks up briefly at a memory of their previous voyage together. 'Goodsir in *Erebus* is a most diligent fellow … he seems much in his habits like Hooker, never idle, making perfect sketches of all he collects very quickly ... He has [the] happy knack of engaging everyone around him in the same pursuit.' But the doubts return with a vengeance. 'James, dear, I am sadly alone, not a soul have I in either ship that I can go and talk to ... I know not what else I can say to you I feel that I am not in spirits for writing but in truth I am sadly lonely and when I look back to the last voyage *I can see the cause* [my italics] and therefore no prospect of having a more joyous feeling.'

Crozier, it seems, was missing James Clark Ross quite as much as he was missing Sophy Cracroft. Franklin must surely have suspected this.

Amongst the senior officers, Fitzjames remained the resolute cheerleader and the one whose eyes were most firmly fixed on the Pacific Ocean. His last letter to John Barrow junior asked him to pass on his kind regards to his parents. 'We intend to drink Sir John's health on the day we go through Behring's Straits,' he promised him, whilst acknowledging that the heavy loads now carried by both ships could bring risks. 'If we get through this season,' he went on, 'we shall have to land somewhere or other to discharge some cargo – for it will not be safe to go into the Pacific laden as we are.' If there were criticisms, they were not those one might expect to have been aimed at a fifty-nine-year-old. In one letter Fitzjames confided that he felt Sir John was taking undue risks by sailing too fast: 'The only difficulty I had was to get Sir John to shorten sail when it was wanted.'

Towards the end of his journal for Elizabeth Coningham we get a hint of other anxieties that underlay the carefully nurtured spirit of optimism and invincibility. Fitzjames reports a conversation with Franklin in which he talks of the 'one great difficulty' awaiting them. And that is the time it might take them to cross Baffin Bay to the mouth of Lancaster Sound, gateway to the Northwest Passage. On Parry's first voyage it had taken him no more than ten days, but on his second he had spent fifty-four days picking his way through the ice.

Fitzjames was not an Arctic man, but he was beginning to learn that the one great unknown was the behaviour of the ice. 'All is conjecture,' he concludes; 'we may do well this year, and again, we may not.'

With the transfer complete, it was time for *Barretto Junior* to return to London, carrying last-minute letters and four crew members who were too unwell to continue. There is no record of why or what was wrong with them, apart from Crozier's breezy dismissal that 'two were ill and two completely useless'. *Erebus* lost one man, reducing her muster-roll to sixty-seven, and *Terror* lost an armourer, a sailmaker and one of her mates, reducing hers to sixty-two.

'We are now full,' Fitzjames wrote on 11 July, 'having three years provisions ... The deck is covered with coals and casks, leaving a small passage fore and aft, and we are very deep in the water.' Indeed, there had not been room for everything. Lieutenant Griffiths, captain of the *Barretto Junior*, reported that he was bringing back '2 Bower Anchors, 2 Chain Cables, 1 Boat, 2 Hawsers, some casks of Rum, Beef and Pork and various stores not required'.

On the morning of 12 July, Lieutenant Griffiths was guest of honour at a farewell meal on HMS *Erebus*. They dined on beef, specially cured for them. Two days earlier he had been asked aboard to sample some of the tinned foods and had been generally complimentary. The carrots 'were as good as if just removed from the ground, the potatoes also were good and sweet, but certainly with little flavour of the potato'.

Emotions must have run high as the lunch drew to a close. Though only a humble part of a great enterprise, the commander and crew of the *Barretto Junior* had played a vital role in ensuring that *Erebus* and *Terror* had come safely across the stormy waters of the North Atlantic without being overburdened. Sir John Franklin showed his appreciation in his last letter to the Admiralty, in which he commended Lieutenant Griffiths for the 'zealous manner ... in which [he] has performed the service entrusted to him', and recommended him for promotion. Griffiths was equally appreciative, and recognised that he and his ship had been part of something quite out of the ordinary: 'A set of more undaunted fellows never were got together ... God speed them! And send them back by Bering's Strait to their native England, covered with imperishable fame. No man in Britain will hail their return with more cordial enthusiasm than myself.'

That same afternoon *Barretto Junior* weighed anchor and turned for home. But her name was not lost to history. By a supreme irony, she was to turn up in Hobart five years later, carrying convicts to Van Diemen's Land, where so many of Sir John Franklin's problems had begun.

At six o'clock next morning, Sunday 13 July 1845, *Erebus* and *Terror* hauled up their anchors and set sail, north by north-west, for Baffin Bay and Lancaster Sound. Finally, they were on their own.

An Admiralty poster offering a £20,000 reward to anyone able to offer 'efficient assistance' to the lost Franklin expedition. The reward for information was £10,000.

CHAPTER 14

NO SIGNAL

———————◆———————

Their initial progress was recorded by a number of vessels that
encountered them over the next two or three weeks. On 19 July 1845,
Captain Stratton of the whaler *Eagle*, calling at the Danish trading sta-
tion at Upernavik, said he had seen two barques that he took to be
Erebus and *Terror*, heading out across Baffin Bay. A few days later they
were positively identified by two whaling ships, the *Enterprise* and the
Prince of Wales, which saw them, hove-to, surrounded by ice in upper
Baffin Bay.

Captain Martin of the *Enterprise* claimed to have spoken with both
Sir John Franklin and some of his officers. Despite the ice, he said,
they were confident of reaching the entrance to Lancaster Sound by
mid-August. In a later, more detailed statement, Martin claimed that
Franklin had told him they had provisions for five years, which could
be made to last for seven.

On 26 July, Captain Dannett of the *Prince of Wales* saw *Erebus* and
Terror at latitude 74.48°N and longitude 66.13°W. Some of their officers
went aboard and talked with Dannett, and Sir John invited him back
to dinner on *Erebus*. The dinner never happened. The weather
improved and, with good visibility and a following wind, Dannett
decided he couldn't delay and they parted company the next day. It is
generally assumed this was the last-recorded sighting of the

expedition other than by Inuit, but Captain Martin, in a later affidavit, claimed that as late as 29 or 31 July he caught sight of the tips of their masts on the horizon.

The arrival of *Barretto Junior* at Deptford Royal Naval Dockyard on the Thames on 11 August, with news and letters from the expedition, together with their commander's upbeat assessment of their mood, was met with great celebration. Lieutenant Griffiths's optimism, later endorsed by the captain of the *Prince of Wales*, meant the Admiralty could breathe a sigh of relief. The ships were on their way, fully provisioned and without serious delay.

Jane Franklin could breathe a sigh of relief, too. But it was typical of her active and agitated mind that she always found something to be anxious about. On 1 September she wrote to Sir James Clark Ross on the subject of their mutual friend, Francis Crozier. Knowing that he had written to Ross from Greenland, she expressed her belief that 'he was to have written to me also, but the letter did not come'. In case this should imply any differences between Crozier and her husband, she was at pains to point out that 'Sir John speaks of him with great regard and with the hope that when they had more time together their intimacy might be of mutual advantage.' And what's more: 'Sir John Barrow spoke to me the other day with such warmth of Captain Crozier ... and he affirmed he was the fittest person possible to be appointed with Sir John in the expedition.'

These were nagging concerns, but with the expedition on its way there was not much more Lady Franklin could do but wait. To take her mind off the Arctic, she spent some of the next twelve months travelling. With her stepdaughter Eleanor for company, she visited France, Madeira and the United States. Towards the end of 1846, when the expedition had been away for some seventeen months, she wrote again to James Clark Ross. This time her anxieties were unconcealed. It was as if she were already preparing herself for bad news.

'I sometimes think,' she wrote, 'it is better perhaps that we should be in happy ignorance of any disaster that may have happened to them, or of any dreadful difficulty they may have yet to overcome than to be viewing as in a magic mirror in a fairy tale their daily vicissitudes. I dare not be sanguine as to their success, indeed the very thought seems to me presumptuous, so entirely absorbed is my soul in aspirations for their safety only.' She, more than anyone apart from James Ross, had lobbied for Sir John to lead the expedition. Now that she had achieved her aim, was there a sense of guilt at having laid such awesome responsibilities on a fifty-nine-year-old who had not commanded a ship for twelve years?

'And should it please Providence,' her letter went on, 'that one should not see them return when we are led to expect them, will you be the man to go in search of them as you did so nobly for the missing whalers [trapped in Davis Strait ten years earlier]? Such a thought, though I do not give it utterance to others, sometimes gives me comfort ... I feel sure that you will spare no pains if need be to rouse Government to prompt and efficient means when the moment arrives that these should not be delayed.'

As 1847 came round, with still no word, there were those who felt that the moment had arrived to do something. Among the earliest to raise the alarm was Captain Beechey, who submitted a plan to the Admiralty in April proposing the despatch of a ship to follow in the wake of *Erebus* and *Terror* to the Barrow Strait. He also suggested sending a boat party down the Great (or Back's) Fish River to the coast. His plan was turned down by the Admiralty as being too much, too soon. They also rejected a rescue proposal from Sir John Ross. Now at retirement age, he had of course pledged to Franklin that he would come after him, if nothing was heard by 1847, but his poor relations with Barrow had continued to influence the Admiralty's view of him, and Ross was told in no uncertain terms that a relief expedition was not yet necessary. He then approached the Royal Society, which agreed with the Admiralty: 'You will go and get frozen in like Franklin, and we shall have to send after you and then perhaps for them that went to look after you,' said its President, the Marquis of Northampton. 'Surely, your Lordship cannot mean that no search will be made for Franklin and his brave companions?' replied Ross.

In June 1847, Dr Richard King – who, like Sir John Ross, had expressed grave doubts as to the wisdom of the Arctic enterprise – made an unequivocal prediction that scurvy and starvation would threaten the lives of the two crews, if they had to survive a third winter in the Arctic, and volunteered to lead a search party. Not just an ordinary search party, either. 'I propose,' he wrote to the Admiralty, 'to undertake the boldest journey that has ever been attempted in the northern regions of America.'

Richard King was a loner, outside the establishment. He alienated people with a manner that was seen as often abrupt and unbendingly egotistical. Yet he could not be ignored. His doom-laden forecasts both exasperated and unsettled the one figure who was to tower above all others in maintaining the search for the missing expedition: Lady Jane Franklin. In December 1847 she wrote to James Ross:

> You will be thinking that Dr. King has been exciting a most mischievous and unjustifiable influence on my mind. Of Dr. King himself I wish to say nothing. I do not desire that he should be the person employed, but I cannot but wish that the Hudson's Bay Company might receive instructions or a request from Govt. to explore those parts which you and Sir J Richardson cannot immediately do, and which if done by you at all can only be when other explorations have been made in vain ... and then does he *not* truly say, it will be *too late*?

James Ross's view, shared by Parry and Sabine, was that both King and John Ross were being irresponsibly alarmist, and that a better course of action would be to offer a £1,000 reward for any information that Hudson's Bay whalers might be able to glean.

There were others, close to the crews, who shared Jane Franklin's worries. John Diggle, who had sailed with James Clark Ross to the Antarctic, and whose daughter, born a few months after they left, was christened Mary Anne Erebus Diggle, had signed on with the Franklin expedition as cook on HMS *Terror*. Hearing that a rescue expedition was to be launched, his father wrote a letter, dated 4 January 1848, to be taken to Diggle:

> I write these few lines to you in hopes to find you and all your shipmates in both ships well ... for it his [is] our fear that wee shall never see you again seeing the Account in the newspaper how you have been situated what with being frozen in and having the dreadful disorder the Schervey [scurvy]. Wee trust God when HMS Plover reaches you our thoughts will be frustrated. Please God it be so. Dear son I conclude with our unbounded gratitude too you, your loving father and mother John and Phoebe Diggle.

A few months later John's parents got their reply. It was a blue envelope, across which was stamped 'Returned to the Sender, There Having Been No Means of Forwarding It.'

By the time John Diggle's father made his abortive attempt to contact his son, the Admiralty was taking a less complacent view and, perhaps embarrassed at its tardiness, proceeded to commission not one, but three relief expeditions in the winter of 1847–8. The first, under Commander Moore of HMS *Plover*, sailed for the Bering Strait, charged with searching the coast of Russian America (soon to become Alaska). Nothing was found.

An overland party set out. It was led by Sir John Richardson, Franklin's close friend and, at sixty, about his age, and by Dr John Rae of

Stromness, who was employed by the Hudson's Bay Company. Rae's statue stands on Stromness waterfront, on a cairn of Orkney sandstone facing out to sea. He's wearing trapper's boots and a fur-lined jacket with a rifle slung over his shoulder – very much the local hero. Rae and Richardson worked their way down the lower reaches of the Mackenzie River to the coast and explored the channels between the Banks, Wollaston and Victoria Islands. A great deal of useful surveying was done, but they found no trace of Franklin and his men.

Sir James Clark Ross, despite his decision to stay at home with his wife and children, faced irresistible pressure from Jane Franklin to join the search. When he finally caved in, she pressed home her advantage with smooth but single-minded determination. In a letter dated 3 August 1847 she thanked him effusively: 'You have given me great comfort by your noble self-devotion. Should it be *you* to rescue them from peril or death, you will have your reward.' But she then went on to make a further request: 'in the event of the expedition returning this autumn without having done what was expected from it, will you not still take the command for a new one ... It is very generous of Government to bear the expense of these 2 simultaneous expeditions. I think it is very likely because it is *you* that they have agreed to undertake it.' And then, having given Ross no wriggle room, she brought the letter to an end with a perfectly orchestrated emotional climax: 'With so happy a home, the sacrifice you contemplate in the service of your friends and your country is great indeed, so great that I think nothing less than your wife's heroic and generous acquiescence would have satisfied you in making it.'

James Ross had no choice but to do the decent thing and return to sea. To help look for *Erebus* and *Terror* – the two ships he knew so well – he took with him three officers who had sailed on them in the Antarctic. Edward Bird, his First Lieutenant on *Erebus*, was given command of the *Investigator*. John Robertson, who had been surgeon on *Terror*, and the man who had so often been Ross's stalwart companion under pressure, Thomas Abernethy, joined Ross on the *Enterprise*. Alongside them was a thirty-year-old Irishman, Francis Leopold McClintock. They were able to cross Baffin Bay and into Lancaster Sound in the summer of 1848, but got not much further than that, as heavy ice barred their way west and young ice was fast forming around them. Their description of the early onset of very severe weather matches meteorological records of the time, which show that the three Arctic winters after the Franklin expedition set out were exceptionally cold ones. The conditions that Ross faced in 1848 were probably very similar to those that Franklin would have faced each year since he set out.

They retreated to Port Leopold on Somerset Island (which Ross had surveyed sixteen years earlier) and, raising tarpaulins over the decks, prepared themselves for the winter. So intense was the cold that it was not until the following May that they were able to get the sledges out and reconnoitre the area. Ross and Lieutenant McClintock worked their way along the north coast of Somerset Island, which formed the southern coast of Lancaster Sound. Ross had not taken dogs, so the sledges had to be hand-hauled, which put great physical pressure on the men. The chances of encountering any evidence concerning which way the expedition might have come were reduced because, at almost every turn, they found the sea passages blocked. Ross and McClintock moved on to survey the west side of Somerset Island, overlooking Peel Sound, and found that the accumulation of ice was so thick and looked so permanent that, after leaving provisions at various points, they withdrew. By the time they reached their ship, they had covered 500 miles in thirty-nine days.

One can't blame Ross for turning back. This was very difficult terrain and, in contrast to his experience in the Antarctic, his men were suffering. On the way back to Port Leopold only four were able to pull the sledges. Two were unable to walk at all. Several were suffering from scurvy, including John Robertson, the surgeon on *Enterprise*.

Everyone on the expedition, apart from McClintock, was on the sick list for one reason or another for the next two or three weeks. Not surprisingly, they reached the conclusion that Peel Sound was an unlikely – indeed, virtually impossible – route for Franklin and his ships to have taken. And Ross, deciding that they were in no fit state to survive another winter, decided to bring the expedition home.

Many, including Jane Franklin, were surprised and disappointed. They had expected Ross to stay and search for a second summer. But leaving aside the state of health of his men, one wonders whether Ross could have faced another year in the Arctic. A sense of obligation to an old friend, manipulated skilfully and single-mindedly by Lady Franklin, had prompted him to agree to undertake this first voyage. But he was recently married, he had two young children, and he also had a publisher waiting for him to complete his account of the Antarctic voyage. Would he really have wanted to take on all the pressures, discomforts and tribulations of a further Arctic journey, when there were much younger men ready to do the job? One suspects that he had had enough.

Lady Franklin made one final appeal. 'I implore you,' she entreated him in a letter dated 12 November:

> by all you hold most dear and sacred to be influenced by what I say. Recall to mind, as I do, the generous earnestness with which you desired ... that my husband should have the command ... Recollect too the earnest part you took in securing for Sir John the services and companionship of your dear and faithful Crozier, and though I know you want no stimulus to arouse your affectionate interest for *both* your friends, yet allow me to plead these facts as additional reasons why I should look to the exertion of your unparalleled energies in devising means for their rescue and to your never *ceasing* to do so till the Arctic seas and shores have been swept in all their branches.

If she had hoped that this bravura piece of emotional blackmail would send him to the Arctic again, she was to be disappointed. James

Ross never again set out to search for Franklin. But Lady Franklin remained indefatigable. Aided and abetted by Sophy Cracroft, who had developed into a campaigner as pugnacious as her aunt-in-law, she turned her sights on anyone of any influence who might be able to help her in the search for her husband. So sustained was the pressure, and so passionate the missives, that her house in Bedford Place became known as The Battery.

Paradoxically, Lady Franklin's campaign received a boost from Ross's lack of success. That such an eminent explorer as James Clark Ross could come back empty-handed added a more sombre, realistic tone to the search for Franklin. His was the most high-profile of three well-resourced search expeditions, and the fact that none of them had found any evidence of Franklin's whereabouts brought home not just to the Admiralty, but also to the British public, the first intimations of disaster. And this produced a powerful, if increasingly desperate, response.

As hopes of rescue began to be replaced by sober awareness of an unfolding tragedy, the fate of Franklin captured the world's imagination. While panoramas of the Arctic wastes were drawing crowds in London and Brighton, and false sightings of the ships and bogus messages in bottles were being reported, the first of thirty-six separate expeditions to be organised over the next decade was heading to the frozen north. The Admiralty despatched *Enterprise* (without James Ross this time) and *Investigator* to the Bering Strait, to search the western end of the Passage. Two sailing ships and two steamers were sent to Lancaster Sound, at the other end of the Passage. The Hudson's Bay Company sent an expedition led by Sir John Ross, and supported by public subscription, in the 12-ton yacht *Mary* (named after his wife). Even the bird-loving ex-surgeon of *Erebus*, Robert McCormick, made a three-week voyage up the Wellington Channel in an open boat, appropriately named *Forlorn Hope*. Lady Franklin, never backward in coming forward, sought help from Tsar Nicholas of Russia and the American President, Zachary Taylor. St Petersburg wasn't forthcoming, but two ships equipped by the US government left New York in May 1850.

This extraordinary concentration of effort at last paid off. On 23 August 1850, the fifth summer since Franklin had left, Erasmus Ommanney, captain of HMS *Assistance*, found the first traces of the expedition at Cape Riley on the south-western tip of Devon Island: 'fragments of naval stores, portions of ragged clothing, preserved meat tins'. As they searched the shore for something more substantial, someone noticed a cairn on the headland of nearby Beechey Island. By this time Ommanney had been joined by the commander of HMS *Pioneer*, a steam tender that was augmenting the rescue expedition. Her captain, Sherard Osborn, later recounted the excitement of the discovery in his book *Stray Leaves from an Arctic Journal*. Men rushed towards 'the dark and frowning cliffs ... too steep for even [a] snowflake to hang upon ... the steep slope was scaled and the cairn torn down, every stone turned over ... and yet alas! No document or record found.'

Other ships in the area converged on the island, including, by fine coincidence, one called *The Lady Franklin*, captained by William Penny. It was one of her sailors who brought the extraordinary news that three graves had been found on the bleak, grey scree-covered beach. The trio of wooden headboards announced them to be the last resting places of John Torrington, leading stoker, 'who departed this life January 1st A.D. 1846 on board of H.M. ship *Terror* aged 20 years'; John Hartnell, able seaman on *Erebus*, 'died January 4th 1846 aged 25 years'; and William Braine, a Royal Marine on *Erebus*, 'Died April 3rd 1846, aged 32 years'. On his grave marker was the text '"Choose ye this day whom ye will serve" Joshua, ch. Xxiv., 15'.

Further along the beach they found traces of sledge-runners in the gravel, deep enough for Sherard Osborn to make the prescient observation as to 'how little Franklin's people were impressed with the importance of rendering their travelling equipment light and portable'. And there was a second cairn nearby. It was 7 feet high and consisted of 600 food tins filled with gravel.

The Beechey Island finds were both revealing and frustrating. Lieutenant Osborn summed up the mood: 'Everyone felt that there was something so inexplicable in the non-discovery of any record, some written evidence of the intentions of Franklin and Crozier on leaving this spot.' The trail that seemed to begin there led nowhere.

The best they could do was follow the route Franklin had been ordered to take by the Admiralty. So Captain Ommanney pressed on westwards to Cape Walker on the northern tip of Prince of Wales Island. He found nothing, but came to the conclusion that Franklin could not have taken the planned line due south from Cape Walker through to the Bering Strait, as it would have been blocked by impenetrable ancient sea-ice. His hunch was right. We now know that Franklin went south, much earlier, down Peel Sound.

The disappearance of the expedition seemed as total as it was inexplicable. Then another possible piece of evidence turned up much further to the south. An overland party led by John Rae was exploring the west coast of Victoria Strait when Rae came across two pieces of what looked like wreckage. One was an oak stanchion and the other looked to be part of the flagstaff of a cutter. A white line had been attached to it by two copper tacks. Both tacks bore the broad arrow imprint with which all Royal Navy equipment was stamped. Because there was no confirmation of the route that Franklin had taken when he deviated from the Admiralty's chosen course, Rae assumed that the fragments had drifted down from the north. It was several years before anyone realised that the two ships might be much closer than he thought.

As the seventh anniversary of the disappearance approached, an increasing amount of head-scratching was taking place. The

Admiralty could not do nothing. Interest in the expedition remained high, and it had taken a jingoistic turn.

Subscriptions were coming in from all over the country. Thanks to the assiduous work of historian Richard Cyriax, we know that one came from Franklin's birthplace, Spilsby in Lincolnshire, another from the Belfast Natural History and Philosophical Society, of which Crozier was a member. A contribution that must have warmed Lady Franklin's heart was the generous sum of £1,872 collected by the people of Van Diemen's Land, 'as the utmost sympathy is felt in this colony in any particular which bears upon the fate of our late respected Lieutenant-Governor'. Lady Franklin used this contribution to fund the *Isabel* expedition of 1852. It was led by Commander Augustus Inglefield, and although it found no trace of Franklin, apart from a handful of relics, it explored and charted previously unknown areas of the Arctic, identifying and naming Ellesmere Island, the tenth-largest island in the world and one of the most rugged and spectacular land masses on the planet.

The findings so far showed that the expedition had almost certainly not gone west of Cape Walker, nor did they appear to have taken any of the heavily iced channels to the south. This left the northern option, the Wellington Channel, between Cornwallis Island and Devon Island. The Admiralty had recommended that Franklin consider this if he found his way blocked by ice, so it was a valid alternative.

An Admiralty expedition led by Sir Edward Belcher therefore took the sailing ship *Assistance* and the steam-driven *Pioneer* up the Wellington Channel, whilst Henry Kellett took *Resolute* and *Intrepid* to investigate Melville Island. Belcher stayed another winter at Beechey Island, leaving a depot of shelter and provisions to which they gave the name Northumberland House, before returning home with only one ship intact, having abandoned the others in the ice. Neither he nor Kellett found any evidence of Franklin, his men or his ships. But

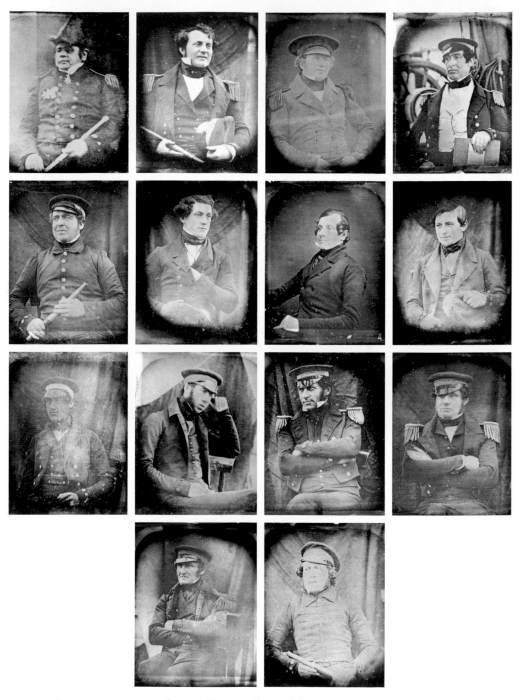

Daguerreotypes of the officers of Franklin's 1845 Arctic expedition.
From left to right: (top row) John Franklin, James Fitzjames, Francis Crozier,
Henry Le Vesconte, (second row) James Reid, Charles Des Voeux, Stephen Stanley,
Edward Couch, (third row) Robert Sargent, Harry Goodsir, Graham Gore, James
Fairholme, (bottom row) Charles Osmer, Henry Collins.

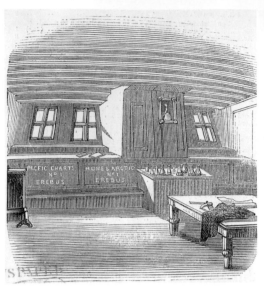

The cabins of John Franklin (left) and James Fitzjames (right), as depicted in the *Illustrated London News*, 24 May 1845.

'Parting company with *Erebus*, 4 June 1845': a sketch by Owen Stanley, an officer on HMS *Blazer*.

'The Arctic Council planning a search for Sir John Franklin' (1851).
From left to right: George Back, Edward Parry, Edward Bird, James Ross,
Francis Beaufort, John Barrow junior, Edward Sabine, William Hamilton,
John Richardson, Frederick Beechey.

The departure of travelling parties from *Resolute* and *Intrepid* to search for the lost
Franklin expedition (1853).

A watercolour by the American explorer Elisha Kent Kane of the graves on Beechey Island (1850).

Above: John Rae, the Orkney man who first pieced together what had happened to the Franklin expedition.

Right: The Victory Point note, discovered by Lieutenant William Hobson in 1859.

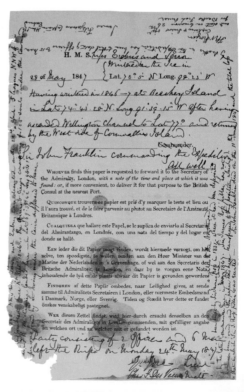

'Man Proposes, God Disposes': Edwin Henry Landseer's pictorial commentary on the Franklin expedition (1864).

Sir John Franklin's memorial in Waterloo Place, London, erected in 1866.

The Franklin expedition memorial at the Old Royal Naval College, Greenwich, erected in 1858.

The body of John Torrington, exhumed by Owen Beattie in 1984.

Relics of the Franklin
expedition: the Guelphic
medal found by John Rae.

A copy of *Christian Melodies*. The letters
'G.G' on the flyleaf suggest it belonged to
Lieutenant Gore.

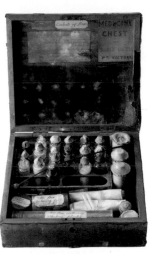

Snow goggles.

A pocket chronometer.

A medicine box
found by Francis
McClintock near
Victory Point.

A plate found aboard
Erebus.

The Beechey Island graves today. Three mark the final resting places of members of the Franklin expedition. The fourth is that of Thomas Morgan, a member of the McClure rescue expedition, who perished in 1854.

The wreck of *Erebus*.

The ship's bell of *Erebus*.

then both were still looking where the Admiralty had instructed Franklin to go, rather than where he actually went.

There had been some collateral successes. The rather magnificently named Robert John Le Mesurier McClure commanding the *Investigator*, and Richard Collinson, commanding the *Enterprise*, had been out on the search since 1850. They had brought their ships safely through the Bering Strait and had come very close to finding their way through to Melville Island when their ships became trapped. In 1853 McClure and his party, having abandoned their ship to the ice, and after surviving two punishing winters, found their way overland from the west to meet up with some of Belcher's men from the east. McClure claimed this as the first crossing of the Northwest Passage, albeit not purely by sea.

With the searches consistently drawing blanks, the Admiralty took the view that since the expedition had now been missing for eight years there could be no possibility of any of its members having survived, and that risking lives and public funds in further futile rescue attempts could therefore not be justified. It is estimated that they had already spent some £700,000 on the search (the equivalent of £28 million / $39 million in today's money). Moreover, they now had other things on their minds: after three decades of peace in Europe, Britain had become embroiled in war with Russia in the Crimea.

On 20 January 1854 the Admiralty let it be known that unless news of the expedition's survival arrived before March of that year, the men of *Erebus* and *Terror* would be removed from the Navy List and declared to have died in Her Majesty's Service. Lady Franklin refused to accept their decision, describing it as 'presumptuous in the sight of God'. She declined a widow's pension and refused to wear black. As far as she was concerned, no news could still mean good news.

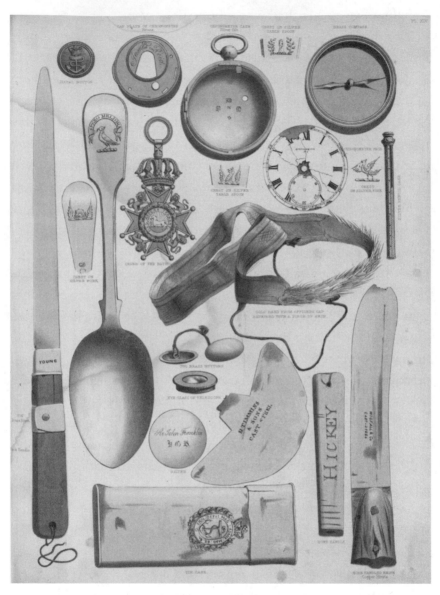

Some of the items from the Franklin expedition recovered by the explorer John Rae as he made his way along the Arctic coast in 1854. They ranged from cutlery to one of Sir John Franklin's medals.

CHAPTER 15

THE TRUTH

Just when it looked as if the end of the road had been reached, news came from the north that would change everything. It involved a figure who had already played a part in the Franklin story.

In 1854 John Rae, the Orkney man working for the Hudson's Bay Company who had found some items on an overland search a few years previously, was making his way along the Arctic coast, trying to complete the first survey of this remote area. He was travelling in Inuit style, building igloos en route. On 21 April he reached the shores of Pelly Bay, where he met up with 'a very intelligent Esquimaux' driving a dog sledge. They were joined by another Inuit, In-nook-poo-zhe-jook (Inukpuhiijuk), who was interested in trading with Rae. In the course of conversation, Rae, through an interpreter, put to him the routine enquiry as to whether he had seen any *kabloonas* (foreigners) in the area. He hadn't, but he had heard others tell of a large group of white men who had died somewhere to the west, 'beyond a large river'. The Inuit had with him an officer's gold cap band, which Rae purchased, before carrying on with his mission. On his return to Pelly Bay, Rae met up again with In-nook-poo-zhe-jook and this time bought more objects from other Inuit who were with him, including a silver spoon and fork embossed with a family crest and with the initials F.R.M.C scratched on them. Rae didn't know at the time that he was looking at the initials of Francis Raw-don Moira Crozier.

Later he was brought other items: Franklin's Guelphic Order of Hanover medal, bestowed upon him for services in the Mediterra-nean twenty years earlier; silverware belonging to seven of the officers from *Erebus*; an under-vest marked FDV 6.1845 (the letters FDV were the initials of Charles Frederick Des Voeux, mate of the *Erebus*).

Gradually, with the help of In-nook-poo-zhe-jook and other visiting Inuit, Rae pieced together the story of what seemed to have been the final days of the expedition. They told of forty men seen travelling southwards from King William Island 'four winters past' – in 1850. They had been dragging sledges, one of which had a boat on it. None of them spoke Inuktitut, but they communicated by sign language that their ship, or ships, had been crushed in the ice and that they had abandoned them to walk south to find food. Most of the men were thin and weak, but their leader was described as being a tall, broad, middle-aged man, a description that would certainly have fitted Francis Crozier. The Inuit called him Aglooka. He purchased some seal-meat from the natives. Then, both sides being unable to commu-nicate further, they moved on.

Later that same season, the Inuit reported, the bodies of thirty men were discovered on the mainland and five corpses on an island nearby. Some of the bodies were found in tents, some under an upturned boat. All were close to what matched descriptions of the mouth of Great Fish River.

This was a revelation. But what came next was a jarring shock. 'From the mutilated state of many of the bodies, and the contents of the kettles [cooking vessels],' Rae reported the Inuit telling him, 'it is evident that our wretched countrymen had been driven to the last dread alternative as a means of sustaining life.'

On his return to London, Rae submitted his report to the Admir-alty. The effect was shattering. A copy was rushed to Lady Franklin and reached her at two in the morning. Sophy broke the news to her. 'No words,' Sophy wrote later, 'can describe the horror of that night.'

Much to Rae's dismay, his Admiralty report was published in *The Times*, and the allegations of cannibalism – 'the last dread alternative' – were picked up in other newspapers. A wave of horror and revulsion spread across the nation. But because the revelations were so shocking and so offensive, people dealt with them by rejecting them. No Englishman could possibly have acted in such a way, it was argued. Rae should not have relied on Inuit testimony. In his weekly journal, *Household Words*, Jane Franklin's influential champion Charles Dickens waded in with a passionate defence of the men, whom he saw as the 'flower of the trained English Navy'. He angrily contrasted them with the Inuit: 'the noble conduct and example of such men, and of their own great leader himself,' he wrote, '. . . outweighs by the weight of the whole universe the chatter of a gross handful of uncivilised people, with a domesticity of blood and blubber'.

Why should people care about such slurs? demanded Dickens. 'Because they ARE . . . dead,' he thundered:

> therefore we care about this. Because they served their country well, and deserved well of her, and can ask no more on this earth for her justice or her loving-kindness . . . Because no Franklin can come back, to write the honest story of their woes and resignation . . . Because they lie scattered on those wastes of snow, and are as defenceless against the remembrance of coming generations, as against the elements into which they are resolving, and the winter winds that alone can waft them home . . . therefore, cherish them gently, even in the breasts of children. Therefore, teach no one to shudder without reason, at the history of their end. Therefore, confide with their own firmness, in their fortitude, their lofty sense of duty, their courage, and their religion.

John Rae, given the opportunity to reply in *Household Words*, defended his Inuit informants and their interpreter from the increasingly common accusation that the Inuit themselves had attacked the Franklin party and that they had been the real cannibals. But his arguments fell on deaf ears. Instead of being given credit for uncovering the first real evidence that the men had died, and more importantly where they had died, Rae was tongue-lashed by the establishment. Lady Franklin tried to block payment of the £10,000 set aside as a reward for the first person to find evidence of the fate of the expedition, and although this was eventually paid, Rae received no public recognition. Knighthoods had gone to so many Arctic explorers – Parry, Franklin, John Richardson, John and James Ross. Why should one not have gone to a man who understood the Arctic as well as John Rae?

He is still remembered with great affection and admiration in the Orkneys. I have seen his statue in Stromness and his old house, the magnificently dilapidated Hall of Clestrain, looking out towards his home town from across the bay. His finest monument is the tombstone in St Magnus Cathedral in Kirkwall. Rae lies on his side in his Arctic furs, arms crooked behind a magnificently bearded head, with an open book and a rifle lying beside him. A man at work. No hint of the heroic. Rae was an explorer in the mould of Amundsen and Nansen, listening to the locals, learning from them what to wear, what to eat and how to survive. In his lifetime he mapped 1,750 miles of unexplored territory, with the loss of only one man. What a contrast with the disastrous expedition whose fate he was the first to discover.

Back in London, Jane Franklin still refused to believe that her husband might not be alive. Rae's report had shaken her badly, but it had not doused her fighting instincts. She continued to write regular, often copiously gossipy, letters to Sir John, sending them out with rescue ships. One of them, which was entrusted to Captain William Kennedy on the *Isabel*, reads: 'My dearest love. I do trust that never for a moment have you thought that your country and your friends had forgotten you or left you to your fate ... Remember me most kindly and affectionately to your friends and companions.' The letter was dated 30 March 1853, almost eight years after Franklin and his companions had disappeared.

Encouraged by further discoveries of wreckage by two Hudson's Bay fur traders, James Anderson and James Stewart, Lady Franklin – who had already ploughed around £35,000 (£1.5 million in today's money) of her own funds into what was now known not just as a search but The Search – tapped her contacts one more time. Charles Dickens spoke at a fund-raiser at the Royal Geographical Society, an occasion that gave him another opportunity, in the words of Franklin's biographer Andrew Lambert, 'to argue that he, not Rae, had been right in 1854 – Franklin and his men died noble Christian heroes, not bestial savages'.

£3,000 was raised from the public, enough to commission and equip a three-masted steam-driven yacht called the *Fox*. At 177 tons, about half the size of *Erebus*, she was a smaller, more manoeuvrable craft than was commonly sent to the Arctic, and her shallow draught made her potentially better able to operate in the silted channels off the North American coast. She had a crew of twenty-five, the majority of whom had previous Arctic experience, and was captained by Francis Leopold McClintock, a thirty-eight-year-old Irishman from Dundalk, the same man who had sailed with Ross in 1848, when the two of them had developed and refined the use of sledges. This time, though, he made sure they didn't repeat the big mistake of having humans, rather than dogs, to pull them. This was no silver-spoon expedition. It was to be fast and light and adaptable, putting into practice lessons learned from natives rather than from naval academies.

The *Fox* left England in July 1857, but became locked in the winter ice in Baffin Bay and was not able to move again until the end of April the following year. Taking their bearings from Rae's report, the expedition ran south down Peel Sound, but ice blocked their progress and they had to backtrack around the top of Somerset Land, which – following William Kennedy and Joseph-René Bellot's discovery of a mile-wide channel bisecting the Boothia Peninsula – was now known to be an island. McClintock tried to take the *Fox* through this narrow channel, called the Bellot Strait after its discoverer, only to find its western end blocked by ice. He therefore made a base at the eastern end of the Strait. It was not until February 1859 that he and his men were able to mount their first sledge-bound reconnaissance expedition.

On their way south along the west coast of the Boothia Peninsula, McClintock and two companions met Inuit with relics to sell and stories to tell. One of them told of a three-masted ship that had been seen to sink off the west of King William Island. In April, with the thermometer showing thirty degrees below, McClintock and his second-in-command, Lieutenant William Hobson, along with ten men and four sledges (two man-drawn and two dog-drawn), therefore set out for the island. On the way they met an elderly Inuit by the name of Oo-na-lee, who told them of a second ship that had been forced ashore by the ice, further south at a place called Oot-loo-lik or Utjulik. Others told of the body of 'a very large man', with 'long teeth', being found aboard the ship. By all accounts, McClintock and his men were closing in on the heart of the disaster. It was time to translate rumour into hard evidence.

When they reached Cape Victoria on the south-western coast of the Boothia Peninsula, the party split. McClintock continued south towards the mouth of the Great Fish River, in the area where three years earlier John Rae had first learned of the Inuit's discoveries. Lieutenant Hobson and his party set off to investigate the report of the wrecked ship on the west coast of King William Island.

Hobson's report, dated 1 August 1859, was never published, and a copy came to light only recently from Library and Archives Canada.

It appeared with a commentary by Doug Stenton in *Arctic* magazine in April 2014. Less formal than a journal or a log, it has a compelling story to tell. It starts with an account of Hobson and his team as they set off due west across the hard-frozen surface of James Ross Strait. Hobson sets the scene carefully and precisely: 'The ice appeared to be of but one year's growth; and although it was in many places much crushed up we easily found smooth leads through the lines of hummocks; many very heavy masses of ice, evidently of foreign formation, have been here arrested in their drift; so large are they, that in the gloomy weather we experienced they were often taken for islands.'

King William Island, the stage on which so much of the tragedy was played out, has been described as a polar desert island. Hobson evokes it as 'a mere shingle bank thrown up by the sea ... a low, barren limestone shore'. Almost uniformly flat and unremittingly gloomy, with no cover from icy winds and driving snow, it must have been the cruellest environment for searchers or survivors.

Early on 3 May 1859, only five days after leaving Cape Victoria, they came across a cairn and the remains of an encampment near Cape Felix on the northern tip of the island. With growing excitement, they opened the cairn, but found only a blank piece of paper folded in a triangular shape, and a fragment of rope yarn. It was a tantalising disappointment. Hobson wrote that 'I have little doubt that this paper had contained some information and that the writing (possibly pencil) had been effaced by exposure.' The encampment looked to have been occupied by some twelve officers and men. There were three small collapsed tents, under which 'bear skins and blanket coverlets were left spread out, to all appearances precisely as their last occupants had used them'.

Scattered along the shore was a trail of discarded items: cooking stoves, a dip circle, badges, the remains of a pair of spectacles, fragments of broken bottles, hanks of twine, brass curtain rods (the historian Ann Savours suggests these might have been intended as gifts for the natives), a mahogany medicine chest and wads of tobacco.

Quite why the camp had been established, Hobson wasn't sure, but he had little doubt that 'it was hastily abandoned and I should think that the party must have been returning to their ship'. 'Under no other circumstance,' he concluded, 'can I imagine that people would leave their tents, sleeping gear and cooking apparatus.'

The pile of evidence continued to grow. On 5 May they came across an 18-foot-long spruce tree that had been cut in half with a whipsaw, presumably for use as fuel. The next day they discovered another, smaller cairn, with a broken pickaxe and an empty tea or coffee canister inside. After spending an hour in a fruitless search for documents, they continued south, where they found a third cairn, with 'a great quantity of gear' strewn about. There was much to investigate here, so they pitched their tent nearby. At midday on 6 May they went to work.

Hobson's description of what happened next is laconic in the extreme. 'A small cylinder was soon discovered among some loose stones that had evidently fallen from the top of the cairn,' he wrote, following this statement with the observation, 'It contained a brief statement of the movements of the lost expedition.' But those few words don't begin to do justice to what he'd found. Now known as the Victory Point note, that 'brief statement' is one of the most significant documents in the history of exploration.

Technically, it's not really the 'Victory Point' note. Richard Cyriax, an expert on the Franklin expedition, has pointed out that the cairn in which the record was originally deposited was actually 4 miles to the north of the spot, first charted by James Clark Ross in 1830, that gave it its name. It was written on a regulation form – one of those issued to expeditions to deposit or throw overboard, to give an indication of their position, and with the instruction, printed in six languages, that 'Whoever finds this paper' should 'forward it to the Secretary of the Admiralty, London *with a note of the time and place at which it was found*: or, if more convenient, to deliver it for that purpose to the British Consul at the nearest Port'.

Though stained with rust patches from the tin cylinder, the hand-writing was clearly legible and was identified as Fitzjames's. It gave a date – 28 May 1847 (almost two years after the ships had left Green-hithe) – and a position: 'H.M. Ships *Erebus* and *Terror* wintered in the ice in Lat. 70°5'N Long. 98°23'W.' It then went on to give a brief account of how they had got there: 'Having wintered in 1846–7 at Beechey Island ... after having ascended Wellington Channel to Lat 77° and returned to the West-side of Cornwallis Island.' It named Sir John Franklin as the commander of the expedition, and offered the reassuring words 'All well', underlined for emphasis. At the bottom of the formal record were a few additional words: 'Party consisting of 2 officers and 6 men left the ships on Monday 24th May 1847'. The note was signed 'GM. Gore Lieut' and 'Chas F Des Voeux, Mate'.

The note might confidently have stated that all was well, but even at this stage there are signs that things were awry. For a start, Fitz-james had got his dates wrong: it was 1845–6, not 1846–7, when they wintered on Beechey Island. Richard Cyriax's explanation is that the mistaken date was simply a slip of the pen and shows that such records were considered of very little importance. But it could be an indica-tion that the members of the expedition had become increasingly disorientated. And the fact that Franklin himself did not write or sign the note was ominous.

But it's the message that Hobson found squeezed around the mar-gins of the note that proved to be of particular significance. Written by Fitzjames some eleven months later, on 25 April 1848, the spidery script describes a desperate change in circumstances:

HM Ship[s] Terror and Erebus were deserted on the 22nd April, 5 leagues NNW of this, [hav]ing been beset since 12th Septr. 1846. The Officers and Crews consisting of 105 souls – under the Command [of Cap]tain FRM. Crozier landed here – in Lat 69°37' 42", long 98°41'. [This p]aper was found by Lt-Irving under the

Cairn supposed to have been built by Sir James Ross in 1831, 4 miles to the Northward – where it had been deposited by the late Commander Gore in June 1847.

The sting was in the tail: 'Sir John Franklin died on the 11th June 1847, and the total loss by deaths in the Expedition has been to this date 9 Officers and 15 men.' This later addition was signed: 'James Fitzjames, Captain H.M.S Erebus' and 'F.R.M Crozier Captain and Senior Offr'. After signing his name, Crozier added, 'and start on tomorrow 26th for Backs Fish River'.

Piecing together what had happened here, it would appear that Gore and Des Voeux set out with more than one record in a sealed container. They mistook the position of Victory Point (named by James Clark Ross in 1830, not 1831, as Fitzjames seems to have thought) and left the record in a cairn 4 miles to the north. They then proceeded southwards and left another identical copy of the record (which was not subsequently amended, but has since been recovered). By the time they returned to their ships, Sir John Franklin had died, only three weeks after Fitzjames had written and underlined 'All well'. From then on, judging from the additional writing on the so-called Victory Point record, all went badly enough for the remaining 105 men to abandon the two ships. They crossed to King William Island eleven months later, after Gore, too, had died. Lieutenant Irving found the first sealed record in a cairn 4 miles north of Victory Point and brought it to Crozier and Fitzjames. They added the latest grim news, and the container was then resealed and placed in the cairn, where Hobson found it eleven years later.

Because of heavy falls of snow, Hobson was prevented from conducting a more thorough search of the site, and so after making a copy, he took the document and an inventory of the items he had found and proceeded south along the coastline. This was easier said than done, since 'There is literally no coastline for a guide.' So disoriented were they by the wind and the driving snow that their next encampment turned out to be not by the sea at all, but beside a lake, 4 miles inland.

On 24 May 1859 they discovered a large boat on the beach. It was embedded in drifting snow and was barely visible. After laboriously clearing away the rock-hard ice and snow, they uncovered one of the ships' cutters, 28 feet long, trimmed down and lightened for overland travel, with a sturdy sledge nearby, on which the cutter had been dragged across the island. The sledge itself weighed 750 lb and it is estimated that it would have taken seven or eight men to shift it, pulling ropes of 3-inch whale-line, which lay discarded nearby. Two rifles were found in the bows, as well as plenty of ammunition. And that was not all. 'In the stern sheets ... was a human jaw bone of great size. Other bones of corresponding magnitude lay near.' A chronometer bearing the name Parkinson & Frodsham found beside the remains led Hobson to believe that it may have been the body of an officer. The bones of another man also lay in the boat.

The boat contained a repository of articles, which the remainder of the expedition must have considered important enough to take with them on the long walk south to the river known to some as the Great Fish River and to others as Back's Fish River. These included eleven dessert forks, eleven dessert spoons and four teaspoons 'bearing the crests of officers belonging to both the *Terror* and the *Erebus*', along with five shot flasks, several small religious books, a copy of *The Vicar of Wakefield*, a small pemmican tin, a great many remains of blankets, bear skins, boxcloth jackets, trousers, gloves, stockings, leather boots, a meerschaum and several clay pipes.

Hobson, crippled with scurvy, brought his sensational discovery back to the *Fox* seventy-four days after he set out. McClintock and his party arrived four days later. They had initially been less successful. They had found nothing from the expedition in the Back's Fish River estuary and few natives to talk to. But then, returning via King

William Island, they had come across a bleached human skeleton, lying face downwards on a gravel ridge. It was partly covered by snow and, from pieces of the uniform, was identified as a steward, probably Thomas Armitage, gun-room steward on *Terror*.

The most intriguing thing about this grim discovery was a small pocket-book lying nearby, which contained a series of near-indecipherable writings and drawings. Among them was a seaman's certificate in the name of Henry Peglar, believed to be a close friend of Armitage. The 'Peglar Papers', as they have become known, continue to frustrate interpretation or translation. Written during the course of the expedition, they read like nonsense; apparently playful scraps of sentences written backwards, and fragments of what look like letters to people. Russell Potter, who calls them 'The Dead Sea Scrolls of the North', has put in much work trying to decipher the papers. On one page Peglar has scribbled down a couplet that begins 'O Death where is thy sting, The Grave at Comfort Cove'. The first line is from the Service of the Burial of the Dead; and Comfort Cove, or Comfortless Cove, was the name of a renowned sailors' graveyard on Ascension Island. So are these words part of a eulogy, and if so, for whom? Two lines later appear the words 'the Dyer was and whare Traffelegar'. The only man on the expedition associated with Trafalgar was Franklin, who fought there. Could these be words composed for Franklin's funeral? And composed not by an officer, but by an ordinary seaman like Henry Peglar? The Peglar Papers remain an enigma, but given the almost total absence of written material from the expedition, a precious one.

Further up the coast McClintock came across the boat that Hobson had discovered. He thought it significant that the boat's prow was pointing north. It suggested to him that the men were hauling it back to, not away from, the wrecked ships.

On 23 September 1859 the *Fox*, the smallest, yet most successful craft to carry a search expedition, arrived at Blackwall Docks in London. With it came final confirmation that Sir John Barrow's great dream had indeed ended in disaster. None of Franklin's men would be coming back.

Five years earlier, Rae's account of the last days of the expedition had been received with horror and outrage. The message of heroism in the face of appalling adversity that *Fox* brought back to port was received with patriotic gratitude. Now the nation could grieve, and talk of sacrifice. Rae had to fight for his reward, but Hobson was promoted without delay, and Parliament voted a £5,000 bonus to McClintock's officers and crew. McClintock was knighted by Queen Victoria and awarded the Patron's Medal by a grateful Royal Geographical Society.

McClintock's subsequent account of the journey, *The Voyage of the 'Fox' in the Arctic Seas*, was a huge bestseller. Of course it had a dramatic and tragic tale to tell. But one senses that it also struck a deeper chord. Despite all the advances of science, the menacing power of nature had been asserted. For all those who felt threatened by Darwin's *On the Origin of Species*, published in the same year as *The Voyage of the 'Fox'*, the fate of the expedition was seen as a classic case of hubris. It inspired Edwin Landseer's gruesome painting of the last remnants of an expedition, flag and all, being torn apart by polar bears on an ice-floe. The title says it all: 'Man Proposes, God Disposes'.

The one comfort drawn from the whole unmitigated disaster was the news that bodies had been discovered far enough south to prove that Crozier had led his doomed men to the last link in the chain of marine connections that made up the Northwest Passage. In the cathartic euphoria that followed the return of the *Fox*, it was a brave man or woman who would contradict the claim that Franklin's expedition – if not the brave captain himself – had achieved its goal. This was what was inscribed on the statues that were subsequently erected, and this is what appeared on the citation that accompanied the award of the Founder's Medal of the Royal Geographical Society to Lady Jane Franklin, the first woman ever to be honoured by the Society.

On 24 May 1859, an expedition led by Lieutenant William Hobson came across a boat on King William Island. It contained the remains of two men, one possibly an officer, the other a young man 'of much smaller size than the other'.

CHAPTER 16

LIFE AND DEATH

By the early 1860s the path of Franklin's doomed expedition had become pretty clear. It was now known that, after leaving Greenland, *Erebus* and *Terror* had crossed Baffin Bay, sailed through Lancaster Sound and that Franklin and Crozier made their winter camp at Beechey Island. In that same year of 1845, or more likely at the start of the summer of 1846, they sailed north-west, up the Wellington Channel, presumably seeking a way round the heavy ice blocking their way through Barrow Strait. Finding no route through, they circumnavigated the previously unexplored coast of Cornwallis Island. (This may have proved to be a cul-de-sac in the search for the Northwest Passage, but it was a remarkable piece of exploration on a part of the map that would not be revisited for another 100 years.)

With ice again piling up to the west, Franklin must have decided to take his ships south to try to find a way through. They seem to have found clear water and sailed successfully down Peel Sound, passing between Somerset Island and Prince of Wales Island and keeping on the move until, towards the end of the summer of 1846, they reached Victoria Strait. Here they would have hit a barrier of impenetrable oceanic, multi-year ice, 40 or 50 feet thick – in Ann Savours's memorably evocative image, 'scouring, churning, groaning and forcing its way down what was later called McClintock Channel'.

Why they didn't take the more sheltered eastern route on the other side of King William Island remains unanswered, but it seems more than likely that it was down to ignorance of the terrain. It needs to be remembered that Franklin and Crozier, bent over their tables in the wide stern cabins, would have been poring over charts of only recently discovered lands, whose details were often sketchy. They might have had monogrammed dinner plates and personalised silver cutlery, but they didn't have very good maps. The charts with which Franklin had been supplied by the Admiralty showed King William Land not as an island at all, but as a piece of land attached by an isthmus to the Boothia Peninsula. Three experienced Arctic explorers – Sir John Ross, Peter Dease and Thomas Simpson – similarly believed that James Ross Strait was joined to the mainland. Franklin and Crozier and their ships therefore continued to sail south into the ice-trap that was to squeeze the life out of them. The Victory Point note names the day when they first found themselves 'beset' as 12 September 1846. They were, we know, still beset in April 1848. Their position, ironically, was on the line where the Atlantic and Pacific tides meet. It was the closest they would get to either ocean again.

Arctic winters are brutal enough, especially as three months are spent in total darkness. By April 1848 Franklin and his men would have endured six months of such darkness. Moreover, their voyage coincided with one of the coldest spells to hit the Arctic in living memory. Even the summers passed with no let-up in the ice's grip.

Sadly, we have no record of life on board *Erebus* during what turned out to be another exceptionally severe winter. What became of Jacko the monkey and Neptune the dog? How much of a blow was Franklin's death, only a month after Gore and Des Voeux set out? With hindsight, we see tragedy staring them in the face, and it's tempting to imagine a scenario of remorseless mental and physical suffering. But the ships were well equipped, and much thought had gone into how the crew might occupy themselves in precisely these circumstances. There were books, carpentry tools, hand-organs and other musical instruments, and we know that Sir John was very keen on religion and schooling and on helping his sailors better themselves. Did Crozier, his successor as leader of the expedition, keep up these activities? How much exercise were the men able to take? How did they pass the time?

The nearest we can get to a picture of what life might have been like aboard *Erebus* and *Terror* during their long confinement is to look at what happened on other ships in similar situations. Perhaps the closest parallel is Parry's expedition of 1819 in *Hecla* and *Fury*. Like Sir John Franklin, Sir Edward was charged with finding a way through the Northwest Passage. Whalers, who were used to the Arctic, would make sure their work was done by the end of the summer. But Parry, with work still to do, had little option but to stay and see out the long months of darkness.

In his book, *Journal of a Voyage*, he captures the bleakness of their winter home: 'the death-like stillness of the most dreary desolation' and 'the total absence of animated existence'. He also gives us an insight into how fearsome the cold could be – a cold so intense it could take your skin off. On a day when the temperature touched -24° Fahrenheit, 'it now became rather a painful experiment to touch any metallic substance ... we found it necessary ... to use great caution in handling our sextants and other instruments, particularly the eye-pieces of the telescopes'.

We know that, as winter came on, Parry prepared his ship *Hecla* by dismantling most of the masts and raising a waggon-cloth cover over the deck, to provide shelter and exercise space. Ann Savours's valuable work on the subject notes that Parry's men 'were ordered to run round and round the deck, keeping step to a tune on the organ, or, not infrequently, to a song of their own making'.

Parry also set great store by amateur dramatics, encouraging the men to build sets and stage plays. He even wrote one himself: *The*

North West Passage, or Voyage Finished – a risky title, I'd have thought. Such theatrical entertainments were popular: 'the effect produced on the minds of men, who have no resource within themselves,' enthused *Hecla*'s purser, William Hooper, in his diary, 'is beneficial to the highest degree'. They also produced a weekly newspaper, the *North Georgia Gazette and Winter Chronicle*, 'composed and edited . . . within fifteen degrees of the North Pole of the earth'. Parry's purpose throughout was 'to promote good humour among ourselves, as well as to furnish amusing occupation, during the hours of constant darkness'.

His example was followed on HMS *Resolute*, one of the squadron of ships sent to search for Franklin in 1852. They had been supplied with a printing press and produced two newspapers, the *Illustrated Arctic News* and the *Aurora Borealis*. Their Royal Arctic Theatre staged a specially written pantomime, entitled *Zero*, and if that wasn't enough diversion, there was also a Royal Arctic Casino. *Resolute*'s captain, Horatio Austin, attended a fancy-dress ball disguised, so one of the officers writes, as an 'odd figure uttering the cry of "old chairs to mend!"' until his 'well-known laugh' revealed 'our ever-cheerful Commodore'.

Of course the Franklin expedition was to spend not one, but three successive winters in the Arctic, and in the later stages their experience could have been more like that described by Henry Piers, the assistant surgeon on *Investigator*, stuck fast in thick ice off Banks Island in 1852:

> . . . let anyone imagine a ship frozen up, with the deck covered with snow a foot or eighteen inches deep . . . a temperature of minus 30 or 40 with strong wind . . . the fine snow drift . . . finding its way through and covering everything, the wind howling through the rigging at the same time: let him picture to himself then this covered deck lit by a single candle in a lantern; five or

six officers walking the starboard side and maintaining some conversation, and twenty or thirty men, perfectly mute, slowly pacing the port side, muffled up to the eyes and covered with snow drift or frozen vapour ... he will then have some idea of many of this winter's day's exercise.

That was *Investigator's* second winter. A third winter in such conditions, as endured by those on Franklin's flagship, seems almost unimaginable. If *Erebus* was indeed named after the darkest depths of hell, it must have felt as if she had come home.

Another subject that has been hotly debated is the state of health of the crew at the time they were driven to abandon the ships.

Writing some fifty years after the departure of the expedition, Sir Clements Markham, an Arctic traveller himself and President of the Royal Geographical Society, laid the blame for their demise fairly and squarely on the quality of the tinned food they had taken with them. He made much of the fact that the company that had supplied tinned food to the Antarctic expedition had been passed over by the Admiralty, in favour of a cheaper bid from a company set up by a Hungarian, Stephen Goldner, whose food was produced to a formula of his own, in a factory at Galatz in Moldavia. Since a new supplier was now involved, Fitzjames had apparently cautioned that before they left London every tenth case should be examined, but Franklin had demurred, probably because time was short and he felt that the authorities had already taken precautions. 'So,' concluded Markham, 'the Admiralty, in perfect ignorance and without a care, went gaily on filling the ships with offal unfit for human food, nicely concealed in cylindrical tin cases painted red. Thus were the brave men condemned to death by slow poison even before they sailed.'

That he should argue this case with such vehemence, a generation later, suggests that Goldner's culpability had been debated for some time, and the allegations resurfaced in a book published in 1939. In *Historic Tinned Foods*, J.C. Drummond, a historian of such matters, speculated that 'It is possible that Goldner's foods prepared for *Erebus* and *Terror* went bad because their preparation was rushed, he being behind with his contracts.' This is also a notion taken up more recently in Scott Cookman's book *Ice Blink*, which suggests that the tinned food contained botulism.

It is certainly significant that it was about the time of the Franklin expedition that 'packs' larger than 2–6 lb were being prepared. And since larger tins would, of course, have required longer processing time to heat the contents and destroy bacteria, Goldner's haste was risky. It therefore comes as no surprise that from 1849 onwards serious reports of faulty tins and bad meat were coming in from many of the victualling yards, and that in 1850 the Royal William Yard condemned no less than 11,108 lb of Goldner's meat. Even so, his tinned foodstuffs won a prize at the Great Exhibition in 1851 and, despite Markham's certainty, there is no firm evidence that Goldner's food was responsible for any loss of life. Had it really been tainted, one would have to ask why so many of the expedition managed to survive for so long.

More recently, a rather different explanation has been floated. In 1984 a party led by Owen Beattie exhumed the first three fatalities of the expedition, who had been buried on the shore of Beechey Island: John Hartnell and William Braine of *Erebus* and John Torrington of *Terror*. Analysis of hair samples showed markedly raised levels of lead. In a groundbreaking and shocking book called *Frozen in Time*, Beattie and John Geiger advanced the theory that the copious quantities of lead used to seal the tinned-food cans had leached into the very things that were supposed to have kept the men alive, and so hastened their deaths.

Other circumstantial evidence would appear to support the poisoned-tin thesis. As Russell Potter emphasises, the diet would have differed quite markedly between decks. Whereas the bulk of the crew would have eaten a fairly basic diet of salt pork and hardtack, cooked by one of the company designated as mess-cook for the week, senior officers, who would have dined with the captain, would have had their own supplies, cooked by their own stewards. We know that Captain Crozier and Lieutenant Fairholme had procured goods from Fortnum & Mason, and they were almost certainly not the only ones. The officers would have had the best-quality tea, tobacco, wines and spirits – and also tinned food, then regarded as something of a luxury item. The Victory Point note records that of the deaths up till April 1848, nine were officers and fifteen were men. Bearing in mind that the proportion of officers to crew was about one to six, this is a startlingly high number of officers, and has been raised as further evidence that the tinned food could have been at fault.

Lead has been advanced as the culprit more recently, too, as more remains have come to light and forensic techniques have advanced. But the argument has also shifted a little. In 2008 William Battersby, James Fitzjames's biographer, while noting the high levels of the toxic metal found in the soft tissue of the dead men, pointed out that food from lead-sealed tins had been safely used on several previous expeditions, including the Clark Ross Antarctic voyage, and suggested that the likeliest source for those aboard *Erebus* and *Terror* was actually the hot-water system, with its lead pipes and tanks, which we know to have been modified for the Franklin expedition. In the interest of balance, it's only fair to mention that this suggestion, too, has been disputed. Peter Carney has argued that the ship was heated by exactly the same Sylvester System that had been used on the Antarctic expedition (in his opinion, the problem lay with the process by which ice was melted for drinking and washing), while research by Keith Millar, Adrian Bowman and others from the University of Glasgow has pointed out that, given the prevalence of lead piping in Victorian England, one would expect to find traces of the metal in human remains from that period.

An alternative theory has its roots in Sir James Ross and Francis McClintock's abortive search for the missing expedition in 1848. John Robertson, the surgeon who accompanied them, not only noted the impossibility of living off the land (they were 'not visited by either deer, hare, grouse,' he noted, 'nor were we able to provide a single fish'), but was highly critical of the provisions they had with them. These he described as being 'bad in quality and deficient in quantity, and the preserved meats were a disgrace to the contractor'. As for the lemon juice provided, this was found to have been poorly prepared and useless in preventing the spread of scurvy – the chronic lack of Vitamin C – the scourge of so many expeditions. Many of those on the expedition, including Robertson himself, were suffering badly by the time they got back to their ship.

It's therefore not surprising that McClintock's belief at the time – taken up later by one of the most respected of all Franklin scholars, Richard Cyriax, whose book, *Sir John Franklin's Last Arctic Expedition*, was first published in 1939 – was that the main cause of death was not food poisoning, but scurvy. Cyriax backed up his argument with testimony from the Inuit that they had seen white men with bad teeth and swollen gums (two obvious signs of the condition). One Inuit woman told the American explorer Frederick Schwatka, who went searching for Franklin remains in 1878, that the men she had met were thin and their mouths were 'dry and hard and black'. The discrepancy between the optimistic tone of the first Victory Point note, dated 28 May 1847, with no mention of any deaths, and that of the postscript, less than a year later, which lists twenty-four, suggests that that last winter in the ice was the killer. This would accord with the known deterioration of anti-scorbutic provisions like lemon juice over a period, and the inevitable diminishing supplies of fresh fruit and vegetables that would have yielded the much-needed Vitamin C. Cyriax also pointed out that scurvy tends to incubate over a long period, not showing itself for eighteen months or so, but that when it takes hold, it accelerates fast. This could account for the rapid increase in deaths in the third and fatal winter, and suggests that Crozier and the others felt they had no option but to evacuate the ships and try for survival on land.

The land journey would have tested the hardiest and fittest, let alone those fatally weakened by scurvy. Admiralty expeditions were not taught how to live off the land. The ships, in Russell Potter's words, 'were seen as powerful, fortified, mobile homes of discovery'. Everything they needed had been provided for them, so long as they stayed aboard. And once scurvy had taken hold, there would have been no chance of reversing it. As they walked, the effects would have worsened. Gums would have swollen and teeth loosened. Bleeding beneath the skin, breathlessness and overwhelming fatigue would have followed. Men would eventually have been unable to stand any longer. They would have fallen as they walked, and would have been left where they fell, by those who had not the strength to bury them.

Doubtless no single theory can be made to fit every fatality. A likely explanation therefore is necessarily also a broader one: that Franklin's men were weakened by the lack of a balanced diet and that this laid them open to infection and disease. In 2016 a team led by Jennie Christensen examined a toenail and thumbnail belonging to John Hartnell, one of the Beechey Island bodies. Nails retain the nutrients in a person's body, giving a record of an individual's health over the last months of their life. They found that Hartnell had died from tuberculosis (one sufferer had, of course, already been removed, soon after leaving Stromness). There was also significant evidence of zinc deficiency, which suggests that the nutritional content of the fresh or canned meat supplies was, from the outset, not at healthy levels. Research by Keith Millar, Adrian Bowman and others, based on the records of contemporary search expeditions, came to the conclusion that Franklin's men would have suffered from common respiratory and gastrointestinal disorders, exacerbated by the harsh conditions.

Scurvy would have been a significant contributory factor in the death-rate and the general lowering of fitness levels. The higher rate of death amongst officers was not due to their greater consumption of tinned food, they concluded, but could probably be explained by the fact that the officers did most of the hunting, and therefore spent more time exposed to the harsh conditions outside the ship.

Ultimately any attempt to find some answer, or some combination of circumstances, that might explain the fate of the expedition is a bit like navigating through the ice. As one lead closes, another opens up. A recent DNA study of skeletal remains, for example, came up with the shock finding that in four cases the bones showed no signs of the Y chromosome, indicating that these were the bones of European females. In fact the most likely explanation for the discrepancy is that studies of old DNA samples commonly fail to amplify the Y chromosome (the male sex chromosome), due to problems of the quantity or quality of material available. But the researchers involved have pointed out intriguingly that 'we cannot discard the ... analysis ... without noting that women are known to have served in disguise in the Royal Navy in the 17th and 18th centuries'; and, as examples, they cite Hannah Snell, Mary Lacy and Mary Ann Talbot – the last-named is said to have served on at least two ships during the Napoleonic Wars, revealing that she was a woman only after she had been wounded and had left the Navy. Whether or not there were women aboard *Erebus* and *Terror,* it's another intriguing twist in the ongoing search for explanations.

In the end, though, all that can be said for certain is that those who served on the Franklin expedition were simply in the wrong place at the wrong time. They ended up in the least hospitable corner of a remote archipelago at a time that even the local Inuit referred to as 'the years without summers'.

Whatever the possible reasons for their fate, the brutality of their predicament once they had abandoned the ships is appalling to imagine. As the masts of the ships that had been their home for three years disappeared from sight behind them, what possible hope could have kept them going? There was, at best, a weak sun above them and hard-packed snow and ice beneath, over which heavily laden sledges had to be hauled. At least on the ships they would have had some protection from the freezing winds. On the low, exposed, treeless island the cold must have been intolerable. Where did the will to live come from? Was there a single inspirational figure whose vision kept them going? Did Francis Crozier rise to the occasion and become that man? What hopes were raised when they encountered a party of Inuit, only to see them disappear after a brief exchange? Was that the moment they lost all hope, or had it gone long before? One hopes that the determination to survive, in-built in us all, was enough to stave off despair. But there is no way around it – theirs was a dreadful way to die.

It could be argued that lives might have been saved if rescue expeditions had been sent out earlier; that better mapping would have helped both them and their searchers; and that Franklin and the Admiralty should have attached more importance to the leaving of cairns indicating their route. There are those who blame Crozier for leading the survivors in the wrong direction after leaving the ship, despite his knowing that there were supplies left at Fury Beach by the Parry expedition in 1825 (supplies that were found to be perfectly good by a party forty-five years later). Instead he headed south and west, for one of the most difficult and dangerous rivers on the mainland, and a Hudson's Bay post that was 1,250 miles away. But then Crozier's options were few. Men, struggling with sledges carrying food and supplies, would have found it hard work in any direction, and Fury Beach was some way off. It is thought they took three boats with them (Hobson found one of them on King William Island and the Inuit said they had found two others), so the plan could well have been to find open water as soon as possible, where boats would have been a more comfortable and much faster means of transport.

The only way we will ever know what precisely was going through the minds of those leading the expedition would be if some new documentary evidence comes to light. The Royal Navy was punctilious in keeping records. Log books kept by the captain and mate, and Sick Books kept by the ship's surgeon, would have been among those routinely maintained on *Erebus* and *Terror* and, unless discipline had completely broken down, would have been maintained to the end. The marine archaeologist Ryan Harris has pointed out that ships' logs were written on linen-based paper that could have survived in the icy water. There are some who hold out hopes that these documents will be found on the ships; there are others who fear that the Inuit, who never had paper themselves, would simply have discarded any records they came across. Most likely they were blown away long ago. But history abhors a vacuum, and as long as we don't know, there will always be those who want to know. A disaster of this scale looks for an explanation of equal magnitude. They must not have died in vain.

Charles Francis Hall's 1864 memoir *Life with the Eskimaux* – for which this illustration forms the frontispiece – recounts the friendships he made with the Inuit as he sought to unravel the mystery of the Franklin expedition.

CHAPTER 17

THE INUIT STORY

Good Friday, 21 April 1848 was the last night the expedition was known to have spent aboard the ship. Article 11 of the Admiralty's instructions, 'The two ships are on no account to separate', had been obeyed to the letter. *Erebus* and *Terror* had stayed together to the end. Now they were left to drift in the ice, empty and deserted, at the mercy of the elements.

Or perhaps not. Research, based on close examination of oral Inuit testimony, backs up a different scenario. John Rae had shown the importance of listening to the Inuit – indeed, that was how he learned the first news of the expedition's fate. Much more information was gathered by two *kabloonas* who came after him, and who, like Rae, lived closely with the Inuit and learned their language.

One was Charles Francis Hall, who believed God was calling him to find remaining members of the Franklin expedition who, he was sure, were still alive and living with the native people. An American of the frontier kind, Hall had been at times a blacksmith, an engraver and a publisher. In 1860 he hitched a ride on an American whaler, which set him down on Baffin Island. He found no Frankliniana, but stayed for two years and made lifelong friendships with two natives, Too-koo-li-too (Taqulittuq) and Ebierbing

(Ipivik). It wasn't until 1869, during a second Arctic voyage, that he reached the holy grail of Franklin-hunters, King William Island. His Inuit hosts were not keen to spend time trawling Franklin sites on the island. There was poor hunting there and they needed to get on with their own lives. Feeling frustrated, Hall never got to all the sites, but he amassed a wealth of stories from his hosts, which provided the groundwork for some very interesting conjectures.

These were added to in 1878 by another American, Lieutenant Frederick Schwatka of the US Army. He led an investigative exped-ition, not as a result of divine guidance this time, but through the sponsorship of the American Geographical Society. After spending a summer combing King William Island and the Adelaide Penin-sula, and working closely with the Inuit, he was able to corroborate many of the stories that had been told to Rae and Hall. Schwatka it was who discovered, among many other relics, a skeleton that proved to be that of Lieutenant John Irving. It was one of only two bodies from the Franklin expedition to be repatriated, and now lies buried in Dean Cemetery in Edinburgh.

David C. Woodman, in his 1991 book *Unravelling the Franklin Mys-tery*, drew on all these records to compile an alternative account of the last days of the ships and crew. It is not definitive – no account of the Franklin expedition ever can be – but it is thought-provoking. As he concludes: 'For one hundred and forty years the account of the tragedy given to Rae by In-nook-poo-zhe-jook and See-u-ti-chu has been accepted and endorsed ... it was a remarkably accurate recital of events. But it was not the whole story.'

Central to Inuit testimony, gathered by Schwatka and Hall, is that they first saw *Erebus* and *Terror* in late 1848, or even 1849, *after* the ships had been apparently abandoned. Not only that, but all their accounts agreed that the ships were manned at the time: there was activity aboard, and indeed some of the Inuit went onto the ships and talked with the crew. Yet the Victory Point note states clearly that all the remaining members of the expedition left the ships on 22 April 1848 to head south. There is no reason, however, to assume that they all stayed together. Some clearly struggled as far the mainland, finally perishing at a place that Schwatka christened 'Starvation Cove', but if the Inuit had seen men on the ships as late as 1849, then it would suggest that at least some others might have returned.

Woodman found a powerful piece of evidence for the idea that there had been a return to the ships. This was the discovery, by Lieutenant Schwatka, of a grave at Victory Point, identified by a medal in the shreds of uniform clinging to the bones as that of Lieutenant Irving of the *Terror*. The grave was properly dug and had heavy boulders around it. It must have been excavated by a party of fit men. But when? Irving was alive and well when he was mentioned in the Victory Point note, so he cannot have died before they left in April 1848. The discovery of his grave is proof for Woodman that Irving, and presumably others, came back and reoccupied at least one of the ships, bearing out the repeated Inuit accounts of meeting white men on the north-east part of King William Island long after they were supposed to have departed. It led Woodman to back up the theory that the party of 105 didn't actually get very far before they split, some going on south to find animals to hunt, some heading east in search of Hudson's Bay Company depots, and others returning to the ship.

Taking all this information, rumour and folk tale together, it looks as if the most likely scenario of the last days of the men and ships of the Franklin expedition goes something like this. In April 1848, ten months after Franklin's death, Crozier and Fitzjames lead the remaining men, with three sledges, some 15 miles across the ice to Victory Point. Here Lieutenant Irving is deputed to go to the cairn a few miles away and fetch one of the two 'All well' notes left eleven months earlier by Gore and Des Voeux. The note's cheerful message is amended by Fitzjames, in the light of the grim events of the last winter. Crozier counter-signs it, in a slightly weaker hand, adding that they are leaving the next day for Back's Fish River. They leave a lot of material at Victory Point, presumably to lighten the load. This would account for the piles of blankets and ropes found by Hobson. They must have made 50 miles down the coast before they stopped, leaving the boat behind, probably as shelter and to further lighten the load. This is where the party first split, with those still fit enough taking some of the provisions and continuing south, possibly splitting again as they headed for Back's Fish River. The others, maybe because they had scurvy so badly they were unable to move, stayed behind, whilst others may have been well enough to stagger back to the ship.

A line of skeletons marks the progress south. One found east of Cape Herschel is probably that of Thomas Armitage, who had Peglar's notebook beside him where he fell. Another body, believed at the time to be Henry Le Vesconte, was recovered by Hall and was later returned to England. Two skeletons were found by the Amundsen expedition in 1904. That the last survivors crossed the Strait, discovering the Northwest Passage as they went, is borne out by the findings of several bodies on the mainland, at Starvation Cove, only a few miles from the Back's Fish River. This was the end of the road for the southern party.

The handful of men who, if Inuit testimony is right, had remained on King William Island and were seen back at the ship almost certainly survived a fourth winter, before leaving the ships – again described in Inuit testimony – to shoot caribou, but never returning.

There is no evidence to suggest that by the end of 1850 any of the 129 men of the Franklin expedition were left alive. Which means that, of all the rescue operations sent out, only the very earliest would have stood any chance of finding them alive.

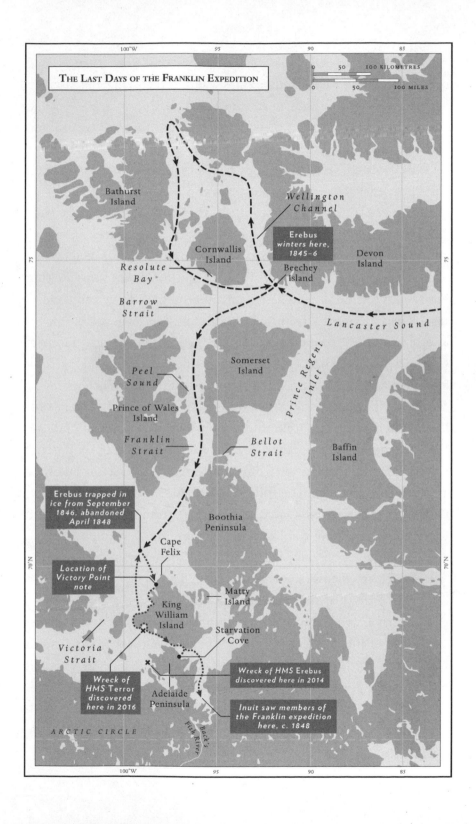

THE LAST DAYS OF THE FRANKLIN EXPEDITION

100°W   95   90   85

0   50   100 KILOMETRES
0   50   100 MILES

Bathurst
Island

*Wellington
Channel*

Cornwallis
Island

Erebus
*winters here,
1845–6*

Devon
Island

Beechey
Island

*Resolute
Bay*

*Barrow
Strait*

Lancaster Sound

*Peel
Sound*

Somerset
Island

Prince of Wales
Island

Prince Regent Inlet

*Franklin
Strait*

*Bellot
Strait*

Baffin
Island

Erebus trapped in
ice from September
1846, abandoned
April 1848

Boothia
Peninsula

Cape
Felix

Location of
Victory Point
note

Matty
Island

King
William
Island

Starvation
Cove

*Victoria
Strait*

*Wreck of HMS Erebus
discovered here in 2014*

Wreck of
HMS Terror
discovered
here in 2016

Adelaide
Peninsula

Back's Fish River

Inuit saw members of
the Franklin expedition
here, c. 1848

ARCTIC CIRCLE

100°W   95   90   85

What of *Erebus* and *Terror*? The presence of a ship, or ships, had been a consistent part of Inuit stories; there is recurring and fascinating mention of men on a seal hunt seeing a ship at a place called Utjulik, 'place of bearded seals', some way south of King William Island. The Inuit boarded it and later told Charles Hall that they had found it deserted, save for the body of a very large white man lying on the floor: 'there was flesh about this dead man, that is, his remains quite perfect – it took 5 men to lift him. The place smelt very bad.' They gave enough detail about the interior of the ship, and the sort of things they found on board, to identify it as either *Erebus* or *Terror*.

A strange twist to the story was the sighting of two ships looking very much like *Erebus* and *Terror*, on an iceberg off Newfoundland in 1851. They were seen from a passing ship, the *Renovation*, but no attempt was made to approach them. In the 1920s Commander Rupert Gould, who liked what he called 'Unexplained Facts', looked carefully at the Admiralty's report on the sighting and, far from dismissing it, came up with some intriguing findings. The two ships were very similar in appearance to *Erebus* and *Terror*, both flush-decked and one slightly bigger than the other. They were close together on floating ice, so they must have come from somewhere in the Arctic, and they appeared to have been carefully dismantled. Neither was a whaler, and both were deserted. Gould studied the currents in the Arctic and found that there were counter-currents running west to east, which could quite plausibly have carried the abandoned ships out into the Atlantic. From what we know from recent discoveries, they could not have been Franklin's ships, but in that case what were they?

Both *Erebus* and *Terror* probably disappeared soon after their crews. Very little of the fabric of the ships, or their contents, was found in Inuit communities. If they had remained afloat for long they would have been stripped, but the likes of Hall and Schwatka found no evidence of this. That they didn't stay above water for long chimes with Inuit stories of one ship sinking after being crushed in the ice, and the other, probably *Erebus*, having been holed by mistake as the natives were prizing out firewood, and sinking in water so shallow that the tips of her masts were showing above the water.

The whole relationship with the Inuit remains a mystery King William Island did not offer much hunting, but there was enough game to attract parties of Inuit, and in the almost two years they were trapped in the ice, it seems odd if no one aboard *Erebus* and *Terror* sought Inuit help, to trade food and glean any information as to where they were and how they might get out. Arctic explorers like Parry and James Ross had set an example in engaging with the local people. We know that some of the officers on *Erebus* were compiling an Inuit phrasebook in Disko Bay, so the intention to make use of any contact with them must have been there. Why then, when they took to the ice in 1848, did they seem so unprepared? Could it be that Franklin, who had been criticised by some after his disastrous Coppermine River expedition of 1819–22 for sticking too closely to Navy orders, still lacked the flexibility of outlook that would have encouraged him to make the most of Inuit expertise?

Tragically, it appears that by the time it was needed, most of the opportunity for local contact had been neglected for too long. The expedition had congratulated itself on being so well provisioned and so well equipped, and yet, where it really mattered, there was a fatal weakness. They thought they had everything they required, and seem to have continued to believe that until it was too late. When they left their wooden fortresses and exposed themselves to the land, what they needed most of all was local intelligence. But by then they were already dying. The Inuit must have known that. The state of the men must have alarmed them, but probably also repelled them. The time for both sides to help each other had passed.

At a celebration dinner of the American Geographical Society in October 1880, Lieutenant Schwatka told his audience that he considered that the destruction of any significant Franklin records had been established beyond reasonable doubt, and in his book *The Long Arctic Search* he concluded that the 'Franklin problem' had been settled 'in all its important aspects'. The Secretary of the Royal Geographical Society in London seemed to endorse his view. Writing in praise of Schwatka's journey 'without parallel', Sir Clements Markham paid tribute on behalf of his fellow Englishmen, who would 'always cherish a feeling of gratitude for the kindly deed of the brave Americans, who tenderly collected and buried some of the bones of our heroes – a task which, we well know, entailed no small amount of peril and hardship'.

The indignation that fuelled the search, the wounded national pride that gave it such an imperative, and the appetite of newspapers, publishers and their readers for the grisly details had all diminished. There was a palpable sense of closure. Thirty-five years after Franklin's expedition set out, the search for explanations had been as fruitless as the search for survivors.

One thing that remained undiminished was Jane Franklin's energy. She may have reluctantly accepted the loss of her husband, but in a way it was easier for her to work on his reputation with him gone. The unpleasantness in Van Diemen's Land had lost its sting. The murky allegations of cannibalism had been tastefully set aside. The suggestion that her husband had been too old or too unfit to lead the expedition had been subsumed by his fate. Her task now was to enshrine his reputation in something more permanent. His body might never be found, but she would make his likeness live for ever in stone and bronze. With the help of some powerful friends, she successfully lobbied Parliament to vote a £2,000 contribution towards a statue of Sir John. It was unveiled in 1866 on Waterloo Place in London, beside the elegant façade of the Athenaeum Club, of which Franklin had been a founder member. The sculptor, Matthew Noble, has Sir John standing tall and defiant with the single word 'Franklin' incised below him. In the words of a modern commentator, Robert Douglas-Fairhurst: 'In life a podgy, balding man of middling height, in death he was transformed into a firm-jawed figure eight feet tall, perched on an imposing granite plinth.'

A relief panel depicts his burial in the ice, his coffin, half-draped with a flag, mourners standing on either side. This is the sculptor's imagination at work, as the place and indeed the cause of Franklin's death remain an unsolved mystery. In an inscription on the marble plinth below, Franklin's rehabilitation is complete. The Man Who Ate His Boots becomes 'The Great Arctic Navigator' who 'with his brave companions ... sacrificed their lives to complete the discovery of the North West Passage'.

This latter claim was never positively established, but Lady Jane defended it with the ferocity of a mother on a nest. She vigorously attacked Robert McClure for his, proven, claim to have been the first to discover the Passage, albeit by sledge and boat, in 1853–4. She was said to have been infuriated by the inscription on the Franklin statue in Hobart, Tasmania, which had the temerity to claim that Sir John had 'lost his life trying to find the North West Passage'. He did not just *try,* he *succeeded,* was her indignant response.

The finest memorial, in my opinion, although it is dedicated only to the memory of the officers, is a marble relief carved by Richard Westmacott that stands at the entrance to the chapel of the Royal Naval College in Greenwich. On either side of it are two figures, in profile. One represents hope and the other despair. Lady Franklin didn't much care for this less-than-triumphant embodiment of the grim realities of the expedition. As Andrew Lambert, Franklin's biographer, writes, 'it fell far short of the heroic image Jane required'. It stands above the resting place of one of only two members of the expedition whose bodies were identified and returned to England. A marble plaque reads: 'Beneath lie the remains of one of Franklin's companions who perished in the Arctic Regions.' These bones, retrieved by Charles Hall, were for a long time assumed to be those of Lieutenant Le Vesconte, but have now been established almost certainly as those of Harry Goodsir, the assistant surgeon on *Erebus*. For a long time this evocative memorial, probably considered a bit morbid at the time, was hidden away behind the altar of the chapel.

By the beginning of the 1880s most of the main players in the great Northwest Passage mission were gone. Not just Franklin and Crozier, but John Barrow, who died in 1848, around the same time as the leaders of his much-vaunted expedition were dying in the ice. Francis Beaufort, Edward Parry and both Sir John and Sir James Ross had been dead for almost twenty years. Of the old guard, only Edward Sabine was still alive. He was ninety-two, the sole survivor of that golden era of exploration that began in the wake of Waterloo.

The febrile atmosphere that had surrounded the search and its dreadful findings had subsided by now. Instead of the horrors, so graphically captured by Landseer, there was instead a weary resignation, laced more with nostalgia than anger. In 1874 the new mood was captured by John Everett Millais in his painting 'North West Passage'. An old sea captain with a sad and faraway look in his eyes sits at his desk, on which a map lies open. His daughter rests her hand on his as she sits on the floor, leaning up against him, reading a ship's log book. This was the late-Victorian image of the Franklin expedition. A little sentimental perhaps, but conveying a sense of haunting sadness – the loss of a dream. But for the energetic Lady Franklin, the confirmation of her husband's death consolidated her status as never before. She was now an international celebrity, universally admired for her persistence, loyalty and dedication. Despite the money she'd spent on the search, she was able to lease a grand house in Kensington Gore, the same road in London on which the Royal Geographical Society was later to set up its headquarters. Here she lived in some style, networking vigorously, giving dinner parties, keeping an eye on the wording of tributes and memorials and on the factual accuracy of the succession of books about the expedition. In his death, as in his life, she continued to manage her husband.

On 18 July 1875, at the age of eighty-three, Jane Franklin, in many ways the central figure in this otherwise all-male drama, finally ran out of steam. She died refusing to the last to take the medicine in which she never had much faith. The obituaries were sententious: 'our regrets will be softened by the reflection that death may reveal to her what remains of that Arctic mystery which was the problem and purpose of her life,' read one. But nothing would have delighted her more than to know that Francis McClintock, Richard Collinson and Erasmus Ommanney had been amongst those who carried her coffin at the funeral, and that Joseph Hooker and William Hobson had been there to pay tribute.

A fortnight after her death the final unequivocal triumph of her campaign for the glorification of her husband came with the unveiling of his bust in Westminster Abbey. It stands just inside the west door, in an alabaster niche. McClintock has a memorial plaque below. Dr John Rae, the bearer of bad tidings, has a stone on the floor.

The memorial bears an inscription written by the man who married Franklin's niece, Alfred Lord Tennyson:

> Not here: the white north has thy bones; and thou,
> Heroic sailor-soul,
> Art passing on thine happier voyage now,
> Toward no earthly pole.

These few lines epitomise the mixed-up emotions that made Franklin such an exemplar of the Victorian spirit. The affirmation of a sacrifice that could never be judged on earth, but only in heaven. A sacrifice that rose above failure to touch the sublime. Something that united a nation in grief, but in that grief was glory.

The same sentiments would surface again to exalt another heroic failure, Robert Falcon Scott, whose death on the way back from the

South Pole in 1912 provoked a similar national trauma. And, a few years later still, on the battlefields of France: *Dulce et decorum est pro patria mori.*

In Waterloo Place in London, across the road from where the first Franklin statue stands, is a memorial to Captain Scott. His failure was to be beaten to the South Pole. Franklin's was to be beaten to the first sea crossing of the Northwest Passage. The man who beat Scott to the Pole was Roald Amundsen. The first man to cross the Northwest Passage by sea was Roald Amundsen. He has no memorial in London.

The first dive on the newly rediscovered *Erebus*.

CHAPTER 18

RESURRECTION

———————⊃●⊂———————

In the 1920s, as the world regained its balance after the First World War, curiosity about Franklin and his fate began to resurface, but it was, as Franklin scholar Russell Potter explains, 'a new kind of curiosity – one not driven by the hope of rescuing anyone or resolving anything, but a sort of restless poking at the edge of the known'.

The impetus for the modern era of Franklin enquiry came not so much from British national pride as from a growing sense of Canadian national identity. When Franklin set out for the Northwest Passage, the nation didn't exist. It wasn't until 1867, twenty years after his death, that a confederation of colonies was amalgamated into the Dominion of Canada. By the start of the twentieth century it had been extended westwards to include nine provinces. In the Great War many Canadians fought and died with the allies, and in 1920 their sacrifice was recognised and the young country was admitted to the League of Nations.

The fate of Franklin fascinated a number of Canadians. Inextricably linked with the fascination they had for the remote and secretive Far North, it was a mystery that had still not been fully solved and therefore required further unravelling. Typical of those who took up this challenge was Lachlan Burwash, a government man working for the Northwest Territories Department of the Interior to help survey the vast agglomeration of lands and islands in the Far North. Whilst exploring on King William Island he heard from the Inuit of a stack of wooden crates found on Matty Island, in the James Ross Strait. This sparked off speculation that one or other of the ships might have taken the eastern route past King William Island.

In the 1930s William 'Paddy' Gibson of the Hudson's Bay Company paid several visits from his base in Gjoa Haven to the area where the last of the Back's Fish River party had died. He scrupulously collected and buried the bones that he found scattered across the surface, among them seven skulls.

In the late 1940s Henry Larsen of the Royal Canadian Mounted Police flew in to King William Island and landed near Terror Bay to drop off fuel. In the days that followed he set out on foot for a careful examination of the western coastline. At Cape Felix he found, embedded between two mossy stones, the remains of a skull, later identified as that of a young white man. It was further north than any other Franklin remains had been found.

Light aircraft and float-planes extended the range of exploration, making best use of the relatively short summer months, and the suitably named Robert Pilot, in his time as Commissioner of the Northwest Territories, set up a group called the Franklin Probe. Among other things, they followed up on the location of a possible Franklin funeral, based on Inuit stories of a man being carried by *kabloonas* onto the Boothia Peninsula and buried with a gun salute.

All these efforts produced new and sometimes conflicting evidence, but nothing that really challenged what Rae and Hall and Schwatka had already discovered. They were largely the work of enthusiastic amateurs who found clues but offered no solutions.

In the early 1980s the approach changed. The scope of the search become more focused and professional, with some breathtaking results. The anthropologist Owen Beattie began an intensive inspection of King William Island. Examining the areas of interest carefully and methodically, and usually on foot, he came up with mute evidence of the horror of those final months. He found femurs with cut-marks that suggested cannibalism and bone fragments that indicated that skulls had been deliberately broken.

It was Beattie's patient examination of the sites on King William Island that led him to one of the most sensational revelations of the entire Franklin search. In 1984 he flew with his team to Beechey Island, with permits to exhume the three bodies buried there since 1846. The first coffin they opened was that of John Torrington, the twenty-year-old stoker on HMS *Terror*. In their book *Frozen in Time*, Beattie and John Geiger describe the smell from the rotted blue fabric covering the coffin, then the easing-off of the lid, as a black thundercloud hung overhead and the walls of the tent they had built to protect the site flapped and snapped in the rising wind. Once separated from the grip of the permafrost, the coffin was revealed to be strong, the box and lid made of mahogany. How many coffins did the Franklin expedition bring with them, I wonder? How could they possibly have been loaded aboard without puncturing the overriding optimism of the enterprise?

Photographs show how disturbingly well the icy conditions had preserved John Torrington. Disturbingly because he looks so young. Disturbingly because he might have died yesterday. His eyes are open, staring back at us from ancient sockets, and his lips are drawn back and his teeth revealed, as if he might have been halfway through a sentence at the moment of death. It took Beattie and his colleague Arne Carlson four hours to complete an autopsy: 'all internal structures were completely frozen. It was necessary to thaw each organ before samples could be collected.'

The next grave to be opened was that of John Hartnell, an able seaman on *Erebus*. The coffin was buried less than 3 feet below the surface, half as deep as Torrington's. Beattie found a shirt cuff that had come free from the body. It was impossible to make out any of Hartnell's features until the ice that had contained him was unfrozen. Warm water was poured gently over the ice, and gradually his face became clear. It looked more grotesque than Torrington's, more like a carnival mask, and more pained. One of his eye sockets was empty and his lips were parted, as if he had died with a stifled scream. He, like Torrington, was exhaustively photographed before being reburied. The photographs went around the world. They were the first direct likenesses of anyone on the Franklin expedition to be seen since the daguerreotype portraits of the officers on *Erebus* went public in 1851. Those had been the confident 'befores'. These were the awful 'afters'.

Two years later, in 1986, Beattie and his team returned to Beechey Island to complete the work of examining John Hartnell's remains and to exhume the body of the third man buried there: William Braine, one of the seven Royal Marines aboard *Erebus*. It took twenty-four hours to dig through the permafrost to reveal Hartnell's coffin. What emerged as they slowly uncovered the body was something no one had expected. From Hartnell's chest to his abdomen there ran a Y-shaped sutured incision, indicating that very shortly after his death an autopsy had been performed: presumably the ship's doctor had been worried about the cause of death and the potential for the spread of infection. William Braine's body when exhumed was estimated to have weighed only 88 lb at his death. Beattie and Geiger described it as 'literally a skin-covered skeleton'. All three men had been taken prematurely, and whatever brought them to their deaths had happened less than a year after they had left London.

Beattie's work on Beechey Island reopened the whole debate on canned food as the cause of the expedition's fatalities, for although the probable cause of death in all three cases was tuberculosis, each corpse was discovered to contain levels of lead that were three to four times what might have been expected. Whilst on the island Beattie examined the cairn of discarded tins and found that the lead-solder used to seal the tins had been applied thickly and sloppily, suggesting that it was this extra amount of lead that could have contaminated the food. Recent research has challenged that theory, but the publicity at the time gave a tremendous boost to international interest in the expedition's fate.

From the 1990s onwards, David Woodman redoubled his energies in searching the area where he hoped *Erebus* might lie. He deployed sonar scanners and metal detectors, but the area to be covered was vast and difficult to work and his best efforts proved unfruitful. Large areas were, however, examined and could be eliminated from any further searches. The momentum continued to grow. *Erebus* must be down there somewhere. It just needed more resources, better equipment and the same sort of determination to recover her that had sent all the Arctic expeditions out in the first place.

In 1994 a CBC documentary entitled *The Mysterious Franklin Disappearance* drew upon the searches made on Beechey Island by a man called Barry Ranford. Margaret Atwood, who wrote a foreword to Beattie and Geiger's book on the Beechey Island findings, took part, as did Pierre Berton, author of *The Arctic Grail*. Their involvement confirmed that Franklin's fate was now a Canadian story. It had taken place in their country, and the fact that so much vital testimony came from their Inuit countrymen needed to be reasserted.

In August 1997 a discreetly produced but significant agreement between the British and Canadian governments moved the process forward. It was called 'A Memorandum of Understanding between the Governments of Great Britain and Canada Pertaining to the Shipwrecks HMS *Erebus* and HMS *Terror*'. By its terms, 'Britain, as owner of the wrecks, hereby assigns custody and control of the wrecks and their contents to the Government of Canada.'

A later clause further defined the ownership issue: 'Once either of the wrecks has been positively located and identified, Britain will assign to Canada everything recovered from that wreck and its contents.' Exceptions were made for any gold recovered or any artefacts identified as being of outstanding significance to the Royal Navy. Canada, for its part, would ensure that anyone dealing with the wrecks would 'treat reverently, and refrain from bringing to the surface, any human remains that are discovered at the sites of the wrecks or in their vicinity'. Meanwhile the creation of a majority Inuit territory in April 1999 underlined the growing concern and respect for their part in the story. From then on, Franklin's graveyard was no longer in the Northwest Territories. It was in Nunavut.

Encouraged by this transfer of ownership, the pace of the Franklin search accelerated through the millennium. Between the mid-1990s and 2008 twenty-one expeditions went north. Most were privately financed. They ranged from the sledge-borne or snowmobile explorations of David Woodman and Tom Gross, to an Irish-Canadian documentary team, and an American Express-sponsored expedition retracing Franklin's route with the motto 'Long Live Dreams'.

A quantum leap came in 2008. The previous year the Russians, whose interest in the Arctic had so alarmed Barrow and the Admiralty, had executed the eye-catching stunt of planting a titanium flag, complete with pole and pedestal, in a capsule on the seabed at the North Pole. It was a highly effective announcement of their intention to claim rights over Arctic waters, and brought a robust response from Canada's Conservative Party Prime Minister, Stephen Harper. He made it clear that the Arctic was to be a priority: 'Canada has a choice when it comes to defending our sovereignty over the Arctic; either we use it or we lose it.' But it was more complicated than it sounded. Theoretically each neighbouring country has a 12-mile offshore area of control. Beyond that, the waters are international. Which means that Lancaster Sound and Barrow Strait are broad enough to have an international, rather than simply Canadian, waterway running through them. And, with the warming of the Arctic, the waters of the Northwest Passage could be ice-free for longer, making it an attractive alternative for Atlantic–Pacific traffic, potentially shaving ten days off the Panama Canal route for some operators.

Nevertheless, Harper went ahead and, as well as staking a Canadian claim to the seabed rights at the North Pole, announced plans to build eight Arctic offshore patrol ships, contesting the American claim that the 950 miles of the Northwest Passage, from the Beaufort Sea to Baffin Bay, were an international waterway. To rub in his message, Harper made a point of visiting the Far North for a few days each summer, taking with him some sweeteners, such as money for a new airport or a new road.

One of the side-effects of the reawakened sensitivity to all matters Arctic was that public money was made available to Parks Canada to fund a serious government-backed search for the whereabouts of Franklin's ships. The area where *Erebus* and *Terror* were likely to lie had been a National Historic Site since 1992. The time had come to find out exactly where they were.

The first expedition, led by Robert Grenier and Ryan Harris, with the Inuit historian Louie Kamookak as consultant, went north in the brief summer window of 2008. It identified sites that might be productively worked on later. The next year no search was funded. In 2010 a wreck was discovered by a Parks Canada team further west at Mercy Bay, off Banks Island. It was neither *Erebus* nor *Terror*, but that of HMS *Investigator*, sent out to find Franklin and abandoned to the ice by Captain McClure.

In that same year, 2010, the enterprise was joined by two multi-millionaire philanthropists, Jim Balsillie, founder and CEO of the company that developed the BlackBerry, and the entrepreneur Tim Macdonald. They announced plans to create the Arctic Research Foundation and fit out a ship specially designed for the search. It was to be named the MV *Martin Bergmann*, in recognition of a Canadian scientist and marine biologist who died in 2011 at the age of fifty-five. The net was tightening.

Parks Canada archaeologists returned to the area for the next three seasons, but bad weather, lack of proper charts and the difficulty of precision-trawling over such a wide stretch of water became increasingly frustrating. The conditions in the summer of 2014, however, were predicted to be good and, christening it the 2014 Victoria Strait Expedition, the Canadian government piled in with resources. The Canadian Navy, Coastguard, Ice Service, Hydrographic Service and even the Space Agency were just some of the government bodies engaged to assist with the search.

The result was an armada reminiscent of the great searches of the 1850s, but with high-tech twenty-first-century equipment. A powerful Canadian Coastguard ice-breaker, the *Sir Wilfrid Laurier*, was at the centre of operations, carrying two self-propelled underwater robots, one of them a 7½-foot-long canary-coloured torpedo called an AUV (autonomous underwater vehicle), carrying sonar equipment that was so state-of-the-art that it had never been tested before. And just to give a nod to historical continuity, one of Parks Canada's smaller auxiliary boats was called *Investigator*. Unlike her 1850s predecessor, she was to be the lucky one.

Despite initially optimistic forecasts, things looked unpromising. Ice filled Victoria Strait on a scale not seen for five years. This confined a number of the ships to the area around Queen Maud Gulf. It was some way south of the proposed search area, but it had at least remained ice-free.

Doug Stenton, an archaeologist on the search, was making the best of the enforced change of plan by reconnoitring a collection of small, wispy islands around Wilmot and Crampton Bay, just off the coast of the Adelaide Peninsula. His plan was to find a good site for a GPS that could receive satellite signals showing water depth and navigability of these trickily shallow channels. Noticing signs of an abandoned Inuit ring tent on one of the islands, he requested the Coastguard pilot, Andrew Stirling, to drop down so that he could take a closer look. Whilst Stenton was taking photographs and measurements of the site, Stirling was wandering along the shore, killing time. He was brought up short by the sight of a rusted metal object sticking half out of the sand. Though his job was that of pilot, he had learned enough about archaeology to know an odd thing when he saw one.

What he was looking at was a U-shaped piece of iron, long and heavy and rusted. He called Stenton over to take a look. The veteran archaeologist was both puzzled and impressed. After photographing it, he took it from Stirling and examined it carefully. He found what he was looking for – the distinctive broad arrow mark denoting Royal Navy property. Nearby, Stirling had found a weathered piece of wood with a rusty nail embedded. All the indications were that this was a substantial piece of equipment, not from a boat or sledge or part of an encampment, but from the deck of a ship. An old ship. Once they were back on board the *Sir Wilfrid Laurier*, fellow archaeologist Jonathan Moore looked on his computer. He found the detailed plans of the Franklin ships, the same ones that I had seen at the National Maritime Museum in Woolwich. It took him about half an hour before he identified that what Sterling had found on the beach did indeed correspond to something on one of the doomed vessels. It was a davit pintle, a piece of the gear used to raise and lower boats off the side of the mother-ship.

What excited everyone on the *Sir Wilfrid Laurier* that evening was not just the discovery of the object itself, but the implications of finding this particular piece of equipment in this particular location. The pintle was too heavy to have drifted far, too heavy to be blown by the wind. Wherever it came from must be close. Probably very close.

They didn't have to wait long. It was 1 September when the pintle was discovered. Sure enough, on 2 September, as the search area was rapidly reconfigured and the laborious business of 'lawn-mowing' the ocean began again, sonar images revealed that they had been right.

There was a ship down there, 36 feet below them. Upright on the sea floor.

Absolute confirmation of the find had to wait until 7 September, when a remote operating vehicle (ROV) with a camera attached was launched into the water. The sea was becoming rougher and choppier, and visibility murkier by the moment. The suspense on the *Sir Wilfrid Laurier* was screwed tight, until the first video close-ups brought absolute clarification that the hulk on the seabed was indeed one of Franklin's ships, her hull broken at the stern, but otherwise looking like it did on the day she was born. Bill Noon, captain of the *Sir Wilfrid Laurier*, was moved to tears. He had thought that the ice in Victoria Strait had kept them away from the discovery area, but in fact it had done exactly the opposite. 'Somebody was pushing us to an answer,' he said at the time. 'Somebody had waited long enough and wanted to solve the riddle.'

As one mystery was solved, a host of others presented themselves. The ship had drifted further than anyone had expected, except the Inuit, who had been right all along. How had she ended up as far south as Utjulik? Was she sailed south or did the ice take her there? Were there men on board to the end, or had the ship been long abandoned by the time she reached her final resting place? And then there were the intriguing possibilities. What items might still be aboard? How well would the freezing Arctic waters have preserved them? Most tantalising of all, if she turned out to be *Erebus*, was it just conceivable that archaeologists might one day find the body of Sir John Franklin, not buried on the Boothia Peninsula as suggested by some Inuit stories, but lying in a coffin deep in the hold of his flagship, awaiting a repatriation that was never to happen?

On 9 September 2014, at a press conference in Ottawa, Prime Minister Harper announced to the world that one of Franklin's ships had been found. It took a few days longer, and a series of dives by the underwater archaeologists, to confirm beyond doubt that it was not just Franklin's, but James Clark Ross's, George Haye's and Philip Broke's ship that had been found.

All who had ever served on her were long dead, but as the glasses were raised in Canada and around the world, *Erebus* was born again.

The ruins of Northumberland House, a shelter constructed for Franklin in the 1850s in the desperate hope he was still alive, serves as a poignant reminder of *Erebus*'s last voyage.

BACK IN THE NORTHWEST PASSAGE

———◁▷◁▷———

'Ah, for just one time I would take the Northwest Passage
To find the hand of Franklin reaching for the Beaufort Sea
Tracing one warm line through a land so wide and savage
And make a Northwest Passage to the sea.'

I'm singing lustily the chorus of this Stan Rogers classic in the bar of *Akademik Sergey Vavilov*, an ice-strengthened Russian survey ship in Prince Regent Inlet, Nunavut, Canada. It's August 2017, mid-evening, and the sun is still some way above the horizon, sending shafts of intense gold light through the thick glass of the windows. Tomorrow we shall make our way through the Bellot Strait, which will take us into Peel Sound and very close to the heart of the Franklin story. Singing along with me, to the accompaniment of Russell Potter's guitar, are some of the ninety-five excited Franklin buffs who are here in this short window of Arctic summer to see for themselves the landmarks they have read about. To see what Franklin and his men would have seen and, hopefully, to make a little more sense of the glory and the disaster.

I was lucky to get on this trip. This is the Northwest Passage and, despite all the advantages of modern technology, the power of the elements restricts most of these cruises to a narrow August–September schedule. And such is the enthusiasm for all things Franklin that the ships are booked up a year in advance. Hearing of my interest rather late in the day, One Ocean Expeditions have done all they can to squeeze me aboard. 'Squeeze' being the operative word, as the only vacant corner they can find is the currently unoccupied pilot's cabin. It's tiny, and the shower in the bathroom is one of those in which you have to run around to get wet, but it's up on the lofty deck-six level, halfway between the bridge and the bar.

> *'Westward from the Davis Strait, 'tis there 'twas said to lie*
> *The sea route to the Orient for which so many died,*
> *Seeking gold and glory, leaving weathered, broken bones*
> *And a long-forgotten lonely cairn of stones.'*

'Altogether now!'

> *'Ah, for just one time I would take the Northwest Passage.'*

Five days ago I was looking at the Davis Strait from 35,000 feet above. I always try for a window seat when I fly, and three and a half hours out of Heathrow I was rewarded with a thrilling view of the Greenland coast. Everyone else was staring at screens or trying to fall asleep, but I couldn't take my eyes off this most majestic of islands. We hurtled across it, clearing the east coast not far south of Disko Bay, where once Franklin and his men joked and wrote their last letters home, and shot ducks and arranged to meet up in Russia in a year's time.

The connecting flight from Edmonton to Yellowknife and Resolute Bay in a plane with a polar bear on its tailfin offered more window-fare. Prairie fields, farmhouses and dotted woodland gave way to lake and forest. Around Yellowknife I could see the scorch-marks of a fierce fire season. On the last lap to Resolute the trees vanished and we were flying over a seemingly endless, forbiddingly inhospitable area of tundra. Glacial flutes – grooves scored out of the rock by ice-action – ran for hundreds of miles in long parallel lines, dotted with ice-lakes. A hard, blank land, aptly named 'the Barrens'.

We land at Resolute Bay less than thirty-six hours after leaving London. I'm on Cornwallis Island, which *Erebus* and *Terror* were the first ships to discover. My ship, the *Akademik Sergey Vavilov*, is solid and stout, rather than sleek – qualities I can't help associating with *Erebus*. Like *Erebus*, her bows have been strengthened for polar work. Like *Erebus*, she was built for something else. No one's quite sure what, but it was probably some sort of quasi-military intelligence-gathering duty. Though the Soviet Union collapsed the year after she was built, there is still something of the old days about the *Vavilov*. Her forty-one-strong Russian crew, who keep the ship going, are rarely seen, except to help us in and out of the Zodiacs that take us to and from the shore. The captain, whose name is Beluga (spelt the same way as the whales we hope we'll see), is tantalisingly aloof. In addition to those who run and maintain the ship, there are twenty-two 'staff'. They include the cooks and waitresses, and lovely people like Tatiana and Maria, who take my laundry and bring it back ironed and washed the next morning. Tatiana has been misled into thinking I'm a famous film star, but can't reconcile this with my cramped little cabin and disordered hair. I daren't tell her, or Maria or Captain Beluga, or any of the Russians, that my most recent starring role is that of Vyacheslav Molotov in *The Death of Stalin*.

The first days on board ship are full of dire warnings. Polar bears can kill, but are less likely to attack a group than an individual. They have a strong sense of smell and can outrun a horse, if they're hungry. Stay close to your guide at all times. Don't go wandering off – like Franklin did. Take the utmost care getting in and out of the landing boats. Never move until your guides are ready. And above all, when you get onshore, don't touch anything. From what I can see of the

treeless, flat-topped rock-stacks in the distance, there won't be much
to touch.

All these warnings increase the tension, ramp up the extraordin-
ariness of where we are: hundreds of miles above the Arctic Circle,
already in the heart of the Northwest Passage.

Around 4 a.m. I wake from jumbled dreams and jetlag-shortened
sleep to find the sun already in the sky. I check my map and see that
we are steaming through Barrow Strait, one of the great highways of
the Northwest Passage. By breakfast time we are off Beechey Island,
which seems strangely familiar to me.

From a straight and soaring bluff of dark rock, the coastline curves
around the bay where *Erebus* and *Terror* took shelter that first winter
out of Britain. We're here in high summer, but chilly winds rise to
thirty knots, ripping up the water and delaying landing for the day.
The next morning it's calmed down, and I'm taken ashore on one of
the first Zodiac dinghies. These usually take up to a dozen people at
a time, but there are only six of us in this first one of the day. Apart
from Russell Potter and myself, there are four guides, all armed with
rifles, who will stake out the area and post lookouts for polar bears.

Russell and I have been granted the priceless luxury of a quiet early
look at the site. At one end of the beach are scattered the remains of
Northumberland House, set up by the crew of *North Star*, one of the
ships on Captain Belcher's expedition sent to try and find Franklin in
1852. The house was built to provide shelter and supplies for Franklin's crew, should they return. Now it's in ruins, but a portion of a
timber partition and a few posts still stand upright, surrounded by the
few remaining courses of a sturdy drystone wall. Scattered about are
planks and rusted barrel hoops, and tins crushed into the limestone
shingle. Nearby are a mast and some planking from Sir John Ross's
yacht *Mary*, in which he came searching for survivors. Russell and I
walk gingerly around the site, boots crunching on the scree-covered
beach. I can understand perfectly now why we have been warned not

to move anything we find. The remains of these little settlements, built in hope, lie about in disorder, but it's a natural disorder. They were built to keep the elements away, and the elements are slowly claiming them back. This is living history. Time and decay are at work and we shouldn't interrupt them.

We walk towards the graves. They look inconsequential: three low humps in the hard ground, each one marked with piles of larger stones, heavy enough to protect the bodies from predators, but not enough to offer them any grandeur or nobility. I think of Franklin's likeness on busts and statues all across the world, and then look again at these rough piles of stones, the only memorials to William Braine, John Torrington and John Hartnell. The memorials back home remind us how John Franklin looked in the prime of life. Thanks to the exhumations on this beach, we only know how William Braine, John Torrington and John Hartnell looked in death. The glory and the disaster.

I'm glad I have had time to pay my respects to the first casualties of the expedition before the crowd arrives. Time to imagine their ships standing out in the bay with the long, silent walls of coastline around them. Time to imagine the bodies being lowered into a boat and brought ashore. The graves would already have been dug (some deeper than others). It would have been hard work digging twice a coffin's depth into the permafrost. Sir John would have said prayers, perhaps given one of his addresses – and that would have been that. Questions come to mind, like why weren't they buried at sea? Why did these three men die so early on, and within such a few weeks of each other? I look out over the bay that bears the name of *Erebus* and *Terror*. It's as bleak and isolated a spot as its namesake in the Antarctic. There are a few ice-floes collecting there, already more than when we arrived. In a few weeks this featureless grey-brown panorama will be all white, like a sheet pulled over a body. I wonder when Torrington, Braine and Hartnell will finally decay. A long time after me, that's for sure.

'Ah, for just one time I would take the Northwest Passage
To find the hand of Franklin reaching for the Beaufort Sea.'

Back on board the *Vavilov*, we cross Lancaster Sound to see the dramatically sheer cliff walls of Prince Leopold Island. Everything makes you feel tiny out here. We transfer into our Zodiacs and pitch around at the bottom of these towering outcrops populated by thousands of birds: murres, northern fulmars, kittiwakes, glaucous gulls, screeching and screaming constantly as they dive down to feed in the rich waters. Every now and then they are not so lucky. We witness a swimming polar bear take out a guillemot bobbing on the water. In fact we have seen a number of polar bears, so many that Martyn Obbard, who is the resident lecturer on polar bears, keeps having to cancel his talk on them, as yet another one is sighted.

I enjoy getting back to the *Vavilov* in the late afternoon, having time to warm up. I sit at the little table by the window of my pilot's cabin, writing up my notes and reading. From what I can remember of the *Illustrated London News* article, my cabin is only a touch smaller than Lieutenant Fitzjames's on *Erebus*.

At night, before I turn in, I take a long look out of the window. It's quite serene out there, in the rosy afterglow of the perpetual Arctic twilight, and the surface of Prince Regent Inlet is lightly rippled as we pass.

The morning after the sing-song there is a heightened air of anticipation in the breakfast queue, as we are given the all-clear to take on the Bellot Strait and cross back onto Franklin's route on the west side of the peninsula. The portents are good. Wind is zero on the Beaufort Scale, and Bellot looks to be clear. But Boris, our young, keen, infectiously enthusiastic expedition leader, is not looking as happy as usual. He draws my attention to the ice-chart, posted outside the dining room every morning. There is a large red blot in the Victoria Strait, hemming in King William Island. Red indicates the thickest, most impenetrable ice, so it doesn't look good. But because we all want, more than anything else, to get to the wreck site, we go along with the plan to get through the Strait and have a look at what we find on the other side. The conditions could change, after all. Except that the absence of any breath of wind, which seemed to be so good at one time, could now be our enemy, because without wind, ice just doesn't move.

The Bellot Strait is a narrow but hugely important channel; strong tidal currents race through it, and the captain has to be confident that navigation is safe. It is, and we're treated to some impressive glacial scenery as we slide through. Franklin wouldn't have known about the Strait. It didn't appear on any charts until Joseph René Bellot, a French explorer who died falling through broken ice whilst helping in the search for Franklin, discovered it in 1852. Had Franklin known about it, it might have been another option for him, both to get in and out of Peel Sound and save the lives of his men.

I'm absurdly excited when Boris points out that the southern shore of the Bellot Strait is the northernmost point of the contiguous American continent. That's quite something: cruising along the northernmost tip of America with a coffee in my hand. I've been to the southern tip at Cape Horn, so now I can say I've seen both ends.

It's not long before we're through into Peel Sound. It's not looking good: apart from a small strip of open water along the shore, the ice stretches off into the distance, all the way across to the hazy outline of Prince of Wales Island. The temperature has fallen noticeably. We have encountered the same kind of ice, in the same kind of place, as when *Erebus* and *Terror* became beset and remained there for years.

After all the talk of global warming, I'd expected something very different. Certainly not to be defeated by ice. I ask Mark Nuttall, another of our resident lecturers, about this. The generally held view, he tells me, is that global warming in the Arctic passed a tipping point in 1999. From that time onwards, people knew that it was no longer a temporary, mercurial phenomenon. In the space of a few years, the sledging and hunting season in West Greenland, for instance, has shrunk from December–June to March–June. Yet it's not quite as simple as it sounds. Because of the rise in temperature, the glaciers have calved off faster, resulting in more – rather than less – floating ice. In the Arctic archipelago there are so many bays and small channels where ice can be trapped and, when that happens, conditions are not so different from the days of Franklin.

As we turn and head back up the Bellot Strait to the safety of the protected eastern shore, I feel cheated – desperately sad to have missed the opportunity to see where Franklin's expedition began to disintegrate. But I have seen enough to strengthen my respect for them and for the forces of nature they were up against.

And one day, God willing, I'll come back to the Northwest Passage, this time with a scuba-suit, to see my ship for myself.

> *'Tracing one warm line through a land so wide and savage*
> *And make a Northwest Passage to the sea.'*

TIMELINE

———————◄►———————

1815   Battle of Waterloo brings Napoleonic Wars to an end

1818   John Ross's expedition to find the Northwest Passage turns back, having mistakenly identified clouds as 'Croker's Mountains'

1819–20   William Edward Parry takes two ships, *Hecla* and *Griper*, through Lancaster Sound to Melville Island

1819–22   John Franklin's near-disastrous Arctic expedition wins him the nickname 'The Man Who Ate His Boots'

1826   Completion of *Erebus* at Pembroke Docks

1828–9   Under the command of Captain George Haye, *Erebus* patrols the Mediterranean

1829–30   *Erebus* continues to patrol the Mediterranean under the command of Captain Philip Broke

1829–33   John Ross's second Arctic expedition. James Clark Ross reaches the North Magnetic Pole on 1 June 1831, but he and his uncle become stranded and nearly starve to death, before they are ultimately rescued by a whaling ship

1839   *Erebus* refitted for James Clark Ross's Antarctic expedition, setting sail with *Terror* on 30 September

1840   *Erebus* reaches Van Diemen's Land (16 August) where Sir John Franklin is Lieutenant-Governor. Sets sail for the Antarctic on 12 November

1841   *Erebus* crosses the Antarctic Circle (1 January) and then sails along the Great Southern Barrier, before returning to Van Diemen's Land (6 April), having reached further south than any previous ship

1842   James Clark Ross's second Antarctic expedition reaches 161°W and 78°9'30"S (23 February), before sailing to the Falkland Islands. Ross's third Antarctic expedition sets sail on 17 December, but is turned back by thick ice

1843   *Erebus* returns to England via Ascension Island and Rio de Janeiro, reaching Woolwich on 7 September. James Clark Ross knighted

1845   *Erebus* refitted for Sir John Franklin's Arctic expedition. Sets sail with *Terror* from Greenhithe on 19 May. Last seen heading across Baffin Bay in late July

1845–6   *Erebus* winters off Beechey Island, where three crew members die and are buried (January–April 1846)

1846   *Erebus* 'beset' in the ice off King William Island (12 September). The crew remain with the ship until 1848

1847   Victory Point note confirms 'All well' (28 May). Sir John Franklin dies (11 June)

1847–8   Three relief expeditions sent out from England, including one led by Sir James Clark Ross, but find nothing. Further relief expeditions follow

1848   *Erebus* abandoned (22 April). Addition to Victory Point note (25 April) confirms that twenty-four men have died and that the survivors will set off to Back's Fish River. Party later splits, with some returning to the ship

1854   While surveying the Arctic coast, John Rae learns from local Inuit that by the end of 1850 all those on the Franklin expedition had perished

1859   Lieutenant William Hobson of the *Fox* discovers the Victory Point note

1866   Statue of Sir John Franklin unveiled on Waterloo Place in London

1984   Bodies of John Torrington and John Hartnell exhumed on Beechey Island

2014   Wreck of *Erebus* discovered

2016   Wreck of *Terror* discovered

ACKNOWLEDGEMENTS

Though my book concentrates on the life of HMS *Erebus*, her story is intimately tied up with that of her sister ship, HMS *Terror*, and it was astonishingly good news to hear that, on 3 September 2016, *Terror* was located less than 50 miles north of where *Erebus* went down. She lies at a depth of 79 feet and is in good condition. That she went down in a place called Terror Bay suggests that perhaps she should have been found a lot sooner, but the fact that both ships that carried the Franklin expedition are now available for examination makes these very exciting times indeed. I'm assured that there are no plans to raise either vessel, and that the marine archaeologists will prioritise work on *Erebus*, as she is at a shallower depth and is more vulnerable to deterioration. Though *Terror* was found by the Arctic Research Foundation, Parks Canada are now in charge of the work on both wrecks.

Which is as good a place as any to start my long list of thanks. Ryan Harris and Jonathan Moore at Parks Canada have been a big help in keeping me informed about the discovery and progress of work on the two wrecked ships.

From the very beginning of the project, John Geiger has been consistently encouraging and supportive. I owe Russell Potter a great debt of thanks for his up-to-the-minute Visions of the North website, and for checking my text and being such good company throughout the adventure. Matthew Betts has generously and promptly answered my endless requests for technical details of the ship and life on board. Mary Williamson, great-great-granddaughter of Franklin's niece, has sent me an invaluable collection of family letters and other details, as has Rick Burrows, great-great-grandson of James Reid, the ice-master on *Erebus*. Claire Warrior and Jeremy Michell at the National Maritime Museum in London have been generous with their time and advice, and Celene Pickard and Julian Dowdeswell at the Scott Polar Research Institute in Cambridge have been equally helpful. Ann Savours entertained me at her cottage and plied me with abundant information, which she augmented in her regular letters to me. Keith Millar has furnished me with useful and relevant updates. I'm most grateful for the encouragement and enthusiasm of Becca Harris, Roz Savage, Leanne Shapton, Andrew Gimson, Linda Davies, Henry Beker and Bob Clarke, whose great-great grandfather Henry Toms sailed on the *Fox* with Leopold McClintock. The staff at the libraries of the Royal Geographical Society, the Athenaeum Club, the Royal Botanic Gardens and the National Archives at Kew were unfailingly helpful.

In my pursuit of *Erebus* locations around the world, I must thank the following for taking the time and trouble to share their knowledge and their hospitality, whilst digging out important information for me: John Evans and Ted Goddard at Pembroke Dockyard; Alison Alexander, Rona Hollingsworth, Annaliese Jacobs, Ian Terry and David Owen in Hobart; Alison Barton, Melanie Gilding, Joan Spruce and Tansy Bishop in the Falkland Islands; the Falkland Islands Historic Dockyard Museum, who kindly shared the manuscript of John Tarleton's letter with me; Norman Shearer in Stromness; and the captain, crew, on-board lecturers, tour organisers and fellow passengers on the One Ocean Expeditions ship *Akademik Sergey Vavilov* in the Northwest Passage, August 2017. And my abundant thanks to

Steve Abbott, Paul Bird and Mimi Robinson at my office, who have guided me through many a book, but none quite like this.

Though, to my great regret, I never met him, the name of Louie Kamookak, the Inuit historian who died in March 2018 at the age of fifty-eight, came up again and again in my research for the book. He wanted, above all, to find Franklin's grave, and it is a huge sadness that time ran out for him. But he won't be forgotten. Everyone who has ever been curious about the fate of the Franklin expedition owes a huge debt of thanks to his dogged and thorough research.

Last but not least, I owe profuse thanks to Susan Sandon at Penguin Random House for encouraging me to write the book, and to my editor Nigel Wilcockson for being such a careful, thorough, enthusiastic and empathetic overseer throughout our long voyage together.

Of necessity I have had to rely on hard work done by previously published authors and researchers. I shall never be able to thank everyone personally, as some are no longer alive, but I offer humble and hearty thanks to all of them, without whose excellent work I could never have started, let alone completed, this book.

Books

Alison Alexander: *The Ambitions of Jane Franklin: Victorian Lady Adventurer*, Allen & Unwin, 2013

William Battersby: *James Fitzjames: The Mystery Man of the Franklin Expedition*, Dundurn, 2010

Owen Beattie and John Geiger: *Frozen in Time: The Fate of the Franklin Expedition*, Bloomsbury, 2004

Captain Richard Campbell, RN (ed.): *The Journal of Sergeant William K. Cunningham, R.M. of HMS Terror*, Hakluyt Society, 2009; https://www.hakluyt.com/PDF/Campbell_Part1_Introduction.pdf

Scott Cookman: *Ice Blink: The Tragic Fate of Sir John Franklin's Lost Polar Expedition*, Wiley, 2001

Richard J. Cyriax: *Sir John Franklin's Last Arctic Expedition*, Arctic Press, 1997 [1939]

J.E. Davis: *A Letter from the Antarctic*, W. Clowes, 1901

Ernest S. Dodge: *The Polar Rosses*, Faber & Faber, 1973

J.C. Drummond et al.: *Historic Tinned Foods*, Publication no. 85, International Tin Development and Research Council, 1939

Jim Endersby: *Imperial Nature: Joseph Hooker and the Practices of Victorian Science*, University of Chicago Press, 2008

Fergus Fleming: *Barrow's Boys*, Granta Books, 2001

John Geiger and Alanna Mitchell: *Franklin's Lost Ship*, HarperCollins, 2017

Barry Gough: *The Falkland Islands/Malvinas: The Contest for Empire in the South Atlantic*, Athlone Press, 1992

Pat Griggs: *Joseph Hooker: Botanical Trailblazer*, Royal Botanic Gardens, 2011

Alice Jane Hamilton: *Finding John Rae*, Ronsdale Press, 2017

Joseph Hooker: Correspondence Project, Royal Botanic Gardens, Kew; http://jdhooker.kew.org/p/jdh

Dean King with John B. Hattendorf and J. Worth Estes: *A Sea of Words: A Lexicon and Companion for Patrick O'Brian Seafaring Tales*, Henry Holt, 1995

Andrew Lambert: *Franklin: Tragic Hero of Polar Navigation*, Faber & Faber, 2010

Brian Lavery: *Royal Tars*, Conway, 2010

Robert McCormick: *Voyages of Discovery in the Arctic and Antarctic Seas, and Round The World*, vols 1 and 2, Cambridge University Press, 2014 [1884]

Ken McGoogan: *Fatal Passage*, Bantam, 2002

Granville Allen Mawer: *South by Northwest*, Wakefield Press, 2006

E.A. (Ted) Michener: *Ice in the Rigging*, Maritime Museum of Tasmania, 2015

Mrs Stuart Peters: *The History of Pembroke Dock*, Elliot Stock, 1905

Russell A. Potter: *Finding Franklin: The Untold Story of a 165-Year Search*, McGill-Queen's University Press, 2016

James Clark Ross: *Voyage of Discovery and Research in the Southern and Antarctic Regions*, vols 1 and 2, Cambridge University Press, 2011 [1847]

John Ross, *Narrative of a Second Voyage in Search of a North-west Passage and of a Residence in the Arctic Regions*, A.M. Webster, 1835.

M.J. Ross: *Polar Pioneers: John Ross and James Clark Ross*, McGill-Queen's University Press, 1994

M.J. Ross: *Ross in the Antarctic*, Caedmon of Whitby, 1982

Ann Savours: *The Search for the North West Passage*, St Martin's Press, 2007

Michael Smith: *Captain Francis Crozier: Last Man Standing?*, The Collins Press, 2014

Tony Soper: *Antarctica*, Bradt Travel Guides, 2013

Tony Soper: *The Northwest Passage*, Bradt Travel Guides, 2012

Barbara Tomlinson: *Commemorating the Seafarer: Monuments, Memorials and Memory*, Boydell Press, 2015

Hugh N. Wallace: *The Navy, The Company and Richard King*, McGill-Queen's University Press, 1980

Chris Ware: *The Bomb Vessel*, Conway Maritime Press, 1994

Paul Watson: *Ice Ghosts: The Epic Hunt for the Lost Franklin Expedition*, W.W. Norton, 2018

David C. Woodman: *Unravelling the Franklin Mystery*, McGill-Queen's University Press, 2015

Articles

William Battersby: 'Identification of the Probable Source of the Lead Poisoning Observed in Members of the Franklin Expedition', *Journal of the Hakluyt Society*, September 2008

William Battersby and Peter Carney, 'Equipping HM Ships *Erebus* and *Terror*, 1845', Newcomen Society, vol. 81, July 2011

Peter Carney: 'Further Light on the Source of the Lead in Human Remains from the 1845 Franklin Expedition', *Journal of the Hakluyt Society*, September 2016

Frank Debenham: 'The *Erebus* and *Terror* at Hobart', *Polar Record*, vol. 3, 1942

Michael Durey: 'Exploration at the Edge', *Great Circle*, vol. 30, no. 2

Ralph Lloyd-Jones: 'The Men Who Sailed with Franklin', *Polar Record*, vol. 41, 2005

Ralph Lloyd-Jones: 'The Royal Marines on Franklin's Last Expedition', *Polar Record*, vol. 40, 2004

Keith Millar, Adrian W. Bowman and William Battersby: 'A Re-analysis of the Supposed Role of Lead Poisoning in Sir John Franklin's Last Expedition, 1845–1848', *Polar Record*, vol. 51, 2015

Keith Millar, Adrian W. Bowman, William Battersby and Richard R. Welbury: 'The Health of Nine Royal Naval Arctic Crews, 1848 to 1854: Implications for the Lost Franklin Expedition', *Polar Record*, vol. 52, 2016

Ann Savours: 'The North West Passage in the Nineteenth Century: Perils and Pastimes of a Winter in the Ice', Hakluyt Society, 2003

Douglas R. Stenton: 'A Most Inhospitable Coast: The Report of Lieutenant William Hobson's 1859 Search for the Franklin Expedition on King William Island', *Arctic*, vol. 67, December 2014

D. Stenton, A. Keenleyside, S. Fratpietro and R. Park: 'DNA analysis of Human Skeletal Remains from the 1845 Franklin Expedition', *Journal of Archaeological Science: Reports*, 2017

Hugh N. Wallace: 'Richard King (1810–1876)', *Arctic* Profiles, vol. 40, 1987

PICTURE ACKNOWLEDGEMENTS

Black and white images are reproduced by kind permission of:

Alamy: x (Pictorial Press), 48 (Chronicle). Bridgeman Images: 176 (De Agostini Picture Library), 248 (© British Library Board). FIMNT Collection: 148. Getty: 18 (Hulton Archive/Stringer), 34 (De Agostini Picture Library), 120 (De Agostini Picture Library), 186 (Illustrated London News/Stringer), 302 (© David Lefranc). © National Maritime Museum, Greenwich, London: 4. © Parks Canada/Thierry Boyer: xviii, 290. Scott Polar Research Institute, University of Cambridge: 210. Victoria and Albert Museum, London: 112. Wikimedia Commons: 162.

Colour images are reproduced by kind permission of:

Alamy: Adélie penguin (520 Collection), Franklin statue (CAM Image). Bridgeman Images: 'Man Proposes, God Disposes' (Royal Holloway, University of London), 'Passage through the ice' (British Library Board), polar chronometer (© Christie's Images). Derbyshire Record Office: ball invitation (ref. D3287/31/8). Getty: Beechey Island graves photo (© Rick Price), cabins of Franklin and Fitzjames (Hulton Archive). National Gallery of Canada: Beechey Island graves watercolour. National Library of Australia: 'Parting company with *Erebus*'. © National Maritime Museum, Greenwich, London:

'Bringing in the year 1842', 'HMS *Erebus* passing through the chain of bergs', 'Part of the South Polar Barrier', Christmas Harbour, relics of the Franklin expedition. © Parks Canada/Thierry Boyer: ship's bell, wreck of *Erebus*. Royal Geographical Society: Francis Crozier portrait. © Scott Polar Research Institute, University of Cambridge: *Erebus* scale model. Tasmanian Museum and Gallery: Rossbank Observatory painting. Wikimedia Commons: 'The Arctic Council planning a search', Franklin expedition memorial, Hooker journal, John Rae portrait, *Pringlea antiscorbutica*, Ross in New Zealand, Victory Point note.

Endpapers show plans of the upper and lower decks of HMS *Erebus* and *Terror* as they were fitted for the Ross Antarctic expedition in September 1839. Reproduced by kind permission of the National Maritime Museum, Greenwich, London.

All other images from author's or publisher's collections.

INDEX